B

Good Neighbors: COMPANION PLANTING FOR GARDENERS

Anna Carr

 Rodale Press, Emmaus, Pennsylvania

Printed in the United States of America on recycled paper,
containing a high percentage of de-inked fiber.

Book design by Jeanne Stock

Illustrations by Pamela and Walter Carroll

Library of Congress Cataloging in Publication Data

Carr, Anna, 1955–
    Good neighbors.

        Bibliography: p.
        Includes index.
        1. Companion planting. I. Title.
SB453.6.C37   1985   635.9   84-24920
ISBN 0-87857-530-8   hardcover

    2   4   6   8   10   9   7   5   3   hardcover

Contents

Acknowledgments

Any work of this sort draws heavily on the work of others. Thanks are due to the scores of scientists whose scholarly research is rapidly expanding our understanding of the ways plants and insects "behave," and particularly to Diane Matthews and other scientists who so willingly reviewed their findings with me.

I am also indebted to Suzanne Nelson for her indefatigable attention to editorial detail and her invaluable help in clarifying some of my thoughts.

1

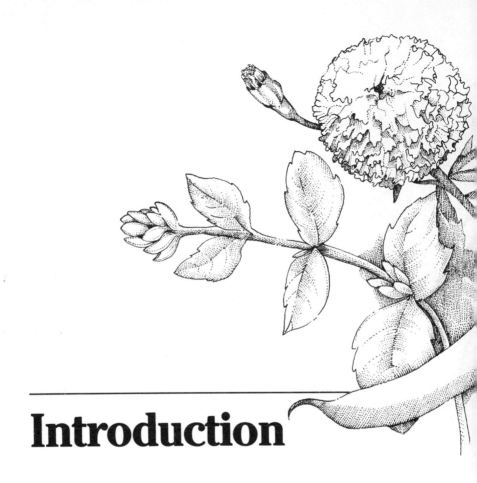

Introduction

Companion planting is an ancient, legendary art. It involves the influence of some crops on others and the arrangement of different species according to their ability to enhance or inhibit each other's growth. To companion planters, a botanical melodrama unfolds wherever two or more crops are grown together. In a magnanimous gesture, some plants protect almost any neighboring plant against the ravages of various pests. Others are more selective; they serve only their best-friend species and will do in their enemies if you give them half a chance. Finally, there are the villains—bad news for lots of different crops. Sound crazy? For centuries, otherwise sane gardeners and farmers have claimed to witness these dramas and have laid out their gardens accordingly. Faithfully, they have planted petunias among potatoes, mustard

in turnip rows and beans in the corn patch. Do you have Mexican bean beetles? They'll tell you to plant marigolds. Are rabbits ravaging your leafy greens? Plant your lettuce in the squash; companion planters claim that the squash will put the rabbits to sleep. Grow yarrow if you want your herbs to have more flavor, keep cabbage away from grapevines, and don't plant anything near a black walnut tree.

Until very recently, scientists responded to these folksy recommendations with a snicker. In their minds it was a quaint but crazy idea–impractical and unfounded. Science recognized only one type of plant interaction–competition for light, water and soil nutrients. Any additional influences were imagined. Besides, companion planting contradicted the gospel according to agribusiness: raise monocultured crops, control pests with insecticides, and supply nutrients by fast-acting chemical fertilizers.

Silent Spring (1962, Houghton Mifflin), the ecological consciousness-raising book by Rachel Carson, and later, the energy crunch, brought changes. Farmers and researchers awoke to realize that many of these efficient, modern methods cause more pest and soil problems than they solve. A new ecological theory of agriculture was born. Researchers took a serious look at the interrelationships of climate, crops and animals. They discovered that modern, monocropping systems aren't necessarily better than some of the traditional, mixed cropping methods still practiced by subsistence farmers and backyard organic gardeners. Interplanting (also called intercropping–they both mean growing two or more crops in a given area at one time) seemed to offer a number of potential benefits. It fared very well in initial comparisons with monocultural methods. Studies showed that intercropping can make more effective use of fertilizers, promote better soil conditions and perhaps even bring higher yields. Where crops are diversified, weed and pest problems are often greatly reduced.

Throughout the late 1960s and 1970s, interplanting was touted by agronomists and garden writers as the "new" technique for increasing world food supplies. Studies raised several important questions. Does intercropping work best in certain climates or with certain soils? How important is spacing and planting design? Can mere diversity explain all the benefits or do certain plant combinations give superior results? In searching for answers, some scientists turned back to the traditions of companion planting.

Today, the notion that plants care who lives next door is seriously studied at most major agricultural research centers. Indeed, companion planting, the practice of interplanting specific crops to make the best use of available resources and to create the healthiest, highest yields, has been recognized as a fledgling science. It has even been given an appropriately awe-inspiring name–agrophytocoenosis. The benefits of intercropping versus monocropping are still debated but mostly in terms of economic feasibility for large farms. For the most part, current research focuses on specific crops and their relations with others. Cornell, University of California at Berkeley, Michigan State, Indiana and other universities in the United States as well as in

4

Europe all boast strong research programs in this field. Some of the most important studies of intercropping and companion planting for increased yields and insect control have been carried out for nearly ten years by Diane Matthews and others at the Rodale Research Center in Maxatawny, Pennsylvania.

Often taking their cue from old herbals and the observations of gardeners and small farmers, scientists are now studying the ways crops interact with each other and with various insects and animals. Some folk tales about garden "defenders" and "villains" are proving to be legitimate. Certain crops do defend others by repelling or at least confusing insect and animal pests. This is their way of protecting themselves, and sometimes the defense also helps their neighbors. Many plants attract beneficial insects that aid in pollination or that prey upon pests. Others may help surrounding crops by supplying necessary nutrients to the soil, creating shade or providing some sort of protection. As for the villains, scores of ordinary fruits, flowers, vegetables, herbs and even weeds have been found to contain substances that, when released into soil or air, inhibit the development of other plant species. Some plants seem to carry destructive diseases, which may not harm them but may infect neighboring crops.

While many studies support companion planting claims, many others challenge them. Some reputedly repellent plants have, under controlled conditions, actually attracted the very pests they're meant to deter. Other plants may deter unwanted pests but are of little practical use since they overgrow surrounding crops or release some phytotoxic substance (one that is poisonous to plants) into the soil.

Such contradictions are a part of any science, particularly one as young as this. Certainly, the jury is still out on companion planting. However, there have been enough positive results to encourage many researchers and to stimulate industries and government-funding agencies to support more work in the field. Although research has just begun, the groundwork has already been laid for revolutionizing the ways we grow fruits and vegetables, both on the farm and in the garden. More and more mutually beneficial cropping combinations are being discovered each year. In related work, substances extracted from a number of weeds and cultivated plants are being tested for use as safe pest repellents and weed inhibitors. Weeds are also being studied as useful intercrops that attract important predatory insects and as valuable green manures and mulches.

For our large-scale farmers, these findings may someday make the use of pesticides and herbicides obsolete and make soil erosion a problem of the past. Already, some farmers are depending less on chemicals since they have switched to interplanting. However, innovations are slow to come.

In the meantime, the value of these practices continues to be proved on a smaller scale—in the laboratory, in test plots and, most importantly, in our own small farms and gardens.

What place could be more suitable for innovations such as companion planting than the home garden—particularly the organic garden? As gardeners, we have been keeping alive a very rich collection of companion planting lore and are well acquainted with crops that are supposed to repel pests or enhance the flavor of their neighbors.

Yet, anyone who has tried to follow some of these old-time planting schemes knows that all too many of these traditions just don't hold true. For years, I've diligently surrounded my cabbage with supposedly impenetrable barriers of onions and garlic but to no avail. Those ubiquitous loopers and imported cabbage-worms still locate my heads of cabbage. At the same time, I've never planted marigolds around my beans, and much to my marigold-planting neighbor's chagrin, have never been done in by Mexican bean beetles.

I've written this book especially for gardeners who, like myself, want to know the facts about companion planting and who want to separate what we *know* from what we *believe* about the ways plants influence one another. I've tried to bridge the gap between tradition and science—between the lore and experi-ences of gardeners and the current research that is being done at universities and independent institutions such as the Rodale Research Center. Throughout the book, you'll find a clear distinc-tion made between what is purely hearsay and the untested experiences of gardeners, and what is factual, having been discovered through formal experiments. I hope that in this way, you'll begin to understand which intercroppings are unpredict-able or harmful and which are reliable and cooperative.

6

Setting the Terms Straight

Just what intercropping or interplanting means isn't always clear since these terms are typically tossed around with others like multiple cropping, mixed cropping and polyculture. Although the American Society of Agronomy and several authors have attempted to define intercropping in a way that distinguishes it from these other cropping practices, there is still a confusing array of terms, with new ones being coined every few years.The most widely accepted definitions are presented below. In this book, an attempt has been made to adhere to these definitions.

Multiple Cropping: Growing two or more crops per year in the same field.

Sequential Planting: Growing two or more crops per year in sequence in the same field or garden. There is no intercrop competition. Growers handle only one crop at a time. This is what gardeners commonly call succession planting. Double cropping (two crops per year) and triple cropping (three crops per year) are types of sequential planting.

Intercropping, Interplanting, Mixed Cropping, Polyculture: Growing two or more crops simultaneously in the same field or garden. Every crop is interplanted during all or part of its growth. Mixed interplanting (growing two or more crops simultaneously with no row arrangements), row intercropping, strip intercropping and relay intercropping are all types of intercropping.

Companion Planting: Selecting certain interplanting combinations in order to achieve a specific benefit such as pest control or enhanced growth. Companion planting is a term coined by horticulturists and not usually found in scientific literature.

Chapter 1

Folk Wisdom or Fairy Tale?

Seen in its broadest sense, companion planting is as old as agriculture itself. Evidence for most mixed cropping practices such as rotation, relay planting and intercropping can be found in archaeological records from prehistoric Europe, Asia and the Americas. Written accounts confirm that such methods were widely used throughout the world from the time of Christ to the nineteenth century.

We can't be sure when farmers and gardeners first noticed that some crops had specific positive or negative effects on certain others. Most early cropping combinations probably originated out of a need to save space. Intercropping let farmers squeeze as many different crops as possible into one cleared area. This satisfied their dietary needs, while maintaining and

even enhancing the health of the soil. Trial and error eventually led them to an understanding of the best combinations of crops that complemented one another with minimal competition for light, water and soil nutrients. Whether the associations were physical, nutritional or chemical, it was clear that some plants seemed to fare better together than apart.

Interplanting through the Ages

Ancient Roman farmers were among the early practitioners of intercropping. They sowed cereal crops between grapes and among fruit trees. The cereals kept weeds under control, protected soil from erosion and may have harbored beneficial insects to prey on potential pests. One well-known Roman, the historian Pliny, recommended sowing chick-peas with cabbage and fitch with rape (the last two were used for animal feed) to repel caterpillars. He wrote that rue is "very friendly" with figs but warned that grapevines "abhor" garden vegetables.

In the Americas, Indians didn't necessarily have a sense of garden "friends" and "enemies," but they did use complex interplanting schemes. They planted corn with squash, beans and sometimes sunflowers and melons. If we take a look at the growing needs of all of these individual crops, it becomes apparent that this is a well-balanced arrangement. Competition for light is minimal since the tallest crop, corn, has the smallest leaf canopy. Competition for water and nutrients is not a problem since the rooting depths of the various plants are somewhat different, and the nitrogen removed by the corn is partially replenished by the nitrogen-fixing beans. And finally, the squash vines act as a living mulch, conserving soil moisture and reducing erosion and possibly even protecting both crops from marauding deer and racoons.

European settlers in the New World adopted this corn-bean-squash interplanting scheme. Later, in the eighteenth and nineteenth centuries, American farmers also learned to interplant other crops. They trained grapes to grow between asparagus beds, which were often interplanted with carrots. According to period farm and garden journals, onions, radishes and lettuces did well among potatoes; spinach thrived between peas; and beets flourished with beans. Tobacco was a well-known insect repellent by the seventeenth century and was interplanted with many vegetable crops to deter maggots.

Early Americans also followed the lead of British horticulturists who, during the sixteenth century, had begun to record garden observations in popular herbals. John Evelyn's *Sylva* recommended interplanting a few vegetables and fruits—radishes with carrots or currants among pear trees—for the overall health of the crops involved. Later, horticulturists John Gerard and Nicholas Culpeper were even more explicit in their assumption that plants influence one another for good or ill. They advised that grapevines and cabbage are "enemies," and sage does well with marjoram but fares poorly with rue. They also counseled

10

that wormwood makes a good overall moth repellent.

During the nineteenth century, the French were the real experts in interplanting and in growing fruits and vegetables in general. The *maraîchers* or market gardeners outside Paris relied on a kind of mixed planting in their year-round intensive production of crops under glass. They selected companion crops more for their complementary shapes, sizes and rates of growth than for any insect repellency or other chemical benefit they might lend one another. Planting and harvesting were carefully staggered so that crops shared growing beds only at certain stages when they would be least competitive. These market gardeners were masters at shoehorning compatible crops into the available space. For example, they would interplant radishes or spinach with lettuce and transplant cauliflower seedlings into a bed of already growing onions or carrots. By the time the root crop was ready to be harvested, the expanding cauliflower was able to fill the empty spaces.

Traditions That Stand the Test of Time

The elaborate French market gardening system died out as trains and trucks began importing produce from the countryside to Paris and manure became less available. (Massive amounts of manure were needed to build and warm the soil for year-round growing.) However, the market gardeners did leave an important legacy. The concept of closely spaced interplantings remains a part of European gardening practices to this day.

In this country, large-scale interplanting went out with the horse-drawn plow. Whereas over half of the Corn Belt's soybeans were grown with corn in the 1920s, today virtually none is intercropped. Although a few stubborn back-country farmers continue to mix these or other crops, organic gardeners and herb enthusiasts are largely responsible for keeping the interplanting and companion planting traditions alive after mechanization took over the farm. Over the years their observations and experiences with various planting combinations have been recorded in many herb and gardening publications. Indeed, a large part of readers' letters to *Organic Gardening* magazine has always concerned companion planting for mutual aid, for insect protection, for soil improvement and for saving space.

Elsewhere in the world where farm holdings are smaller and less mechanized, companion planting methods remain today as important to farmers as they were centuries ago. Interplanting has been continually practiced among subsistence farmers in each hemisphere. In the tropics, intercropping is the most common planting technique, and several effective cropping companions are used extensively. Cotton is intercropped with cowpeas, alfalfa, sorghum or maize; tomatoes and tobacco are mixed with cabbage; peach trees are ringed with strawberries; and corn is paired with peanuts, beans or other legumes. Ninety percent of Colombia's bean crop is grown with potatoes, corn or other companions. Seventy-eight percent of Africa's staple cowpea crop is raised in intercropped fields. In India, intercropping is also widespread. Sorghum is grown with soybeans, cucurbits or onions, in the midst of fields of sugar cane, and wheat is grown between potatoes.

China and Japan remain the countries with the finest examples of continuous intercropping. Forty centuries of trial and error have resulted in elaborate companion planting schemes in both these countries and in many others in southeast Asia. Composting, mulching and manuring build the soil so that land can support many closely spaced crops in an almost nonstop relay of interplantings. The Chinese have a saying, "wheat and legumes are never parted" so they intercrop beans with nearly every grain crop. Whether in a small garden or a large farm field, at least two crops share every row or bed. Asian gardeners grow radishes between rows of rice or trefoil, and they raise millet with beans, cabbage with eggplant, and cucumbers with beans. All this on land that, by most western standards, should have been exhausted 30,000 years ago!

The Biodynamic Movement

Twentieth-century Westerners have been slow in recognizing the importance of these complex plant interrelationships so fundamental to Asian agriculture. One exception was Rudolph Steiner, founder of the Biodynamic movement. In the early 1920s, this Austrian scientist anticipated many of the problems we're now experiencing with chemical agriculture. In his lectures on agriculture, he stressed the importance of understanding the farm or garden as a complete organism composed of plants, animals and man, with all of these parts interacting. His biodynamic methods are based on what science now calls agroecology. They include very specific guides for making compost, applying mulches and rotating crops in order to return lost nutrients to the soil and improve soil structure. Interplanting is done with companion crops having complementary physical demands. Light-loving crops grow with shade-tolerant ones, deep-rooted plants with shallow-rooted ones, nitrogen feeders with legumes, and so forth, just as the French *maraîchers* and Asian farmers had done. In addition, biodynamic gardeners are convinced that plants influence one another in more subtle ways—through various leaf and root exudates, which may repel or attract insects or otherwise affect the health of nearby crops, and through electromagnetic or even mystical means.

Many of these ideas promoted by Steiner were tested by his student, Dr. Ehrenfried Pfeiffer. Pfeiffer used laboratory methods called chromatography and sensitive crystallization to compare various plants' responses to one another. By these methods, plant extracts could be mixed and tested for effects on each other. Today, scientists use similar but much more sensitive and accurate chromatography methods for analyzing plant exudates.

Steiner's philosophy continues to form the basis of work carried on by the Biodynamic Soil Association. The association is very active in Britain and Germany but has only a small membership on this continent. Despite its small ranks, the association's philosophy has permeated American horticulture and to some extent agriculture. Alan Chadwick, a Shakespearean actor turned gardener, made biodynamics popular among organic gardeners. In his impressive demonstration gardens at the University of California at Santa Cruz, he combined Steiner's philosophy with the French Intensive methods developed by the early *maraîchers*. The resulting gardens, still maintained after Chadwick's death, demonstrate the best of both philosophies.

On a farm scale, biodynamics is not quite as well known. A few biodynamic farms scattered around the country apply Steiner's theory of agriculture and healthy living. At Kimberton Hills in

Pennsylvania, 350 acres produce enough organically grown food to feed a community of over 100 individuals, with additional income earned through the sale of baked goods, cheeses and produce. Like other followers of the Steiner philosophy, Kimberton people believe in biodynamics and see no real need to formally test it. They know it works, and their healthy, productive gardens go a long way toward convincing most skeptics.

In the eight years he gardened at Kimberton, horticulturist Joel Morrow learned to watch the crops he grew. He took care to record what worked each season, so the best ideas could be repeated and refined. Morrow planted many of the Kimberton vegetables in intercropped beds, but some of the same crops were also grown in field rows for market harvest. Every year, he found that the intercropped gardens were healthier and more productive than the solo-cropped fields. His experiences showed him that the more diverse the garden, the fewer the pest problems that arose. For instance, he observed that Mexican bean beetles tended to be half as damaging in the interplanted gardens as in the single-cropped ones, and flea beetles were almost nonexistent in mixed plantings. Aromatic companion plants seemed to contribute special benefits, so he always planted onions, yarrow and other herbs around and throughout every bed.

Convinced as he is of its benefits, Morrow is quick to point out that he doesn't have any raw data to "prove" the value of companion planting. What works for one gardener may not work for another. In different areas, plants may behave differently. They may in some mysterious way even respond to the gardener himself. Says Morrow, "A garden is an orchestra. Depending on who is conducting, the same piece sounds very different."

The Role of Research

Testimonials of skilled gardeners like Joel Morrow are an invaluable source of information, but they certainly won't convince a farmer to redesign his entire spread for companion planting. Indeed, even gardeners may be justifiably skeptical. For one thing, it's often very hard to know what you're seeing. One bean plant may *look* better than another, but is it really producing more? How do you know? Did you count the beans or weigh the total output? If it really has produced more, is its marigold neighbor the cause or could it be receiving more light or water than the other plants? Perhaps the roots happen to be growing in a pocket of rich compost.

Direct observation isn't really very dependable. It may be the source of interesting ideas, but their value is only really known once the ideas have been subjected to the rigors of the scientific method. Now, finally, research on companion planting is being conducted in a systematic manner. Horticulturists, agroecologists, entomologists, biochemists and plant pathologists are studying various plant interactions in an effort to find the most effective systems for growing specific crops—whether alone in monocropped systems, or if in mixed or interplanted systems, then in what specific combinations.

Monocropping versus Intercropping

Intercropping makes good common sense to millions of subsistence farmers who rely on it throughout the world. Based on the results of dozens of studies, it makes good scientific sense, too. Although a few respected researchers continue to debate its merits, intercropping is recognized by most as a method with decided advantages over monocropping. Indeed, it has even become the darling of many agricultural research centers. Workers at the Rodale Research Center and at Cornell and Michigan State Universities, in particular, are trying to explain just why it works so well for those subsistence farmers and to learn how it might be applied here at home. What we do know at this point is that intercropping offers three potential advantages: it may increase yields, improve soil quality and reduce pest and disease problems.

Increased Yields

In some traditional systems, intercropping raises yields some 60 percent per unit of land area. In other words, if you were to divide the same intercropped field into several smaller fields to accommodate monocultures of each species, the total amount you harvest would be smaller. Not all studies demonstrate such great increases, and indeed some have shown yield reductions from interplanting.

However, where interplanting does boost yields, there are lots of possible explanations, most of which relate to the use of resources. First, studies have shown that two or more crops growing together seem to make better use of the sunlight in a given spot. As long as their heights and leaf angles differ, shading will be minimal, and more sunlight will be intercepted and put to use by the plants. High yields might also be due to what goes on underground—how the plants use soil nutrients and water. It is clear that more nutrients are taken up from the soil by intercropped plants than by those grown "solo." One reason may be that each intercrop has a different rooting pattern and draws from a different soil layer than its neighbor. Several workers have suggested that the mere presence of intercrops causes certain plants to "avoid" their neighbor's root area. If this is the case, deep-rooted crops, for example, may be forced even deeper when you grow them with a shallow-rooted neighbor. In other instances, it may be that the crops have different nutrient needs to begin with or require the same nutrient but at different stages of growth.

Improved Soil Quality

Where polyculture has been practiced for centuries, it seems to have protected the soil from total nutrient exhaustion. Many of the reasons given above also apply here. In addition, when you intermix crops with different rooting systems, they often help to aerate the soil and even disperse nutrients throughout all layers of the soil. The thickened root systems of some tree crops help drain the soil, making it fit to support other types of plants.

Reduced Pest and Disease Problems

By far the most research has been done in this area. Studies show that monocropping tends to attract fewer types of diseases and insects but in such large numbers that they end up causing considerable damage. In mixed plantings, a greater variety of insects and diseases are present, but the damage isn't likely to be as significant. For example, a monocropped cabbage field may not have many cabbage webworms or diamondback moths or fall armyworms or cutworms or maggots, but the cabbage loopers can do a very nice job of destroying the crop on their own. In a mixed cabbage planting, small numbers of all these pests may be present, but the total damage will be much less extensive.

This idea that more (in terms of a greater variety) pests can cause less damage may strike you as rather odd. Entomologists offer several explanations. First, a diversity of plants provides shelter and food for insect predators and parasites that help to control potential pests. This creates a more stable environment where no population is likely to get out of hand. Secondly, the color, shape, height and smell or other qualities of the interplants may confuse pests so that they can't find their host crop or at least don't choose to colonize on it. Tall crops might even act as a physical barrier that helps keep out wind-borne diseases and pests. Finally, reduced pest and disease problems may be due to the way interplantings change microclimates in the field or garden. Usually a mixture of closely spaced crops of varying heights creates a damper, darker area beneath the leafy canopy. This low-light, high-humidity environment may not be favorable for the pests' reproduction.

Critics of intercropping as a means of pest control point out that undesirable insects and diseases may actually be encouraged by a wide diversity of plants. They contend that more crop plants mean more food and refuge for the pests. This and other arguments will be discussed later in chapter 3. For now, it is enough to say that in most cases, interplanting tends to create a more stable environment so that no insect population is likely to take over.

Finding the Right Combinations

While plant diversity in the garden has some decided advantages, it can also cause some problems if you intercrop the wrong species. Instead of complementing one another, some crops may compete for space, light, water or nutrients. The presence of certain plants tends to increase the incidence of pest and disease problems in their neighbors. It has even been shown that a number of crops release toxic substances, which inhibit the germination and growth of other species.

In order to make wise interplanting choices, we need to understand each plant's needs and the ways it interacts with the environment—with soil, with other plants and with insects. In these areas, recent studies have led to some exciting discoveries that help explain the effectiveness of some traditional companion plantings and that suggest many new schemes as well. Most of the landmark work is discussed in the chapters that follow. In this chapter, you'll find an overview suggesting the directions research has taken.

The Plant-Nutrient Connection

This has always been a focus of agricultural research, but now it's taking on a new dimension in the study of compatible intercrops or companions. The nitrogen-fixing properties of beans, peas and other legumes are well known for the important part they play in most rotation systems involving heavy feeders like corn or cabbage. Studies in the 1930s showed that legumes could actually excrete nitrogen *during* growth. More recently, researchers have found that some legumes might even be stimulated to fix more nitrogen when growing beside nonlegumes. Since legumes will only fix nitrogen if it's not readily available in the soil, the presence of high-nitrogen feeders could encourage the process. This relationship is complicated by other plants' abilities to affect soil chemistry in different, often opposing ways. For example, while legumes are busy building nitrogen levels in the soil and some crops are encouraging them, other crops and weeds are undoing that work by dramatically inhibiting the work of nitrogen-fixing bacteria. Similar relationships have been noted involving other soil nutrients as well.

Obviously, we as gardeners and farmers need to know which combinations are nutrient-enriching and which are nutrient-inhibiting. It's not enough to rely on the mere variety of plants to enhance crop growth and increase yields. Indeed, some of the crops we interplant out of habit may be competing for nutrients or slowing their absorption. We need to understand the specific way each crop feeds and to apply our knowledge as we design our gardens.

Plants against Plants

Billions of dollars are spent on chemical herbicides each year. Yet, until recently, few researchers have seriously examined the natural herbicides quietly exuded from scores of weeds and crop plants. Many, perhaps most, plants release substances that slow or stop the growth of certain other species. Ecologists call this phenomenon allelopathy and have long recognized it as a part of the dynamics of natural ecosystems. Allelopathy helps the plant stake out its territory and protect itself while it becomes established. For example, goldenrod produces allelopathic substances, which keep many different trees from growing up around it. Black walnut trees keep many plants at a distance. Only certain plants can thrive under its canopy, no matter how much light, water or food is available.

Only recently have agricultural scientists begun to appreciate the role allelopathy plays in the way crops interact with other crops and with weeds. Often the effects are overshadowed by more dramatic problems caused by out-and-out competition. Nevertheless, allelopathy can make the difference between a small harvest and no harvest at all. Some studies suggest that plant-produced toxins can reduce crop growth by up to 90 percent.

In the laboratory, efforts are being made to isolate allelopathic substances. In the field, workers are demonstrating many forms of allelopathy. The tremendous number of variables makes work in this area more than a little challenging. Weather, soil type and other factors all influence the production and release of these chemicals. Then, there is the problem of actually noting how and under what conditions they are released. Sometimes the substances are stored in a nontoxic form and change into poison only when the plant is injured. In most plants, chemicals are released by living roots, but in some, the strongest toxins are released by decaying leaves or other residues. Such information could be important in selecting rotations, green manures and mulches, and in the timing and handling of intercrops.

The best known studies of allelopathy involve common weeds that show up in most of our gardens. Their competition for water, light and food brings obvious harm to crops, but their silent, unseen biochemical influences may be even more troublesome. As little as 0.5 percent nutsedge foliage in the soil can reduce the yield of corn by 20 percent, and foxtail roots may have an even more harmful effect. But crops aren't totally defenseless—some have been known to retaliate with phytotoxins (plant-produced toxins) of their own. Cucumbers, sunflowers, rye, sorghum, barley and other cultivated plants possess potent "plant killers." These crops pose an especially attractive research avenue for breeders. Imagine a crop that weeds itself!

Plants against Pests

In the past two decades, agricultural researchers have devoted time and energy toward identifying specific interplanting combinations that reduce insect and disease damage. Scientists have long realized that certain plants contain potent poisons or deterrents. Indeed, some of our most familiar repellents and insecticides have been derived from plants since ancient times: pyrethrum from chrysanthemum species, rotenone from the derris plant, nicotine from tobacco and citronella from a fragrant Asian grass. Now it appears that many other plants—mostly weeds and herbs—also produce useful chemicals. In addition to the repellents, there are attractants, which lure insects to their hosts, and stimulants and deterrents, which cause them to start or stop some behavior such as feeding or laying eggs. All of these substances could have practical significance in agriculture. In the future, some may be available as safe pesticide sprays or dusts we can use in our gardens.

Companions to Fight Pests

Some of the most interesting work, however, involves companion planting with these plants themselves. This is a big part of the traditional companion planting practiced by so many gardeners. When you include repellent weeds, flowers or herbs in an interplanting scheme you create a naturally stable ecosystem. Ideally, this means you'll spend less time dealing with pests and diseases. If repellent food crops or other interplants with real economic value could be identified, then the practice would be even more appealing.

While it's true that science has affirmed that many of the traditional repellent plants do protect themselves from certain target pests, it isn't clear yet how much effect they have on their neighbors. Furthermore, even if these repellent plants can be interplanted to help control pests, other problems may develop, such as allelopathy or competition. In some cases, the repellent plant becomes such a pervasive, uncontrollable weed that its effectiveness as a repellent is overshadowed. Much of the work carried out at the Rodale Research Center is aimed at identifying not only the most effective repellent companions but the most practical ones as well.

While some scientists concentrate on repelling the pests, others are focusing on companion plants that attract beneficial insects. For example, certain plant families are especially good at drawing predatory and parasitic wasps. By identifying the beneficial insects for target pests and then finding plants they like to feed on, you can prevent a lot of pest damage. Already, interplanting with insectary plants (ones that attract insects) has become a valuable part of integrated pest management for certain economic crops in this country.

Research Can Be Tricky

Difficulties associated with research on interplanting are manifold. In the laboratory, test plants can be grown in artificial media, fed nutrient solutions and kept under artificial lights, so variables are fairly easy to control. However, results from such studies must ultimately be tested in the field if they are to have any practical value for farmers and gardeners. There it is impossible to equalize completely the factors affecting all the test plants. Variations in surrounding vegetation, soil type and the like can only be noted and accounted for. In addition, there are the factors related to the study itself, such as spacing, culture and placement of crops. When it comes time for the researcher to analyze the data, decisions made in those areas become especially critical.

Such complications often muddle the entire issue of interplanting. Because the science is so new, few "rules" have been set down for experimental work. There is room for critics to challenge the way data is interpreted. For example, a researcher may find fewer eggs, larvae and adult pests on his interplanted beans than in the monocropped control plot. Is the effect due to diversity or to the specific intercrop tested? What about the quality and yield of the harvested crop? If the crop of green beans is being damaged by pests—even if fewer pests are causing the damage—then the treatment isn't a very practical means of control. If the beans are healthy but their yield is only half that of the monoculture control, then the method is again suspect.

By the same token, proponents of interplanting often debate negative conclusions. Where companion plantings don't "work," it may not be the plant's "fault" at all. Experimental design is often the culprit. Most certainly, different spacing, moisture, nutrition levels and even cultivation give different results.

The Gardener's Role

Gardeners rarely swallow this scientific stuff whole. We temper it with the suggestions from our gardening friends, our own firsthand observations and a healthy skepticism about all three. No one who has had anything to do with plants believes that science can entirely unravel the secrets of growing them. There will always be one more mystery to confound and delight us just when we smugly believe we've got the whole thing figured out.

When I consider some of the new research findings, I am amazed that plants forced to grow in my garden not only survive but thrive. For years I have successfully grown lettuce between early broccoli, unaware of possible allelopathic effects and unconcerned about nutrient competition in my well-manured soil. It's a pleasing combination, and you might say that what the plants don't know won't hurt them. My Brussels sprouts grow fine without the benefit of a weedy intercrop, and it's hard to find more than a few Mexican bean beetles on my snap beans, although the nearest potatoes are only a half-mile up the road.

Yet, how much better could my garden be if I *did* consider these effects? By understanding a little of the chemical and physical interaction among plants and animals, we can all make more intelligent choices in the design, planting and cultivation of the crops we grow. If we are serious about raising fruits and vegetables, then we can't afford to ignore information that suggests more efficient, ecologically responsible ways to do so.

For years, the organic farming and gardening movement remained well outside mainstream scientific investigation. While researchers were busy developing technologies for chemically dependent agribusiness, organic growers were pining for the past and following the traditions of a prechemical, premechanical era. Now, finally, science has begun to realize the limitations and dangers of chemical agriculture. Research has undergone a profound shift in the direction of a more sensitive, resource-conserving approach to raising food. Agroecology is the new frontier, and intercropping, along with green manuring, mulching and loads of other good sensible methods, has come of age.

Organic gardeners can smile quietly as science "invents" the intensive, interplanted garden and "discovers" the pest-repellent powers of marigolds. We've known these things all along! But, on second thought, have we? Sure, we've been practicing many of these methods but often without knowing why. When modern science examines companion planting, it brings a new depth and objectivity to the subject. It provides some of the whys and wherefores and even some of the why nots. Sometimes, the latest word from the scientific community can provide just the information we need to overcome a pest or soil problem. Often, scientific research simply gives us the insight we need to devise our own solutions. Ultimately, this deeper understanding of garden ecology may lead us to our own discoveries of better cropping combinations, of effective repellent plantings and of techniques for building soil and boosting yields. Companion planting is not a panacea for all garden ills. But, it is one of dozens of sound practices that can contribute to the overall stability and health of your garden. If you use it in conjunction with green manuring, composting, mulching and crop rotation, it may well mean the difference between a good garden and a great garden.

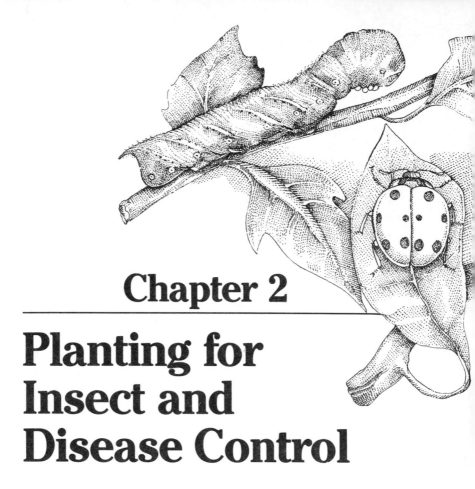

Chapter 2

Planting for Insect and Disease Control

Most ecologists agree that the practice of monocropping is largely responsible for the growing pest and disease problems we face today. Scores of studies have demonstrated what has almost become a truism: Fewer kinds of plants means fewer kinds of pests, but they come in such great numbers as to cause considerable damage. In other words, where one crop covers an area of ground, a few species of plant-eating insects and wind-borne disease organisms seem to take over.

Explanations for this phenomenon abound. Cornell entomologist and a leader in the field of interplanting, Richard Root, has put forth one of the most convincing theories. He has suggested that pests that feed on only a small variety of host plants are more likely to find that host when it is growing in nearly pure stands,

with no other crops mixed in. Insects that might ordinarily feed on wild plants turn to the monocrop because there is nothing else available for them to eat. Patches of host crops act as traps, luring certain pests and encouraging them to colonize. They meet with little opposition since few insect predators and parasites are active in the simple microclimates created by sole cropping. With relatively few enemies to speak of, pests tend to stay around for a long time. Given this ideal environment, it's no wonder that they reproduce at phenomenal rates.

The Chemical Merry-Go-Round

All in all, the monocropped field is an unnatural, unstable ecosystem, which requires chemical pesticides, herbicides and fertilizers for its existence. Ironically, these very materials have made problems worse in recent years. The widespread use of pesticides in particular has proven to be a painful lesson in economics and ecology. Pesticides work quickly but often indiscriminately. Their end result is all too often an increase in the very pest they were meant to control.

According to Robert van den Bosch, a researcher at the University of California at Berkeley, 24 of California's 25 worst pests were encouraged by pesticide use. Crop losses due to agricultural pests have doubled, despite a tenfold increase in pesticide use over the past 40 years. The scenario goes something like this: In destroying target pests, pesticides wipe out other animal life including beneficial insects, which are particularly susceptible to poisons. When pest populations recover and return, as they inevitably do a few days or weeks after the spraying, there are no enemies to discourage recolonization. Worst of all, the pests themselves come back stronger than ever; after repeated exposures over several generations, they develop genetic immunity to the poison. This in turn leads us to create new, more potent substances, which control the insects for a few years until they again develop resistance. Again, we respond with new potions, and again these most adaptable creatures get used to our chemical concoctions. It is a crazy, insidious merry-go-round rapidly spinning out of control.

Organic gardeners have long advocated a return to interplanting as a way to break this cycle. It has been mostly an intuitive argument, with history, tradition and personal experience to back it up. Common sense suggests that interplanting would protect against major pest damage since it sets up conditions that mimic nature, and in natural environments, insects only rarely wipe out plants. Nature has a system of checks and balances, which can be recreated in the garden.

Maintaining the Balance

For centuries, traditional farmers from Peking to Peoria have practiced interplanting with the simple objective of maintaining this natural balance. Often, although pest control is not the first objective, it's such an important benefit that some crops' survival may depend on it. In the tropics where the moist, warm climate supports so many insects, chemical spraying and dusting could never control all the different pests likely to arise in a monocropped system. Interplanting is a subtler, less drastic approach. Outbreaks may still occur, but they are less frequent and more manageable.

Traditional farmers in cooler climates have also reduced insect damage through interplanting. In ancient times, Roman farmers were able to maintain healthier orchards when grains were planted alongside fruit and nut trees. In more recent times, some nineteenth-century American farmers advocated similar, natural, no-till orchards, where a floor of wildflowers and grasses was maintained. Japanese, Chinese and Korean farmers from as early as the fifteenth century consciously intercropped all sorts of grain and vegetable crops to control specific pests.

Today's organic gardeners look on these as early examples of responsible agriculture. Ecologically minded growers continue to practice interplanting because they believe it prevents many of the disease and pest problems that chemical farmers and gardeners solve by spraying. Besides that, it is a logical complement to other sound gardening practices. Used in conjunction with mulching, green manuring, composting and the selection of resistant varieties, interplanting seems to make the garden less dependent on you, the gardener. Many pest and disease problems take care of themselves when you orchestrate the process by handpicking, trapping or occasionally using natural sprays and dusts such as botanical feeding deterrents made from garlic or safe biological insecticides such as *Bacillus thuringiensis.*

The Scientific Viewpoint

Many researchers, like gardeners, also recommend intercropping as at least one practical alternative to the heavy use of pesticides. Although they don't usually paint so rosy a picture, they too are looking at traditional mixed cropping systems with the realization that crop diversity does indeed reduce insect damage. These researchers are quick to point out that intercropping isn't "feasible" for large-scale operations, but they concede that it makes perfect theoretical sense. Their explanations give depth and meaning to what the organic gardener and traditional farmer may have guessed but "ne'er so well expressed." Diversity and stability are the two main contributions that many scientists believe intercropping brings to the garden.

Diversity

More plant species within the same plot seems to mean more insect species. It also means a decrease in the overall numbers of pests but often an increase in the numbers of beneficial insect predators and parasites. According to Cornell University's David Andow, who has carefully reviewed the considerable literature on the subject, this is due to two basic factors: available food and habitat. Food comes in the form of the plants themselves and the insects feeding on them. Obviously, all sorts of plant-eating insects will seek out the diversity of crops in an interplanted area. The diversity of insects in turn attracts parasites and predators to feed on them.

This same variety tends to confuse most pests, however. Chemical, physical or visual stimuli from the interplants make it difficult for one-crop feeders to find their host plants. Just as gardeners have suspected, fewer pests tend to find their way into the interplanted field or garden. Many insects rely on sight to find their host plants. Plants growing against a background of bare soil stand out prominently. But in a dense interplanting or a weedy patch, the host plant is camouflaged. A 1976 study by Judith Smith at Imperial College, in London, showed that aphids had trouble finding Brussels sprouts when a weed cover was allowed to grow between plants. Similar findings have been noted with other vegetable crops and with many pests.

It may also be true that insect pests that do manage to find their hosts among a mixture of crops, don't stay for long. Movement from one host plant to another is not as simple as in the monocropped plot—sluggish insects may have a hard time making their way over to the next row! There's also the factor of microclimate. Mixing plants with very different growth patterns creates a basically humid, dark, cool environment. While this is ideal for many insect predators and parasites, pests usually prefer to colonize and reproduce in drier, sunnier spots. Given their preferences, the beneficial insects stay in the interplanted plots, and the pests move on.

Stability

All this diversity of plants and insects gives the intercropped field a certain stability and balance. The gardener's hunch that interplanting mimics nature is correct. The ecosystem of a garden with mixed plantings bears a fairly close resemblance to that of the natural environment. Pest outbreaks are less likely to occur since so many natural constraints are at work. The interplanted field is able to more or less police itself.

Examining the Experimental Evidence

Whatever the theoretical reasons, plenty of strong experimental evidence supports the organic gardener's contention: Insect damage can indeed be decreased by using crop mixtures. Much of the research deals with cotton, alfalfa and other agricultural crops since these are most dependent on pesticides. Some research is also underway with the fruit and vegetable crops commonly found in home gardens. Strawberry plants grown near peach orchards have helped to control oriental fruit moths. Fewer flea beetles were found on collards intercropped with tomatoes, tobacco or even ragweed than in monocropped plots. Leafhoppers were reduced on beans when corn was the companion. The incidence of striped cucumber beetles, and hence disease, was lower when cucumbers were planted with corn or broccoli. The list goes on and on.

At the same time, there is a body of experimental evidence indicating that mixed cropping may sometimes encourage pests. These researchers look on interplanting as a clumsy, almost primitive practice, which in the past 50 years, has been happily replaced by pesticides and soil fumigants. Their point cannot be easily dismissed. If intercrops are susceptible to the same pathogens or pests, the chances of infestation are greatly increased. In France, intercroppings of melons and some vegetables actually increased root-knot nematodes on young peach trees.

Further, interplanting some crops may draw the very pests it is meant to control. Work carried out by M. A. Latheef at Virginia

State University seems to suggest that French marigolds and certain herbs actually attract imported cabbageworms to feed on cabbage. Experiments at the Rodale Research Center resulted in more cabbageworms on broccoli interplanted with catnip and tansy than on broccoli plants growing by themselves.

Under some conditions, a mixture of crops may provide

(continued on page 32)

Good Bugs to Have in the Garden

How can you distinguish the helpful insects from the harmful ones? It's not always easy unless you actually observe them as they go about their business, and even then you can't always tell whether they're eating the plant or some minuscule pest on the plant. To help you, here is an overview of some of the more common beneficial insects. They fall into three basic groups: the predators, which actually hunt and kill other insects; the parasites, which lay their eggs on other insects so that, upon hatching, their young may dine on the host's life blood; and the pollinators, on which we depend for the all important transfer of pollen among fruits and flowers.

Beetles: Ground beetles and lady beetles stand out as the most effective predators in this group, although blister beetles, fireflies, soldier beetles, tiger beetles and rove beetles are also good bug-eaters. Ground beetles like the shade of low vegetation such as clovers and low-growing weeds. They are also associated with nightshade and amaranth. Lady beetles like to lay their eggs on tansy and yarrow.

Flies: Hover flies or syrphids are the brightly colored flies we see flitting about the garden. Their larvae parasitize aphids and other small, soft-bodied pests. They need the pollen provided by flat, open flowers such as daisies or marigolds. Tachinid flies are important parasites of European corn borers, Mexican bean beetles, gypsy moths and other caterpillar pests. Sweet white clover and most flowering plants in the carrot family attract them.

Lacewings: These are lovely light green creatures that, as larvae and adults, prey upon small, soft-bodied pests such as aphids and mealybugs. Tree of heaven (*Ailanthus* spp.), sorghum and various evergreens are favorite shelters for lacewings.

Wasps and Bees: These are by far the most beneficial of all garden creatures, for they are pollinators as well as parasites. Braconid wasps are small (half an inch or less) wasps that attack corn borers, sawflies and all sorts of larval pests. The tiny white cocoons you find on the back of a tomato hornworm were put there by a braconid wasp. Flowering carrot family plants such as Queen Anne's lace and yarrow attract these insects.

The even smaller chalcid wasps (less than a quarter inch long) parasitize lots of caterpillar pests. The trichogramma egg parasite you can buy for biological control is a type of chalcid wasp. Like most other wasps, it can be encouraged to stay around the garden if you provide a border or strip of yarrow, wild carrot and other flowering plants. Wasps also seem to benefit from nearby evergreens.

Ichneumonid wasps are varied in their appearance and size, but most species are important parasites of larval pests. Fennel, rye, wild mustard and some evergreens feed and shelter ichneumonids during part of their life cycle.

To encourage bees, our best garden pollinators, plant clovers, fennel, buckwheat and all sorts of flowering carrot family plants.

pests with just the alternative hosts or habitats they need to survive from season to season. In the nineteenth century, rocky mountain locusts destroyed crops on small farms that grew more than one type of crop. As modern agriculture took over and meadows and natural ecosystems disappeared, the pest all but disappeared, too.

If intercropping achieves its pest control through a kind of camouflaging act, it could be that close spacing of a monocrop would have the same effect. Studies with corn and other crops have shown that denser plantings do, in fact, reduce pest populations. This could be because no individual plants stand out against a background of bare soil.

In light of all these negative findings, you may start to wonder whether interplanting is such a realistic way to control pests. While some researchers are ready to dismiss the entire practice, many investigators remain convinced of its worth. It is true that the field is still quite young, and few hard and fast rules have been set down as yet. Nevertheless, what information we do have is valuable, fascinating and quite useful to gardeners and small-scale farmers. Advocates of interplanting stress that its success as a pest control measure definitely depends on the way it's carried out. The choice of crops, how and when they're planted and even climate and geographical location all affect the outcome.

Timing and Arrangement

Planting the intercropped garden isn't simply a matter of tossing handfuls of seeds into the air and letting them fall. There's an optimum time to plant some intercrops and a preferred spacing that minimizes competition but maximizes pest control. Scientists have only begun the huge task of determining when, where and how to interplant common garden crops, but they have already given us some useful pointers. For aphid control, early planting is a good idea so that the ground is covered and the newly planted main crop is less visible. In other cases, the intercrop may be more effective if you set plants out later. In a 1978 study of bean-corn intercrops, Miguel Altieri, a professor at the University of California at Berkeley, found that planting corn 20 to 40 days before planting beans reduced leafhoppers by 66 percent when compared with simultaneous planting. He also saw that if *beans* were planted 20 to 30 days before corn, fall armyworm damage to the corn could be reduced by 88 percent.

When it comes to spacing, some companions have different preferences. For example, you must plant marigolds very densely, well ahead of the main crop in order to protect it against nematodes. Other companion plants, like tansy, seem to perform better when you give them more room.

Geographic location might also affect pest control plantings. It is possible that companion plants that are beneficial in one locale may be harmful in another. For example, corn and cotton intercropping helps control the caterpillar *Heliothis virescens* in Peru, but the same system actually increases the pest in California.

Selecting Companions

By far the most important factor in controlling pests through interplanting is your selection of crops. In general, any mixture is better than a monoculture, but some combinations can have downright negative effects. With certain pests and crops, the selection of interplants means the difference between virtual devastation and abundant, healthy harvests.

This is where *interplanting* in a general sense leaves off, and *companion planting* takes over. Every gardener's dream is to have a garden of Eden that takes care of itself with little attention from the grower. Companion plants could theoretically bring us one step closer to that goal. It's certainly an appealing notion, this idea that the mere presence of one plant might somehow protect its neighbors against insect attacks. But is it true? A good deal of our lore and hand-me-down words of gardening wisdom suggest that it is. Herbals and farm manuals, gardeners' letters and anecdotes are filled with recommendations of herbs and aromatic companions that, planted here and there, will chase bugs away. These various sources tell us to grow leeks to get rid of carrot flies, raise mint to repel aphids, plant marigolds to drive away Mexican bean beetles and grow petunias to discourage potato bugs.

The Earliest Companions

Lots of these maxims originated in ancient history or even

33

before. They grew out of people's observations of the native plants that seemed relatively free of pest problems and out of their trial and error experiences in using these plants. Most of the recommended plants are aromatic because early growers reasoned that strong, bitter flavors are distasteful to insects. As early as 300 B.C., the Greek philosopher Theophrastus pointed out that caterpillars eat sweet plants but leave pungent ones alone. Pliny reiterated this and went on to recommend that bitter crops or wild plants be planted among those that insects prefer. He advised that interplanting a type of vetch with rape, and cabbage with chick-peas would repel larval pests.

In native cultures of the Americas, India, Africa and Asia, growers made similar discoveries. The bitterest, most persistent herbs were recognized for their insecticidal or repellent properties. Some of these plants even held religious importance; their boughs were used as charms against crop failure and the like. In Africa, a species of spurge was grown as an ant repellent, and the flowering four o'clock was planted by doorways to keep away mosquitoes. Indian farmers interplanted a member of the mallow family among cotton as a pest repellent.

These few examples may give you the impression that companion planting was widespread in ancient and native societies. In general, this doesn't seem to be the case. *Interplanting* was, and is, an important part of many native agricultural systems. It boosts yields and, as we have seen, certainly helps reduce pest damage. But as for *companion* planting aromatic herbs or other plants with the primary intention of repelling insects—that is a different matter. With limited space, traditional growers only cultivated crops that had high nutritive or medicinal value. Most would not waste tilled land on repellent plantings. Wherever possible, they seemed to choose the route followed by modern farmers—sprays and dusts. Repellent plants were gathered in the wild, then dried and ground or steeped in water. The resulting repellents or insecticides were then used on plants, soil, clothing or people themselves.

Companions Chosen by Herbalists

For the most part, the art of companion planting as pest control belongs to herbalists and gardeners. They have contributed much of the lore concerning the repellent properties of plants. Aside from a few ancient references, these traditions have their roots in the writings of early European herbalists. Judging from some of these books, Europe, and later the New World, were hot beds of repellent plantings from the fifteenth to nineteenth centuries. Herbalists recommended all sorts of companions for pest control. They all seem to have sworn by wormwood, claiming it could repel flies and flea beetles. Heliotrope was said to work against ants, and geum against clothes moths. Burning stalks of loosestrife were recommended as deterrents against fleas, snakes and gnats. During the eighteenth and nineteenth centuries, growers shared their remedies for various plant ills through letters published in farming magazines such as *Gardeners Chronicle* and *New York Farmers* and *American Garden Magazine*. It is through these sorts of writings that the concept of repellent planting received attention. One farmer wrote in that tomatoes keep aphids off his cabbage. Another gardener suggested rhubarb against clubroot in cabbage. Sage was recommended as a good toad repellent, and mint was supposed to keep mice at bay.

Current Companions

Today, the banner of pest control planting is waved by organic gardeners repeating many of the same claims. Organic gardeners advocate companioning as one of the more natural forms of insect management since it usually involves deterring, not killing pests. Many of the recommended repellent plants are useful herbs or attractive flowers, so it seems reasonable for gardeners to tuck them into vegetable gardens or orchards where they can serve double duty by providing culinary and medicinal herbs and repelling pests.

Organic Gardening, Mother Earth News, The Furrow and other periodicals are filled with testimonials of growers ready to swear by their discoveries. "I planted pennyroyal and got rid of cabbage butterflies," writes one organic gardener. Peppermint worked for another. Someone recommends sowing radishes around vine crops to control squash bugs, and someone else uses pink petunias in the same way. A gopher plant hedge protects one garden but seems to turn another into a groundhog's paradise.

The result is a tangle of sworn statements, which even Perry

Mason would have trouble unraveling. Each gardener claims to be right, yet each has such different results. Of course, few of these amateur researchers have systematically tested their companion planting schemes. Most "results" can be explained by factors other than the companion plant—variables such as a change in crop location, natural fluctuations in pest populations, surrounding vegetation and the like. Still, there are too many of these success stories repeated for too many years for them to be entirely discounted. An awful lot of gardeners swear that they work. Visit thousands of country gardens in the South, and you'll find castor beans grown to keep away moles. Growers from the West Coast to the East Coast, myself included, seem convinced that garlic reduces aphids on roses and other plants. Marigolds have found their way into just about every vegetable garden, as a cure for just about any horticultural ill.

Probably because of our strong convictions as gardeners, some researchers have begun to investigate these claims. In their search for new pest control methods, they have turned to many traditional companion plants. Yet, where traditional pest control plantings almost exclusively involve plants with strong scents or other obviously repellent qualities, scientific research covers a whole range of mechanisms based on the complex chemical and physical interactions of plants and insects.

How Insects Feed

Before companion planting can become an effective tool for pest control, researchers must examine the ways pests identify and locate their host plants. Already, much work has been done in this area, and some of it is particularly interesting to gardeners. The more we can discover about insect-plant relationships, the better able we will be to predict which plants can interfere with this process.

Most insects rely on three senses to locate their food— sight, smell and taste. The colors and shapes of flowers help pollinators find the entrance to receptacles containing nectar. In general, however, an insect's sense of smell and occasionally taste are much more important than sight in locating and feeding on host plants.

Insects have very sensitive receptors on their feet and mouthparts. This gives them a keen chemical sense, so they are often able to detect certain odors several miles away. This sensitivity varies from species to species and even between the sexes. An insect's sensitivity to some substances may be quite high, while to others it's almost nil. An understanding of each pest's sense of taste or smell may be crucial in the search for an effective companion planting deterrent.

How Plants Fight Back

It's no wonder insects have developed such sensitivity. Plants are sophisticated chemical factories—they've had to be in order to survive and prevail over these past 350 million years. While insects chew and suck and scrape away at their tissues, plants fight back with some pretty sophisticated weaponry. Each species produces a whole line of substances Du Pont would be proud of. A tiny bit of plant tissue may contain not only nutrients and water but also insecticides, fungicides, antibiotics, antivirants (substances that work against viruses) and dozens of more subtle defense chemicals. Many plant-produced substances are very similar to insect pheromones—those chemicals produced and released by insects to cause a certain behavior (for example, egg laying, flying, feeding, mating) in other insects.

Research with secondary plant chemicals includes some of the most exciting work in biochemistry. Developments over the past 20 years have led to a whole new understanding of plants not as passive victims of their environments but as active, responsive organisms able to practically manipulate the insects that associate with them. Not only do plants manufacture these powerful chemicals, but it seems that they're even able to control their release and strength. The plant's age, the season, the amount of stress they're undergoing and sometimes even the health of other nearby individuals of the species all affect the balance and availability of secondary plant chemicals. This gives plants a very active defense system against insects, foraging animals and diseases. Of the many types of chemical substances plants produce, four are of major importance in companion planting. These are attractants, stimulants, deterrents and repellents.

Attractants

These are the substances that draw insects toward the plant. As early as 1910, E. Verschaffelt discovered that cabbageworms and the adult moths are attracted by the mustard oils in their host plants. Since then, much research has been done with cole crops and other plants. We now realize that once cabbage plants have been even slightly injured, more mustard oils are produced, attracting more and more pests. One of the sulfur compounds that gives onions their pungent, tear-producing odor attracts female onion maggots just before egg laying. Likewise, codling moths respond to an attractant in apple skins.

Stimulants

These encourage insects to feed or lay eggs. Cucumber beetles respond to bitter chemical stimulants in melons, cucumbers and squash. Female Mexican bean beetles will not lay eggs unless bean plants are present to stimulate the process.

Deterrents

Insects are inhibited from feeding or egg laying by these substances. The same mustard oils that attract cabbageworms sicken or even kill various flies, mosquitoes, spider mites, pea aphids and Mexican bean beetles upon contact.

Repellents

When insects are forced to move away from the plants,

(continued on page 40)

Sophisticated Weaponry

Within hours after Colorado potato beetles begin their nibbling, the injured potato or tomato plants start mustering their defensive forces. They begin manufacturing a powerful inhibitor—a chemical that presumably gives the beetle a bad case of indigestion. This substance, discovered by

Clarence Ryan at Washington State University, appears not only in the chewed leaves but throughout the entire plant, even on untouched leaves.

Major commercial crops (wheat, rice, corn, clover, alfalfa, soybeans and all solanaceous crops) and lots of trees respond to insect attack with the same sort of chemical defenses. Although some plant-produced chemicals, such as growth inhibitors, have delayed effects on pests, all help keep insect populations in check.

Plants fight disease in a similar way. When infected by a fungus or bacterium, they begin manufacturing antibiotics (called phytoalexins) in cells adjacent to the diseased ones. Rice, potatoes, beets, carrots, beans, wheat, peas, barley, cotton and possibly many other plants are able to heal themselves in this way.

Someday, farmers might be able to spray their crops with a substance to make them disease or insect resistant. Already, Peter Albersheim, a University of Colorado biochemist, has identified some of the ways phytoalexins might be released without a disease being present. Monsanto Agricultural Products Company is looking at commercial applications.

Fantastic as it sounds, at least some plant species are able to alert their neighbors about invading pests. A discovery by University of Washington biochemist David Rhoades and subsequent work by Dartmouth's Jack Schultz have shown that some airborne chemical message is released by leaves or perhaps the unwitting pests themselves. Whatever the mechanism, neighboring plants of the same species take note and set up the appropriate chemical defenses before they're even attacked. Studies of willow trees showed that just two weeks after the first trees were attacked by caterpillars, nearby willows produced identical chemicals, which slowed the insect's growth. Sugar maple and poplar trees have been found to behave in the same way.

repellents are at work. These are so closely allied to deterrents that it's often impossible to tell whether a certain plant chemical is driving the insect away (as a repellent would do) or whether it is a deterrent, which discourages feeding or egg laying. Repellents have, however, been identified and isolated from numerous cultivated and wild plants. Some, such as citronella, have important commercial uses (you'll find citronella in pest-repellent candles and sprays). Applications for other repellent plants have yet to be discovered, although current research suggests some possibilities. In one laboratory study, a single compound extracted from catnip repelled some 17 species of insects. Juglone, in the black walnut, keeps elm bark beetles from lighting on or eating that tree. A species of wild potato (*Solanum berthaultii*) repels aphids by releasing a substance, similar to aphid alarm pheromones, from sticky hairs on its leaves and stems. Air several inches above the plant's leaves contains enough of the volatile compound to keep aphids from landing.

Chemicals in each of these groups have obvious agricultural applications. They are largely responsible for many plants' evolutionary survival, and if we understood them better, these chemicals could possibly improve the survival of our crop plants. Plant breeders have focused on these chemicals in trying to develop resistant varieties. Many of our most important pesticides and herbicides have been developed from actual plant extracts or synthetic versions of them.

How Insects Respond

For their part, insects have developed complex ways to handle this amazing assortment of plant chemicals. They may respond by altering their feeding patterns—perhaps chewing on a leaf just until the chemical response is initiated, then moving on to a fresh one. Sometimes pests develop a genetic resistance to a plant-produced chemical, just as they would to a man-made pesticide. Occasionally, as in the case of aphids, the insects become so tuned in to the way their host functions that they respond to changes in its composition, or even influence the movement of nutrients within the plant to their own advantage.

How does all of this relate to companion planting? For gardeners and farmers, it remains to be seen which of these plant-produced substances can affect neighboring crops. With factors of allelopathy and cultural methods clouding the issue, it's difficult to draw any conclusions, but some studies are encouraging. Field experiments with different cropping combinations have produced interesting but mixed results. Some researchers have found that plants with powerful attractants may be used to draw beneficial insects or to trap pests. A few traditional repellent plants have performed well under experimental conditions, but some have demonstrated no pest protection, and still others have actually attracted the very insects they were meant to deter.

Plant Defense Guilds

A landmark study by ecologists Peter Atsatt and Dennis O'Dowd in 1976 pointed out the many ways plants use mechanical as well as chemical means to help each other in the war against insects. Atsatt and O'Dowd coined the phrase "plant defense guilds" to mean a kind of good neighbor policy by which plants of all shapes and sizes, from the largest trees to the smallest weeds, protect one another. These defense guilds function in three ways: as nursery plants that attract and harbor beneficial insects; as repellent plants that use toxins, odors or physical barriers to deter pests; and as decoy or trap plants that lure pests away from crops.

If, as gardeners, we are aware of this idea of guilds involving our crops, we can manipulate them to our advantage through intercropping or by using hedgerows or cover crops. In some instances, guilds extend over such great distances that we may need to manage surrounding vegetation as well as plants within the garden's borders.

Companions as Repellent Plants

Lots of well-documented examples demonstrate how various wild plants protect themselves and others with physical barriers such as thorns and shade, and chemical ones such as toxins, repellents and feeding deterrents. These findings are just now being applied to cultivated plants with some interesting and revolutionary results.

Physical Repellents

The physical fortresses some plants create are easy to spot. Spines, thorns or hairs repel animals, protecting not only the plant that has them, but those growing nearby as well. Grasses and weeds growing in the shadow of a prickly cactus or thorny bush obviously enjoy protection from birds and even some insects. As Atsatt and O'Dowd summarized in their discussion of plant defense guilds, fescue and other grasses that associate themselves with the noxious buttercup weed are saved from grazing cattle. Another example, a parasitic plant, *Pedicularis densiflora*, grows only in the shade of oak trees in order to avoid the checkerspot butterfly, which would otherwise feed on it. This butterfly, like most, seeks out warm, sunny areas to feed.

It seems reasonable to suspect that these sorts of physical relationships are also at work among cultivated plants and pests. Tall crops or hedges that border gardens often serve as combination trap and repellent for aphids and other wind-borne insects and disease. These windbreaks create a turbulent strip on both sides where aphids are deposited. Such zones typically measure one times the hedgerow height to the windward side and three to six times the height to the leeward side. In some studies, the effect is so dramatic that aerial photographs of fields show brown borders where aphids have been dumped by the wind. Of course, small beneficial insects as well as pests are among the insects deposited, so the overall effect might not always be as positive.

A familiar garden crop may have a beneficial windbreak effect similar to hedges. In a study by Stephen Risch, sweet potatoes were interplanted with corn. Two beetles (*Diabrotica* species) were effectively controlled on the sweet potato vines. Repellency was most effective where the corn was taller than 20 inches, indicating that a change in air currents may have discouraged the pests.

There are other ways plants may serve as physical repellents. Some researchers feel that the lower soil temperatures created by short, dense crops may slow the development of certain harmful fungi. By this reasoning, companion plantings of clover, beans or squash might be expected to prevent smut or root rot in corn. Yet by the same token, the same cool, humid conditions

Insect Interceptor: *Although you can't actually see it, tall crops and hedges create a strip of air turbulence on both sides. When you surround the garden with a windbreak like this, aphids and other wind-borne insects are deposited in the hedge, instead of in the garden.*

might encourage mildew or other diseases. More work needs to be done before any recommendations can be given.

Researcher Judith Smith's study of aphids on Brussels sprouts showed that weedy ground covers make it harder for pests to locate their host plants. Any low-growing companion crop that thoroughly covers the ground (such as cress or lettuce) might similarly protect Brussels sprouts or other garden cole crops. If you decide to try this in your own garden, plan to get the ground covered early in the season, before the aphids become active.

Chemical Repellents

Indisputable proof of actual chemical repellency from companion plantings is hard to come by. We do know that many plants use chemicals to protect themselves. Extracts of some of these plants repel certain insects when they're sprayed on crops. One study showed that cabbage butterflies laid fewer eggs on plants sprayed with an extract of either thyme or sage. Odors of both dandelion and meadow grass have repelled Colorado potato beetles.

We also know that many, perhaps most, insects rely on smell and taste to find their host plants. It seems reasonable to suspect that certain other volatile plant chemicals could mask those attracting odors or actively repel insects just as companion planting lore suggests.

The testimonies of organic gardeners regarding repellent plants have no doubt inspired much of the field work being done in this area. More often than not, these experiments have been inconclusive at best and negative at worst. The fact that mixed plantings interfere with pests' ability to sniff out their host plants is well documented. The extent to which a specific aromatic or other companion plant actually repels insects is another matter. Still, several important studies have shown some promise for this method.

Companions That Show Promise

Repellent plantings that have performed well in controlled experiments include nasturtiums against whiteflies, southernwood against egg-laying cabbage butterflies, potatoes against Mexican bean beetles and tomatoes and tobacco against flea beetles.

Diane Matthews, entomologist at the Rodale Research Center, has looked at some of these as well as a number of other aromatic companions. Her results are inconclusive but encouraging nonetheless. Against Colorado potato beetles, interplants of catnip, coriander, nasturtiums and tansy each had some effect. Catnip and nasturtiums also repelled green peach aphids on bell peppers. Interplants of catnip and tansy each caused significant reductions of squash bugs infesting zucchini squash plants.

Cornell entomologists Jorma Tahvanainen and Richard Root studied a particular species of flea beetle in collards intercropped with ragweed or tomatoes. Pure stands of collards had more adult beetles, and the insects colonized there more rapidly than in mixed plantings. Follow-up work done in the laboratory showed that chemicals given off by the tomatoes and ragweed interfered with the pest's ability to find and feed on its host crop.

Tomatoes may repel whiteflies and diamondback moths from cabbage. Work carried out in the Philippines by R. P. Buranday and R. S. Raros demonstrated that fields planted in alternate rows of cabbage and tomatoes had fewer eggs and adult moths. They concluded that volatile compounds given off by tomato plants probably repelled the moths. For optimum pest control, the researchers recommend planting two cabbage rows between every two rows of tomato bushes.

The Power of Marigolds

Probably the best known, yet also most misunderstood, work with repellent plantings concerns marigolds. These flowers have long been interplanted among vegetable crops in India, they're included in very old European lists of beneficial herbs, and today are given a prominent spot in most organic gardeners' hearts. Nevertheless, until fairly recently, the powers of the humble marigold were little understood.

In the 1940s, African (*Tagetes erecta*) and French (*T. patula*) marigolds were found to resist root-knot nematodes. These early studies showed that larvae that penetrated the roots would not lay eggs. Turning under a cover crop of marigolds increased yields 141 percent by reducing nematode populations. In the home garden, this means that you plant the nematode-infested area with nothing but marigolds, let them grow all season, then turn them under at season's end so the roots can decay. Once the plant matter has broken down, you can then resume planting your usual vegetable crops.

Through further investigation, toxic chemicals and some feeding deterrents have been isolated. These substances take effect quite rapidly, even before roots decay. In one study, nematodes were reduced to low levels 42 to 70 days after planting.

Furthermore, the control seems to last. Tomatoes grown in soil previously planted entirely to marigolds had 75 percent fewer nematode cysts. Some researchers have suggested that the marigold's controlling influence on certain nematode species can remain effective as long as three years after the marigold cover crop has been turned under.

Interplanting with marigolds also offers good nematode control since some toxic chemicals and feeding deterrents are released by growing roots. However, you may not realize the benefits as rapidly or as dramatically as in rotation plantings, where you plant an area entirely to marigolds for a season. In a Rhodesian study, tomatoes interplanted with marigolds enjoyed considerable protection. In India, marigold companions protected cabbage, cauliflower, tomatoes, peppers, eggplants and potatoes. A Japanese study showed that sowing marigolds 24 inches apart virtually eliminates the effects of nematodes. This makes it possible to interplant them between all sorts of crops.

Other work with marigolds suggests that they may also be effective repellents or deterrents against other pests. In a 1982 study at Brookhaven National Laboratory, R. P. Cort studied Colorado potato beetles' response to interplantings of beans and marigolds. Fewer beetles moved into intercropped fields so that it appeared that the companion marigolds masked the attracting odors of the bean plants. Cort stopped short of suggesting that these interplants actively repelled the beetles. After carefully examining movement patterns, he concluded that neither the marigolds nor the beans released effective repellents.

There's a lot of evidence to warn us that marigolds aren't the wonder plants some would have us believe. Garden traditions maintain that marigolds will protect our crops against Mexican bean beetles. Several experiments by M. A. Latheef have shown this to be true, but Latheef warns that all marigolds don't necessarily make ideal interplants. While French marigolds do indeed repel the beetles and are very effective against corn earworms on beans, they also seem to exude toxins, which harm the bean plants. As an interplant with cabbage, French marigolds provided no protection against cabbage loopers, imported cabbageworms, diamondback moths or cabbage webworms. It's even possible that the marigolds themselves attracted egg-laying moths.

Summing Up Repellent Plants

These are not the only studies to which critics of the repellent planting theory turn. Matthews found that several traditional aromatic companion crops had no effect on pests. In fact, she observed that catnip and tansy interplants encouraged imported cabbageworms to feast on broccoli. Latheef drew similar conclusions about interplantings of many aromatic herbs among collards. It may be that imported cabbageworms actually prefer to lay eggs in environments created by these companions over those created by monocroppings of their host plant.

In some cases, companions effectively repel the target pest but not enough to fully protect crops. Researchers Koehler, Barclay and Kretchun at University of California's Deciduous Fruit Field Station in San Jose evaluated several companion plantings as repellents against cabbage and bean pests. After studying anise, marigolds, nasturtiums, catnip, summer savory and basil, they concluded that while many of these plants significantly reduced pest populations, they competed with main crops and therefore reduced yields. Furthermore, their powers of repellency weren't great enough to prevent all damage to plants; worm injury to cabbage was still a problem, even where catnip, nasturtium and marigold interplants reduced larvae and egg numbers. Again, this conclusion echoes work by Latheef; in one of his experiments, flea beetles were repelled by southernwood, tansy and wormwood, but the collards still suffered serious pest injury.

These findings shouldn't totally discourage growers interested in companion planting. Repellent plantings *do* have potential. While large scale growers might not wish to rely wholly on these repellent plantings to protect their crops, repellent companions may prove useful as part of an integrated pest management program, along with cultivation, rotation, and the use of safe sprays and dusts. Used in this way, repellent plants can significantly reduce the costs and dangers of using chemical insecticides. This is especially true with companions such as tomatoes, which have an economic value.

In the home garden or on a small farm, where plots are carefully tended by hand, companion plants that significantly reduce pest populations make sense. When insects do find crops and begin laying their eggs and munching away, you can easily remove them with occasional hand-picking or dusting with relatively safe biological insecticides such as *Bacillus thuringiensis*, rotenone and pyrethrum.

Companions as Nursery Plants

Nursery plants are species that attract and harbor beneficial insects. In an important study by Stephen Gliessman and Miguel Altieri, collards intercropped with beans had many more wasp parasites than monocropped collard fields, resulting in four times fewer aphids. With less aphid damage, the mixed plots had the greatest number of harvestable collard leaves per unit of area.

Companion plants like the beans offer predators and parasites nectar, pollen, shelter and/or the alternative hosts they need at some point in their life cycles. (Alternative hosts can be either plants or pests.) Almost all types of plants function as nurseries for some insects. In some cases, a mixture of various weeds can serve the purpose quite well. In other instances, insect-plant associations are more specific and limited, with only a certain species of plant satisfying a finicky beneficial insect. In gardening and farming, the key is to cultivate the most appropriate plants for maintaining the beneficials best able to control target pests.

Flowers for Nectar and Pollen

Gardeners are familiar with the many flowering plants that draw butterflies and honeybees to the vegetable patch and orchard for pollination. Bee balm, various mints, hyssop, salvia, loosestrife and dozens of other brightly blossomed plants come to mind. These flowers and many less flashy species play even more important roles as nursery plants. Their scents and colors attract trichogramma, braconid and chalcid wasps, hover flies, predatory mites, lady beetles and other beneficial insects as well. Many predators and most parasites need nectar and pollen to supplement their diet of mealybugs, aphids, and the like. These plant sources supply carbohydrates, amino acids or other compounds missing from their main hosts. Without these plants, the insect species can't survive. Farm fields, orchards and home vegetable gardens that don't include any flowering plants have low populations of these beneficial insects. Even if you buy a quart of lady beetles or lacewings or other predators and parasites to release in your garden, they won't stick around if there are no flowers. In Puerto Rico, a wasp introduced to control mole crickets failed not because there weren't enought crickets to eat, but because two important weeds were not present.

Although lots of work remains to be done on this subject, it is clear that flowering plants are an important component of a healthy garden ecosystem. Sometimes, flowers from the crops themselves or from ornamental plants provide nectar and pollen; for example, cotton and peach trees are good sources for some insect species and alyssum, yarrow or marigolds attract others. Showy, hybrid flowers don't always fill the nectar niche, however. They've been bred to please our senses, not the insects' senses. More often, insects seek out wildflowers. Insects don't share our aesthetic tastes and often prefer a lowly weed with modest flower clusters over the most gorgeous, sweetest smelling cultivated flower. When nearby weeds are in flower, braconid wasps are more efficient in parasitizing alfalfa caterpillars. In an apple orchard, wildflowers attracted enough parasites to increase by 4 to 18 times the number of tent caterpillars and codling moths that were destroyed.

Favorite Flowers

Certain botanical families seem to appeal to specific groups of insects. Members of the carrot family, including dill, celery, parsnips, coriander, ginseng and Queen Anne's lace, are favored by most of the wasps and tachinid and ichneumonid flies. Studies of cabbage fields in the Soviet Union showed substantially more parasites in fields where flowering carrot family plants grew nearby. In New Jersey, stands of wild carrot plants were necessary to sustain parasites of the Japanese beetle. A Canadian report on wasps that prey on white cabbageworms, tent caterpillars and pine-shoot moths showed that wasps live five times longer, and hence lay scores more eggs, when Queen Anne's lace, milkweed, buckwheat and catnip are present. These plants provide nectar during a critical period when the prey the wasps feed on is unavailable.

Hover flies go for the daisy family. Some well-known members include black-eyed Susans, coreopsis, asters, goldenrod, chamomile, bachelor's buttons, Joe-pye weed, yarrow and marigolds. Hover flies also like flowering cole crops like mustard. The females need to fill up on nectar just before depositing their eggs, one-by-one, in aphid colonies.

Diane Matthews tells me that lady beetles like tansy. At the Rodale Research Center, females in the greenhouse and field seek out tansy as a place to lay their eggs. They're also attracted to yarrow.

Flowers aren't the only nectar source for beneficial insects. They can also get a drink from the leaves, stems and stalks of plants that have special structures called extrafloral nectaries. These tiny glands ooze nectar, attracting not only aphids and ants but many parasitic wasps as well. Extrafloral nectaries are found in all kinds of plants, from cherries and elderberries to Jerusalem artichokes and pokeweed. The unlikeliest of species may be a critical food source for the beneficial insects that keep certain pests under control. Watch for beneficials in and around your garden or yard, and notice where they feed. These plants may be worth keeping in a hedgerow or weedy border.

A Source of Alternate Hosts

In addition to nectar and pollen, nursery plants also supply alternate prey for beneficial insects. An outstanding example of this function has been noted in wild grapes and successfully put to use in California vineyards.

Grapes can be devastated by the grape leafhopper. The egg parasite *Anagrus epos* is an effective control, but it needs an alternate host to feed on, particularly in early spring before grape leafhoppers emerge. Nature has the answer. In February, another leafhopper, *Dikrella cruentatu*, emerges and lays eggs on new blackberry leaves. *Anagrus epos* moves in, parasitizing the eggs and building up its own numbers so that its population peaks just when nearby grapes leaf out. This is the time when grape leafhoppers wake up from their winter sleep to begin laying *their* eggs. Temperatures might change the emergence dates from one year to another, but the sequence of events remains the same. Genetic selection seems to have favored later grape plants over those that might leaf out earlier. Grape leaves and the grape leafhopper's first round of egg laying always seem to wait until blackberry leaves appear and *Dikrella cruentatu* has laid its eggs. This gives the egg parasite a chance to digest its first big meal before it starts on the grape leafhopper eggs.

In light of this relationship, researchers suggest that grape growers leave a border of wild or cultivated blackberry plants around their fields so that this same defense guild can join forces in cultivated vineyards. Studies have shown that blackberry plants can be up to four miles away from the grapevines and still provide effective control of the leafhopper, although closer plantings are obviously better.

There are other examples, as well, of companion plants for orchard and vegetable crops that harbor alternative hosts. Altieri has shown that interplantings of soybeans, bush beans or even low-growing weeds provide alternate hosts for predators of fall armyworms that attack corn. In an orchard experiment with pest management consultant Kate Burroughs, Altieri found that winter cover crops of bell beans (similar to fava beans) or weeds provided aphids for hover flies, lacewings and lady beetles to feed on in early spring and summer. Once the beans dried out and aphid populations declined, insect predators moved into the fruit trees. Burroughs and Altieri found twice as many predators in the trees that were growing in the cover crop as they did in orchards without cover crops.

For the most part, studies stop short of explaining an increase of beneficials as due to any single factor. It seems clear, though, that the presence of alternate hosts is important.

An Attractive Habitat

Some companion plants serve as nurseries by offering shade and shelter to beneficial insect species. The dark, cool, moist conditions created by dense plantings and ground covers especially appeal to ground beetles and spiders. It's interesting to note that the very conditions that beneficials seek out are the same ones that most pest species flee. This keeps the balance of good bugs to bad bugs tipped in your favor. In a study of imported cabbageworms on Brussels sprouts, F. P. Dempster found that weedy plots had more predators and fewer caterpillars. Other studies showed that white or red clover companion plantings among cabbage provided shelter for spiders and ground beetles. A peanut interplanting in corn also helped spiders control corn borers, and a band of moss or weeds around peach tree trunks offered shelter to numerous predators and parasites.

Using Nursery Plants to Your Advantage

Ideally, gardens and agricultural fields should be surrounded by nursery hedgerows that include a mixture of flowering plants, as well as various perennials, trees and shrubs. You should select species on the basis of flowering cycles so that a variety of plants are blooming throughout the growing year. In the typical backyard, where open space is at a premium, you may need to plant some nectar plants in the garden itself and possibly allow a few scattered vegetable plants to go to seed. Among the carrot family, dill, anise, cumin and coriander all interplant fairly easily and bloom readily. Parsley, carrots and celery are biennials, but they're easy to overwinter for early blooms the following summer. Don't forget that as relatives of the carrots, all of these plants host the same disease organisms and pests, in addition to the beneficial wasps they attract. Don't plant them alongside other family members especially where carrot flies, carrot weevils or other family pests and diseases have been present, or you're likely to compound your problem.

Hover flies and lacewings are drawn to the daisylike flowers of the composite family, so you should plan on including some of these plants in your backyard, if not in the vegetable garden itself. Marigolds, particularly the dwarf or low-growing types, interplant easily and bloom all season long. For other flowers in the same family, choose from small chrysanthemums, single asters, chamomile and all the various kinds of daisies. You may even want to allow a few lettuce plants to finish out the season in the garden after they have bolted. Their limp tufts of flowers add whimsy to the midsummer garden and attract plenty of wasps and syrphids since lettuce, too, is a composite plant.

Companions as Decoy and Trap Plants

Trap plants serve as alternate food for pests, luring them

Nursery Hedgerow: *Create an attractive habitat for beneficial insects by surrounding the garden with a hedgerow of appealing plants. Include flowering ones like chamomile, asters, chrysanthemums and daisies. You might even have room for a dwarf fruit tree, like the small apple tree at the corner of this hedge. Be sure to leave enough room between garden beds and the nursery hedgerow so there's no stressful competition or overcrowding.*

away from the main crop, where you can then destroy them. Decoys do this and more. As pests feed on decoy plants, they get sick or lose their ability to lay eggs. Traps and decoys are time-honored techniques for managing insects. In India, a species of hibiscus is grown as a trap crop around cotton plants. Eighteenth-century garden books recommended radishes or spinach among cauliflower as a trap for "the fly." Mullein is often suggested as a trap for stink bugs in apple orchards, and borage is recommended for use against Japanese beetles. Organic gardeners through the ages have suggested all kinds of trap crops—borders of goldenrod for cucumber beetles, lamb's-quarters or pigweed for gophers, nasturtiums for aphids and sunflowers for corn earworms.

Research has confirmed only a few of these associations, but many studies have shown that decoy and trap relationships among plants do indeed exist and can be used effectively. Today, decoy or trap cropping is widely practiced by some of the most chemically oriented farmers. Soybean growers often plant a small trap area of soybeans one to two weeks before they sow the main crop. These diversionary plots are located near bean leaf beetle hibernation areas so the overwintering adults tend to stay there when they emerge. Although most farmers then use pesticides to destroy the trapped pests, it is also possible and practical to eliminate them by releasing a parasite or predator into the infested area. Mexican bean beetles are trapped in a similar fashion by small plantings of lima beans.

Other crops that have been tested include wild squash vines as traps for corn rootworms on corn, and spiny amaranth as a trap for black cutworms on beans, cucumbers or tomatoes. Often, only a very small amount of the trapping companion is needed. For example, narrow strips of alfalfa in cotton fields effectively trap lygus bugs even when only 5 percent of the total acreage is in alfalfa.

Some plants send out chemicals or other attractants that draw pests. Then, once they've lured them in, the plants finish off the insects with toxins or hormones. Marigolds work in this way with some pests and as repellents against others. While most nematodes seem to be repelled by marigold roots, some of these worms do penetrate and feed on the plant tissue. Once they've feasted away, however, they don't develop properly. Other plants, including castor beans (*Ricinus* spp.), rattlebox (*Crotalaria spectabilis*) and certain *Chrysanthemum* species also make good nematode decoy crops.

Black nightshade (*Solanum nigrum*) is a proven decoy plant for potatoes infested with Colorado potato beetles. For some reason relating to chemical attractants, adult beetles prefer to lay eggs on the nightshade rather than on the potatoes. When the eggs hatch, the larvae feed on this poisonous weed and die.

It's important to realize that these companion plants may be quite difficult to manage. Trap and decoy cropping is a tricky business. You need to know exactly how and when insects feed, move and colonize in order to properly manage your companion plantings. You can learn this by consulting books such as *Rodale's Color Handbook of Garden Insects* (Rodale Press, 1979) and by watching insect behavior in your own garden. Pests may be attracted to a given plant just because there's nothing better to eat. Like a kid looking at a plate of broccoli when the apple pie appears, some pests quickly move on to the main crop as soon as it is available.

What to Do about Weeds?

In the face of all this evidence of weeds as nursery, repellent and trap plants, it may appear that pulling out a clump of weeds is a horticulturally criminal act. Some people would say it is—at least if you haven't identified the plants. No one is advocating a complete surrender to the plants that invade and often overrun the garden or field. Every gardener knows that weeds' competition for nutrients, moisture and space can destroy a crop. Many weeds harbor disease organisms or insect pests, and to give these plants the run of the garden is likely to spell trouble for any food crops you're trying to grow. But not all weeds are villains— some do offer advantages in certain situations. Completely clean fields and gardens, with virtually no weeds in or around them, are highly susceptible to pests and diseases. We have seen that many flowering weeds provide food and shelter for valuable predators and parasites, others trap pests, and still others emit powerful feeding deterrents. Weeds penetrate the soil to bring nutrients up to the plow zone, and they break up and aerate the soil to the

(continued on page 58)

Read Your Weeds!

Weeds (or wildflowers, depending on your point of view) can offer all kinds of clues about the health of the garden and the species of pests and beneficial insects most likely to frequent it. Before you pull them up or plow them under, take a few minutes to identify the weeds in your garden. One good guide to consult is *Peterson's Field Guide to Wildflowers* (Houghton Mifflin, 1968). Learn to read what they tell you about your soil, and find out what beneficial insects they may host.

Weed	Soil Condition	Remarks
Barnyard grass (*Echinochloa crus-galli*)	Any	Residue reduces corn growth.
Black nightshade (*Solanum nigrum*)	Any	Decoy to Colorado potato beetles.
Butterfly milkweed (*Asclepias tuberosa*)	Any	Good host for parasite of cabbageworms, tent caterpillars and codling moths; extract applied to corn seed before planting deters wireworms and rootworms; substance in leaves may harm crops.
Canada thistle (*Cirsium arvuse*)	Nitrogen deficiency	Good pollen source.
Cattail (*Typha latifolia*)	Poorly drained	Supports alternate host for predator of Willamette mites on grapes.
Clover (*Trifolium* spp.)	Nitrogen deficiency	Shelters ground beetles; attracts pollinators; some species support parasite of woolly apple aphids.
Daisy (*Chrysanthemum* spp.)	Acid	Attracts wasps; good pollen source.

Weed	Soil Condition	Remarks
Dandelion (*Taraxacum officinale*)	Acid, poorly drained	Attracts wasps; good pollen source; repels Colorado potato beetles; encourages fruit and flowers to ripen quickly.
Foxtail (*Setaria faberii*)	Any	Residue or live plants enhance soybean growth but reduce corn growth.
Goldenrod (*Solidago* spp.)	Any	Supports alternate hosts for beneficial insects; reduces growth of black locust and sugar maple to some extent.
Goosegrass (*Eleusine indica*)	Any	May reduce leafhoppers on beans.
Johnson grass (*Sorgum halepense*)	Any	Hosts predator of Willamette mites on grapes.
Lamb's-quarters (*Chenopodium album*)	Any	Reduces soybean yield.
Larkspur (*Delphinium* spp.)	Acid	Roots toxic to bean leaf rollers, cabbageworms, cabbage loopers.
Lawn grasses (many different species)	Any	Turf suppresses growth of trees, shrubs.
Nutsedge (*Cyperus* spp.)	Any	Roots decrease nitrogen availability to corn.
Pepperweed (*Lepidium alysoides*)	Alkaline	Supports alternate hosts for many beneficial insects.
Pigweed (*Amaranthus retroflexus*)	Dry	Supports many potential pests and beneficial insects; extract of pigweed on corn increases parasitization of corn earworms.

Weed	Soil Condition	Remarks
Quack grass (*Agropyron repens*)	Acid, wet	Reduces growth and yields of corn, alfalfa and possibly other crops.
Ragweed (*Polygonum* spp.)	Any	Provides alternate hosts for parasite of strawberry leaf rollers; may repel cabbage flea beetles and other pests.
Spurge (*Euphorbia* spp.)	Dry, sandy	Even small amount of litter reduces tomato growth.
Spurry (*Spergula* spp.)	Light acid	Shelters many predators and parasites.
Wild blackberry (*Rubus procerus*)	Any	Hosts parasite of grape leafhoppers.
Wild mustard (*Brassica hirta*)	Alkaline	Provides food for beneficial wasps; supports parasite of some aphids and larval pests; produces substance that attracts diamond-back moths and inhibits emergence of cyst nematodes.
Yarrow (*Achillea* spp.)	Any	Excellent nectar and pollen source for wasps.

benefit of other crops. They are also outstanding at controlling soil erosion. Despite their lowly status in the minds of most gardeners, weeds can be excellent helpmates.

You may be a bit skeptical about the idea that weeds have a rightful place in the garden, but in many cases, higher yields have been obtained in weedy plots than in those that were clean cultivated. Work done with corn, beans and other crops has shown that weeds can be maintained at tolerable levels with minimal competition and maximum pest control benefits. Taking into account their possible advantages and disadvantages, the ideal solution is to control but not eliminate weeds. Studies have shown that interplanting, particularly with close spacing and the use of ground covers, keeps weed growth to an optimum level for insect control. When crops are grown in close quarters they form a tight canopy, shutting out light from the low-growing weeds.

Of course, some weeds are more easily tolerated than others. A lot depends on the weeds themselves and on the crops being grown. Altieri found that, in most cases, weeds threaten crop plants only during the first two to four weeks after crops emerge. After that initial period when the seedlings are becoming established, weeds contribute more to the crop's well being than they detract from it. As long as air can circulate and soil nutrients and water are in good supply, disease problems aren't likely to occur. You can control the weeds by regular clipping so foliage remains at or below the height of the main crop. If that offends your sensibilities toward a "clean" garden, then strip cropping weeds in bands within the garden may be more appealing.

In fact, it's not always necessary or even preferable to let weeds grow *in* the garden in order to enjoy their benefits. If you carefully plan your companion planting so there's a wide variety of herbs and food crops, the resulting mixture of plants should provide a good ground cover and diversity of plant species. Pest populations should remain fairly low, and at least some beneficial insects should be present. Nearby weedy hedgerows or borders (the closer to the garden the better) can then provide the extras— nectar, pollen and alternate hosts—for a large population of beneficials until they are needed in the garden.

The key to making this sort of weed-crop association work is timing. Weeds must provide the beneficial insects with alternate prey when garden pests aren't available, and the alternates must be *less* attractive when the garden pest population starts to climb. If the weeds' alternate prey and the garden's pests are available simultaneously, the beneficial insects may just decide to stay where they are, on the weeds, and let the pests devour your crops.

One technique for handling this is to let weeds grow until the beneficial population builds up, then mow them down. This leaves the insects no choice but to move on to the food crops. This strategy is used in orchards where a permanent ground cover of clover or mixed grasses is maintained. Timing in such strategies is crucial—you must understand not only what the beneficials like to eat but also their life cycles. Experiments with stinging nettle (which harbors nearly a dozen species of beneficial insects) showed that destroying the weed at just the right time could force predators into nearby bean fields.

The time when insects emerge and their feeding patterns are different for each geographic area. Check with the local agricul-

(continued on page 62)

Weeds Associated with Disease

In general, most weeds and other native plants belonging to the same genus, or even the same family as a cultivated crop, host the same pests and diseases. We have seen, however, that this is not always true. Wild potatoes repel the very pest that our cultivated species seem to attract from miles around. It seems likely that many of our "thoroughbred" crops have had the fight bred out of them. Somehow, in selecting for sweetness, succulence and the like, we've lost the genes for pest resistance.

As far as disease goes, many weeds are capable of serving as carriers while exhibiting few, if any, signs of the disease. For this reason, it's sometimes a good idea to keep cultivated varieties away from wild ones. For instance, keep domestic cucumbers away from wild cucumbers, cultivated brambles away from wild ones, and so on. In the well-tended home garden, disease is rarely the problem it becomes in large, monocropped farm fields. Most researchers feel that intercropping, as long as it doesn't mix two crops susceptible to the same disease, tends to diminish the incidence of disease.

However, no garden can ever be entirely disease-free. Running water, birds, insects, wind and gardeners themselves all carry infection. To cut down on the damage such infection does, take care to use resistant varieties, and rotate crops every season. Maintain good soil health by adding organic matter and balanced organic fertilizers. Destroy any diseased plant material, and when in doubt, don't add any you suspect to be diseased to the compost pile. When you water, do a thorough job, but don't water more often than necessary. A soggy garden is the perfect breeding ground for a host of disease problems. Don't handle wet leaves, and never touch solanaceous plants if you've been smoking. (This group includes potatoes, tomatoes, peppers and eggplants.) There's a chance that you may inadvertently infect these crops with tobacco mosaic virus. Be a meticulous gardener and clean up garden debris between relay plantings and at the end of the season. Finally, make some attempt to keep away weeds that might aggravate any disease problem that has already developed.

Below you'll find a list of some of the common weeds capable of spreading disease to garden crops. Just because they are present doesn't mean that diseases are, too. If air circulates and a variety of other weeds are present, you probably won't have any troubles. If, however, garden crops do show signs of infection, eliminate the associated weeds.

Weed or Native Plant	Disease	Susceptible Garden Crop
Bittersweet, chickweed, ground-cherry, horse nettle, jimson weed, mints, nightshade, pokeweed, ragweed, wild cucurbits	Mosaic virus, verticillium wilt	Cucumber, pepper, tomato
White pine	Rusts	Currant, gooseberry
Wild blackberry	Anthracnose	Raspberry
Clover, cotton, cow pea, lupine, tobacco	Root-knot nematodes (nematodes carry the disease called root knot)	Peach
Wild cherry, wild plum	Black knot	Cherry, plum
Hawthorn	Fireblight	Apple, pear, quince
Juniper	Cedar apple rust	Apple
Chokecherry	X-disease	Cherry, plum

tural extension agency and with state or province agricultural schools to learn the egg-laying, flight and feeding schedules of the pests and beneficial insects you're dealing with in your garden. Rely, too, on your own observations and experience, for ultimately they may well give you the best clue to managing your garden's ecology.

Botanical Pesticides and Repellents

Companion planting isn't the only way that plants can fight pests. In addition to strategically locating certain plants in the garden, you can also take advantage of their pest-controlling powers by using plant-derived sprays and powders.

Long before the advent of chemical pesticides, traditional farmers had a number of plant-derived poisons and repellents they relied on for pest control. Although the repellents have mostly been forgotten, the more effective pesticides are still in use today. Farmers from China to Britain have long recognized the powerful poison of *Strychnos nux-vomica*, which we now call strychnine. Nicotine sprays made from tobacco leaves were used by American Indians, and by the late seventeenth century, these sprays had become important pest controls in European gardens. By the early nineteenth century, hellebore or bear's foot was a well-known insecticide. Pyrethrum, found in several species of chrysanthemum, was familiar to Asian and European growers. Rotenone from the Malaysian derris plant is a relative newcomer, not discovered until the early nineteenth century.

The high cost of many chemical pesticides coupled with the consumer demand for substances that leave fewer residues and have less drastic environmental effects, have led to renewed interest in these botanical materials. Yet, ecologically minded growers often use these botanicals without realizing that they are, in fact, *poisons*. Like any pesticides, they have harmful effects on the environment. They may destroy beneficial insects and even mammals. Pyrethrum poisons just about all caterpillars, aphids, thrips and many beetles—regardless of whether they are plant-eaters or pest-eaters. Rotenone is also broad spectrum and is highly toxic to fish, although it loses its toxicity rapidly when exposed to sunlight. It acts as a stomach poison, while pyrethrum and nicotine destroy an insect's nervous system.

Far safer than these kinds of botanical poisons are some of the feeding deterrents and repellents extracted from plant material. Rather than kill the insect on the spot, these send the pest off in the other direction or reduce its feeding, mating or egg-laying capabilities. These plant-derived deterrents and repellents are usually quite species-specific, working only against the pest without harming beneficial insects. University research in this area is flourishing. The United States Department of Agriculture (USDA) and industrial researchers are even searching for new botanical repellents and deterrents by looking closely at traditional pest control methods and by examining other likely sources. Although the work is progressing, results are slow in coming. Out of some 3,000 plant species, which have already been studied, only 10 new substances show promise.

Often, feeding deterrents and repellents are found in the very plants that pests feed on but in such small amounts that they don't ordinarily affect the insects. When these substances are extracted and sprayed on crops, they can sometimes give protection just as complete as that given by chemical insecticides. Cotton, for example, contains a feeding deterrent that's effective against the boll weevil, a notorious pest.

Most of the work done with feeding deterrents involves nonhost plants or those plants that the insects don't normally feed on. Peppermint contains a deterrent effective agianst Colorado potato beetles. Substances in apple, cottonwood and black locust trees deter elm bark beetles. There are plenty of other examples, involving all sorts of ordinary and exotic herbs, trees, vegetables and weeds. Elwood Rice's book *Pest Control with Nature's Chemicals* (University of Oklahoma Press, 1983) gives a complete rundown on the research done up to 1983.

New discoveries are being made every day. Mike Villani at North Carolina State University has done some exciting work with feeding deterrents to control soil pests. He believes that plant substances might easily compete with the chemical seed coats and other soil pesticides that are so widespread today. Since protection against soil pests is needed only for a short time and just a small amount of material is required, botanical extracts could be practical and affordable even for farmers. In preliminary tests of 82 different plant extracts, Villani found that butterfly milkweed (*Asclepias tuberosa*) and English ivy (*Hedera helix*) extracts significantly reduced corn wireworms. Further tests with butterfly milkweed showed, however, that treated seed corn suffered some allelopathic effects such as delayed germination and lower growth rates.

(continued on page 66)

Recipes for Botanical Pesticides and Repellents

Here are a few suggestions for various botanical repellents, deterrents and pesticides that you can make from common native and cultivated plants. Most of them have only the recommendations of organic gardeners and a few ancient sources, for they haven't yet been subjected to the rigors of scientific examination. Test them under controlled conditions in your own garden. Where soap is called for, be sure to use soap such as Ivory flakes and *not* detergent, which could harm plants. Be sure to keep all these substances away from children.

Plant	Recipe	Pest-Control Claims
Anise	Cover anise leaves with water. Boil. Cool and strain. Add a touch of soap and spray on infested plants.	Said to repel aphids.
Catnip	Cover leaves and stems with water and emulsify. Strain. Add a touch of soap and spray on infested plants.	Said to repel many pests. Rodale Research Center tests showed spray possibly deters Colorado potato beetles.
Garlic	Chop 3 cloves and add to 2 tablespoons mineral oil. Soak 1 day or longer. Add 2 cups water. Emulsify in blender. Strain. Spray on infested plants.	Toxic elements have been identified. Harmful to various larvae, as well as aphids, mildew and many mammals.

Plant	Recipe	Pest-Control Claims
Nasturtium	Cover leaves and stems with water and emulsify in blender. Strain, add a touch of soap and spray on plants.	Said to repel Mexican bean beetles and cabbageworms. Rodale Research Center tests showed spray possibly deters Colorado potato beetles.
Pyrethrum* (*Chrysanthemum cinerariifolium*)	Pick flowers at full bloom. Dry completely and grind. Use as dust or mix with water to spray.	Proven to paralyze many different pests. Wait 1 week before using plant that has been sprayed.
Rhubarb*	Boil 1 pound leaves in 1 quart water for 30 minutes. Cool and strain. Spray on infested plants.	Said to kill aphids, leafminers, spider mites; controls clubroot disease; contains oxalic acid and is very toxic.
Tobacco*	Cover stems and leaves with boiling water. Let cool for several hours. Dilute 1 cup brew to 4 cups water. Spray on infested plants.	*Very* toxic to man and insect. Wait at least 2 weeks before eating plant parts that have been sprayed. Don't use on potatoes, tomatoes or eggplants because spray may spread mosaic disease.
Tomato	Chop stems, leaves, roots. Blend with a small amount of water and strain. Add a touch of soap and spray on infested plants.	Antibacterial and antifungal substances have been isolated. Hairs of wild tomato plants contain proven pest repellent.
Tree of heaven*	Boil bark in water. Strain, cool and add some soap. Spray on infested plants.	Said to repel many insects. One compound with insecticidal properties has been isolated.

*Indicates extremely toxic extracts, which should be handled with care.

Over the course of work at the University of California at Berkeley, Isao Kubo has isolated a feeding deterrent for use on cotton plants. The bitter-tasting chemical is extracted from grapefruit seeds and, when sprayed on cotton leaves, deters fall armyworms and cotton bollworms. This finding comes hot on the trail of a similar substance found in the Indian neem tree. Already well known to Indians, neem extract contains toxins and feeding deterrents. USDA researchers have found it to be effective on over 60 insect species, including cucumber beetles, Mexican bean beetles, Colorado potato beetles, aphids, mealybugs and other serious pests.

Make Your Own Botanical Pesticides

Most of us don't have a neem tree handy, but we can make our own sprays and dusts from garden plants. This is an excellent opportunity to learn about weeds and flowers and to experiment with different pest control agents. However, it shouldn't be done carelessly. Many homemade sprays are safer than chemicals you might buy at the garden shop, but some are downright dangerous. Nicotine kills just about any kind of insect, and pyrethrum is only slightly safer. Always be sure to allow two weeks to pass before harvesting a crop that you've sprayed with nicotine, and wait one week before using a pyrethrum-treated one. Don't automatically reach for the poisonous sprays or dusts when a problem develops— use these materials *only* as a last resort.

Plant-derived repellents and deterrents are safer, but you should still use them only when absolutely necessary. They do no damage to your crops and in most cases, deter only specific species so that most beneficial insects will not be affected. Still, they're not to be taken lightly. Before you reach for the sprayer, try less drastic strategies such as handpicking, companion planting and the like. Once you realize how time-consuming the task of concocting sprays and dusts can be, you'll probably be more inclined to try simpler, faster methods first, then turn to the sprays and dusts only when they're absolutely necessary.

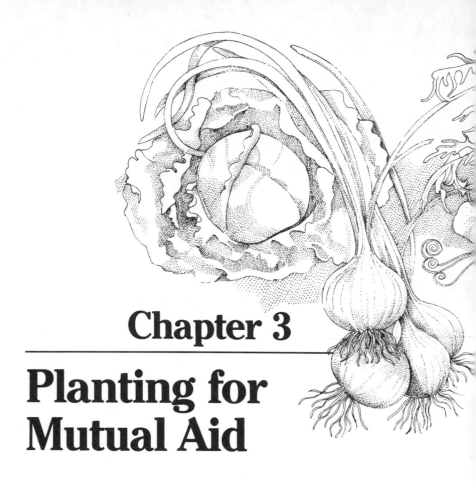

Chapter 3

Planting for Mutual Aid

Nongardeners are quick to mock the eccentric ways of the horticulturally inclined. Nowhere do they get as much ammunition as from those gardening books and articles where we growers tell all: how we sing to our roses while spreading ground banana peels and rabbit dung on the roots; how we leave a note for the groundhog, warning him politely, but in no uncertain terms, to stay away from the vegetable beds. Scattered among these gems is usually at least some mention of plant friendships. The idea is to arrange your garden so that plants can spend the season in the company of their botanical friends. They'll be happier if you try to accommodate them, and they'll reward you with bigger, tastier, more plentiful harvests. According to certain gardeners, carrots and potatoes get on famously, while tomatoes

like parsley. Lettuce loves radishes. Cabbage likes beans. Loves? Likes? The unenlightened find this hilarious. Not even a gardener who corresponds with groundhogs could be *that* nutty, they say. Either the gardener is off his rocker, or some imaginative writers are desperate for something to fill their pages.

The interesting thing is that gardeners have been talking and writing about these botanical romances for years and years in dozens of languages and on several continents. Furthermore, while much of it is nonsense, there *is* enough valid evidence of chemical and physical interactions among plants to at least make scientists give an interested nod in the direction of such "love affairs."

The benefits attributed to plant pairs vary from bigger harvests to the more specific claims of earlier harvests, faster growth rates or even improved flavor. Peppermint, yarrow, chamomile and several other herbs fall into this last category. Dr. Ehrenfried Pfeiffer, the biodynamic gardening pioneer, did some work with herb companion plants, and according to the Biodynamic Gardening Association's publications, he found that many herbs did indeed influence the amount of essential oils in neighboring herbs.

Although mainstream scientists had all but dismissed this notion, they couldn't entirely rule it out. A plant's nutritional status has a lot to do with its flavor, and we know neighboring plants can influence nutrition in profound ways. There may even be some chemical activity involved. The chemicals responsible for fruit and vegetable flavor are often the same ones that plants use to defend themselves against pests and disease or to respond to injury. Perhaps one day we'll discover that some chemical conversation goes on between plants such as yarrow and its next door neighbor.

Elroy Rice, in his reviews of the research done with plant chemicals, *Pest Control with Nature's Chemicals* (University of Oklahoma Press, 1983), points out that a few modern studies have shown that some plants actually produce chemicals that enhance their neighbors' growth. In a Yugoslavian study done in 1974, corn cockle (*Agrostemma githago*) stimulated the growth of wheat seedlings. The compounds responsible were isolated from the weed seeds, and when these compounds were applied to the wheat field, grain yields increased appreciably.

Weed scientist Jerry Doll and agronomist P. C. Bhowmik found similar benefits from residues of corn and giant foxtail. In a field test, they discovered that decaying debris from these crops seemed to stimulate soybean production.

These studies stand out as two of the few showing positive chemical interactions. Their results certainly can't be interpreted as evidence that all the traditional claims for plant "likes" are valid or even that mulches of those decaying plants would be, under all circumstances, beneficial. However, the studies do suggest that we ought to consider the possibility that plants may release chemicals that stimulate other plants' growth. It's a fascinating thought—one for which there's just not enough unbiased evidence to draw any sweeping conclusions.

As far as we know, plants aren't capable of "loving" or even "liking" one another, but it is true that certain species benefit from the presence of certain others. Every high school biology student knows about symbiosis, in which two different species of plant or animal grow together for the benefit of one or both. The lichens you see growing on trees or rocks are really two plants–an alga and a fungus. The alga contributes food produced by photosynthesis; the fungus returns the favor by providing shelter and water for the alga. In the soil, a similar relationship exists between nitrogen-fixing bacteria and roots of legumes.

Companion planting is really nothing more than setting up a kind of large-scale symbiosis between the crops in your garden. We have seen in chapter 2 under Plant Defense Guilds how some plants form defense guilds to protect one another from pests. You can take advantage of these relationships by planning your planting patterns and weed management accordingly. In a similar way, you might devise other schemes in which plants provide the shelter, nutrients or physical support their neighbors require. For example, when peas grow next to lettuce, the pea vines provide shelter and shade for the sun-shy, cool-loving greens. Radishes keep the ground shaded and moist with their leaves–the very conditions slow-to-germinate parsley seeds crave.

Perhaps, then, there really is something to the idea that tomatoes grow well with parsley. The two plants have very different shapes, sizes, and light and nutrient needs, so competition shouldn't be an issue. Parsley would certainly benefit from the shade provided by the tomato bush, and maybe the tomato enjoys some of the benefits of a living mulch created by the parsley.

Complementing Not Competing

Seen in this light, the notion that plants have "friends" doesn't seem quite as ridiculous. Every living organism in the garden affects every other living organism around it. Common sense tells us that certain planting combinations are better than others. Sometimes this is because of a specific benefit provided by the companion crop such as shade, food or pest defense. Sometimes it occurs simply because the two crops have complementary, not competitive, needs. In monocropped fields or garden beds, every single plant is fighting for the same light, water and nutrients at the same time. If you were to plant the right combination of noncompetitive crops, they might make better overall use of those available resources.

Agronomists have devoted considerable energy to identifying the least competitive cropping combinations. While they don't talk of plant friendships, they do refer to the complementarity of species. Size, shape, growth rate, maturity periods and nutrient, water and light needs all influence how well two or more crops perform together. The more we learn about these factors, the better we'll become at selecting companion crops for our gardens, fields and orchards.

Food and Water

The wrong cropping combination can very quickly exhaust soil nutrients and water. The right one, properly managed, can conserve and even build up these essential resources. There are a number of factors you should keep in mind when judging whether or not the nutrient needs of certain crops will complement each other.

Legumes as Companions

In America, interest in interplanting for good crop nutrition is growing in proportion to escalating fertilizer costs. Farmers and gardeners have long recognized the role of beans and peas in replacing soil nitrogen. Legumes are an important part of most crop rotation plans. They're planted, allowed to mature, then turned under so the nitrogen-rich nodes on their roots can enrich the soil as they decay. What isn't as well known is that some nitrogen is released to the soil even as the plants grow. It isn't necessary to wait for legumes to be plowed under. When you interplant legumes, they provide their companion crops with a steady stream of nitrogen, and there's still some left over for the next year's crop.

Research on this topic has been going on for some 75 years, but no one is ready to etch the findings in stone. Scientists know that legumes release nitrogen while they're growing, but they aren't sure how much is absorbed by companion crops; what, if

(continued on page 74)

Vegetables in the Sod

Certain grasses and clovers may be pretty good companions for some vegetables, as long as competition can be kept to a minimum. In hillside gardens, where erosion is a serious problem, sowing a sod cover crop around vegetables can be an invaluable way to keep the garden soil from washing away with every rainfall. If the cover crop is then tilled under as a green manure at the end of the season, its benefits are compounded even more. The cover crop might even fulfill a third function as a very effective weed control. But the bottom line is this—just how well do garden crops and neighboring sod co-exist in such close quarters?

Eileen Weinsteiger at the Rodale Research Center has conducted preliminary studies to observe how well several garden vegetable crops interact with overseeded sod crops. These were seeded in early summer, after an early pea crop had been well established. Second crops of potatoes, lettuce or beets were then planted directly in the sod.

Weinsteiger found that rye formed the densest ground cover with its thick mass of roots and grass. White Dutch clover (*Trifolium repens*) was disappointing—because it germinated poorly in dry summer months, it didn't establish a good cover. Both crops required frequent mowings in order to prevent shading, reduce competition with the main crop and keep weeds in check. When it became apparent that the sod crops needed to be controlled even more, a 6-inch band of bare soil was left around each vegetable. Still, even with all of these management techniques, the rye and clover reduced vegetable yields.

As more formal experiments get underway, workers at the Research Center will be testing various ways of handling sod overseedings with a variety of vegetable crops. They hope that these future studies will uncover specific vegetable crops and sod species that might be grown simultaneously to control weeds and erosion and enrich the soil—without diminishing yields.

any, special conditions are required; and which legume-nonlegume combinations make the best use of this arrangement.

In several tropical studies, main crops of maize, sorghum or other nonlegumes have been interplanted with soybeans, groundnuts or other legumes. Most results have shown significant increases in the main crop's yields—presumably because of the nitrogen contributed by the companion. One study in particular, done at Iowa State University, showed that a companion soybean crop boosted corn yields over 10 percent.

Still, the issue of legume companion crops remains controversial. Some scientists argue that while legumes transfer nitrogen during growth, the amounts simply are not substantial. These researchers believe that legumes are better used in monocrop rotations; plant cowpeas one season, harvest or plow them under as green manure, then follow them with a crop of corn the next season. So far, few studies have been done to show us exactly how legume interplanting should be managed for the best results. However, at least one researcher reports that some legumes work harder when grown alongside nonlegumes and in soil already low in nitrogen. Since the neighboring crop is depleting the available nitrogen, the legume has no choice but to produce its own.

Legumes in the Garden

For the gardener, it's really a moot point as to when legumes release the most nitrogen. As long as you leave behind the healthy legume roots to decay at the end of the season, nearby crops can enjoy the nitrogen benefits both now and later. Many legumes have more to offer neighboring crops than free nitrogen. Alfalfa and the clovers host all sorts of predators and reduce erosion. They also improve soil aeration and contribute organic matter for a nice, loose soil texture. They make excellent companions for heavy nitrogen feeders such as corn and tomatoes simply because they won't compete for that vital nutrient.

Which legume you pair with which crop can make all the difference in just how beneficial the partnership is. Competition is a major problem with some legume-vegetable mixtures. Cover crops of alfalfa, clover or other dense legumes tend to seriously hinder seed germination and growth of their companion crops.

(continued on page 76)

Legumes for Companion Planting

Dozens of native and cultivated legumes will thrive in North America but not all are particularly well suited to interplanting. Those listed below are best able to hold their own in mixed plantings, without overrunning the main crop. To make the most of their nitrogen-fixing abilities, don't apply any nitrogen fertilizers.

Plant	Remarks
CULTIVATED LEGUMES	Legumes are aided in their nitrogen gathering by special bacteria; when you purchase seeds, be sure to inquire about the appropriate bacteria inoculant to use; not all legumes respond to the same inoculant.
Alfalfa (*Medicago sativa*) Perennial	Expensive but good companion to grasses or as strip interplant in vegetable garden; unable to tolerate shading from dense plantings; requires frequent mowing.
Bean and pea (various genera)	Include broad beans, soybeans, garden peas, chick-peas; excellent soil-building edible companions; require no mowing.
Clovers	
Crimson (*Trifolium incarnatum*) Annual	Good winter cover crop; use as a sod interplant or strip crop; tolerates shading well.
Red (*T. pratense*) Perennial	Good companion cover crop for wet, acid areas.
White (*T. repens*) Biennial	Has performed well as sod cover crop for corn and soybean interplanting at Rodale Research Center; may do well in the home vegetable garden if you manage it carefully.

Plant	Remarks
Lupine (*Lupinus* spp.) Annual or perennial	An attractive, if cumbersome companion crop; large flower spikes come in blue, pink, red, yellow and purple; grows 3 to 5 feet tall and may need staking; scatter a few through the garden or orchard for beauty and soil building.
Peanut (*Arachis hypogaea*) Annual	Good companion for corn in warm climates.
Vetch (*Vicia* spp.) Annual or biennial	Excellent green manure, cover or companion crop for fruit and nut crops; fava bean (*V. faba*) typically companioned with potatoes.
NATIVE LEGUMES	Any of these wild-growing plants make a good ground cover. Some will attract beneficial insects; allow them to grow in a border alongside the garden; because they are legumes they won't rob crops of nitrogen.
Bird's foot trefoil (*Lotus corniculatus*) Perennial	Some gardeners consider this a weed, while others grow it as a ground cover or for forage; has yellow flowers; reaches 2 feet tall.
Burr clover (*Medicago hispida*) Annual	Leaves are finely toothed at the ends; bears yellow flowers.

Frequent mowing is the best way to keep these competitive legumes under control in a garden setting. When these crops are paired with orchard trees or sturdy grasses and agricultural crops, they need only intermittent trimming.

Chemical Interactions

Russian studies suggest that some legumes interact chemically with companion crops to their own benefit or detriment. This interaction goes beyond nitrogen availability to affect other nutri-

Plant	Remarks
Canada tick-clover (*Desmodium canadense*) Perennial	The seed pods attach themselves to the clothing of whoever brushes by; flourishes in sandy, dry soil; grows 3 to 5 feet tall.
Crotalaria (*Crotalaria* spp.) Annual or perennial	Also called rattlebox; plants produce attractive yellow flowers, somewhat akin to common garden pea flowers; grows 4 feet tall.
Partridge pea (*Cassia fasciculata*) Annual	Vining growth stretches from 1 to 3 feet; leaves fold shut when touched; flowers are deep yellow; does well in sandy soil.
TREES AND SHRUBS	When you plant low-growing companion crops around any of these trees, you won't have to worry about the tree depriving the companion of nitrogen.
Black locust (*Robinia pseudoacadia*)	Hardy, quite tall; prime specimens can reach 75 feet.
Carob (*Ceratonia siliqua*)	Requires warm, somewhat dry coastal climate.
Honey locust (*Gleditsia* spp.)	Suited to almost any climate; in excellent location can soar to 135 feet; gives only very light shade.
Redbud (*Cercis canadensis*)	Very hardy, easily grown; reaches 36 feet tall; purple-pink flowers in spring; leaves turn yellow in fall.

ents and plant growth activities. Little research has been done to identify the harmful combinations of crops commonly grown in this country, so we gardeners must run our own trials. What we do know is that some legumes can be harmed by certain crops. Roots of field pea (*Pisum arvense*) and hairy vetch (*Vicia villosa*) exude substances that stimulate photosynthesis and phosphorus uptake in barley and oats. At the same time, barley and oats release chemicals that *inhibit* photosynthesis and phosphorus

(continued on page 80)

Rooting Patterns of Some Common Garden Crops

Don't judge companion crops solely by what's growing above ground—consider the shapes and depths of their roots, as well. This is particularly important in the intensive garden, where plants are very closely spaced and competition for soil nutrients and water could be a problem.

Here you'll find a brief description of the rooting patterns of some common garden crops. As you divide and transplant perennials or uproot vegetable plants in the fall, take note of their root size and shape. Eventually, you'll have a pretty clear picture of what your garden plants look like from "head to toe."

Soil texture and water and nutrient availability can greatly alter rooting habits. Obviously, a hardpan layer will stunt root growth, while a lack of water or nutrients could force roots to grow deeper than they normally would. So too, the way you garden can promote certain types of growth. Transplanting drastically changes root shape. Tomatoes grown from seed and never transplanted develop long taproots. When tomatoes are transplanted, as they almost always are, they develop fibrous, shallower root systems. Also, if you water frequently and lightly, you'll promote shallow roots among all your garden crops.

Even walking in the garden can effect plant roots. If your garden is laid out in single rows with paths beside each row, your footsteps will compact soil around every plant and reduce root growth considerably. Plants grown in beds where there's a minimum of foot traffic tend to have much deeper, healthier root systems.

As a general rule, you'll want to select plants with complementary rooting patterns for intensive intercropping within rows. Pair shallow-rooted plants with deep-rooted ones, and match those that have taproots with plants having broader fibrous ones.

Crop	Rooting Pattern
Alfalfa	Very long, rapidly growing taproot reaches some 6 feet in the first year and ultimately grows up to 20 feet deep.
Beet	Short taproot with fibrous roots reaching down as far as 5 feet; most roots limited to the upper 1 foot of soil.
Cabbage	Shallow, fibrous roots, mostly confined to the upper 1 foot of soil.
Carrot	Short taproot with fibrous roots reaching down as far as 5 feet; most roots limited to the upper 2 feet of soil.
Celery	Transplanted celery develops shallow, fibrous roots mostly limited to the upper 6 inches of soil.
Corn	Deep, fibrous roots reach down as far as 7 feet; most are confined to the upper 3 feet of soil.
Flax	Long taproot reaches down some 3 feet.
Lettuce	Fast-growing taproot can reach up to 5 feet long; usually stays in the upper 2 feet of soil.
Onion	Small bulb with fibrous roots that grow 6 to 8 inches deep.
Pepper	Fibrous, spreading roots mostly confined to the top 8 inches of soil, sometimes extend 4 feet deep.
Potato	Early growth is shallow but late in the season; fibrous roots may reach 1 to 2 feet deep.
Pumpkin	Taproot usually draws nutrients and water from the upper 2 feet of soil; may possibly extend 6 feet deep in some gardens.

Crop	Rooting Pattern
Spinach	Fast-growing taproot measures up to 5 feet long; usually limited to the upper 1 foot of soil.
Squash	Taproot usually confined to the upper 2 feet of soil; can possibly extend 6 feet deep.
Tomato	Transplants develop fibrous, spreading roots 3 to 4 feet deep, but most remain in the top 8 inches; roots may spread out to a diameter of 5 feet.
Wheat	Fibrous roots probe as deep as 5 feet; most roots confined to the upper 2 feet of soil.

---

uptake in the legume.

It seems likely that many different crop plants—nonlegumes as well as legumes—release chemicals that stimulate others. Elroy Rice reports in *Pest Control with Nature's Chemicals* that a Russian study demonstrated the positive chemical interactions of buckwheat, lupine, mustard and oats.

Rooting Patterns

It seems that rooting patterns also influence nutrient uptake and ultimately growth. If companion crops feed in different soil layers, they make better use of the available resources. In other words, nutrients, whether already present or applied in the form of fertilizers, seem to go a lot further in an interplanted plot than in one that contains the same type of crops. One explanation may be that the presence of a shallow-rooted species might encourage a deep-rooted one to go even deeper in order to avoid the other's territory.

For this reason, it's important to consider not only a crop's nutrient needs but its rooting pattern as well when you devise a companion planting scheme. With a legume-nonlegume this isn't as important as with other combinations in which the crops share roughly the same appetites. Even though corn and squash

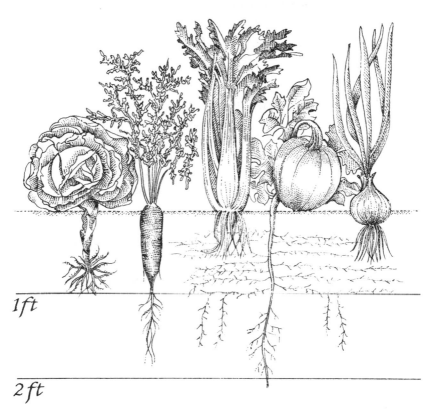

1ft

2ft

Companions Underground: *Don't forget to consider rooting patterns when deciding which plants to grow as neighbors. Pick plants that grow to different depths underground so they won't compete for nutrients and water in the same soil level. For example, alternate the shallow fibrous roots of a cabbage plant with the more probing roots of a carrot, or surround a deep-growing pumpkin plant with shallow-growing celery or onions.*

both require fairly stiff doses of nitrogen, the fact that they feed in such different zones makes them fairly compatible companions. The corn plants will pull nutrients and water from the top 18 to 36 inches of soil, while the squash roots will probe deeper, going down 36 inches or more.

81

How Much Light Do Plants Need?

Light is most likely to become the limiting factor in interplanted gardens. Nearly all garden plants need intense light in order to develop properly. Seeds of certain crops such as lettuce need light in order to germinate. The flowering, fruiting and seed production processes of most plants only occur if the right amount and intensity of light is available. Even root crops like carrots and beets need sunlight, for the underground portions grow only after the leaves have received enough light to produce adequate food to fuel root development.

You can tell when plants haven't received enough light—they look lanky and weak, with very succulent tissue. In some crops such as celery, endive, leeks and some lettuces, these are desirable qualities, and we purposely blanch or shade them from the light during part of their growth.

However, most summer vegetables and fruits are firm, compact plants that won't thrive unless given adequate light. Without it, they become so weakened that they are very susceptible to drought, heat, pests and diseases. Fortunately, the intensity and quantity of required light isn't the same for all garden plants. While most do best basking in direct sunlight all day long, many crops tolerate partial shade, and some can even be grown in fairly deep shade, if only for part of their lives.

Refer to this listing of light needs as you select companion vegetables, fruits, herbs and flowers for all the different nooks and crannies of your garden.

Demand Full Sunlight: These sun-loving plants only perform well if given eight or more hours of full light each day. Less light will certainly reduce their yields and may even make them sickly.

Vegetables: amaranth, beans, chicory, corn, eggplant, Jerusalem artichoke, melons, okra, peas, potatoes, pumpkins, squash, sunflowers, tomatoes, watermelons

Fruits: bramble fruits, gooseberries, quince, strawberries

Herbs: most herbs

Flowers: most annuals, asters, daisies, flax, geum, spurge, thistles, yarrow

Tolerate Partial Shade: These plants will grow well in filtered light or if they receive only 5 hours of direct sunlight each day. You can interplant these among taller crops that partly shade them, as long as sunlight isn't completely cut off. Cool-weather crops actually prefer shady areas during the hot summer months.

Vegetables: asparagus, broccoli, cabbage, carrots, celery, chard, cress, cucumbers, garlic, kale, kohlrabi, leeks, lettuce, onions, parsley, parsnips, spinach, turnips

Fruits: blackberries, chokecherries, grapes, nuts, most fruit trees

Herbs: mint, tarragon

Flowers: alyssum, bee balm, begonias, lupines, marigolds, pansies, snapdragons

Tolerate Deep Shade: These plants are for the darkest corners of the garden that receive few if any hours of direct light and only moderate filtered light. These are good companions to set under trees or hedges. Most plants will germinate and grow fairly well in these areas for the first few weeks of life, so you might consider planning nursery space here as well.

Vegetables: celery, lettuce, watercress
Fruits: no fruits do well in deep shade
Herbs: sweet woodruff
Flowers: impatiens, nicotiana (flowering tobacco),
          lobelia

Timing

Timing is also a crucial factor in choosing nutrient-complementary plants. In general, you should make sure that the crops' critical periods (when they need the most food and water) don't overlap. By juggling planting dates, you can make most crops compatible. For example, bush beans are a fine companion crop for corn, but you'll get the best results if you time it so the bean's flowering and the corn's tasseling don't coincide. Both crops need plenty of water at that time, and unless supplies are unlimited, you may reap a poor harvest as a result of the competition. To avoid any possible competition, plant beans in the early summer, just a week or two after the corn has emerged, or in the fall, just before you harvest the corn. Unfortunately, there hasn't been any more research done to date that can help us figure out when these critical periods occur for most of our common garden crops. Once again, observations in each of our gardens will have to fill the gap left by the lack of scientific evidence.

Sun and Space

All garden plants need light but not necessarily in the same amounts or at the same times in the growing season. Fruit producers like tomatoes, eggplants and peppers practically worship the sun—the hotter and brighter, the better. For spinach and other greens, strong light is almost an enemy. These crops prefer filtered sunlight. Somewhere between the two extremes are a host of crops that do pretty well under a variety of light conditions; carrots, cabbage, onions and others fit in here. Common sense suggests that low-light plants might grow nicely in the shadows of the sunloving ones. Perhaps this is the logic behind some of our traditional pairings—onions between heads of cabbage or carrots tucked in among pea vines.

Science has carried this common sense idea of maximum light use one step further by studying plant leaf angles to determine which cropping combinations absorb the most light without shading each other. Most of this research is rather esoteric, involving theoretically perfect grass mixtures in which no leaves at all would overlap!

Of more interest to those of us who have gardens are the suggestions for grouping plants with inherently different heights and shapes to take advantage of the available light. Think of tall, sparse crops, such as corn, as the top of a canopy. They need lots of light, yet they won't significantly shade bean, squash or potato crops that grow down below. You can plant compact, lower level crops quite densely to take advantage of the reduced light intensity on the garden floor.

Practice Crowd Control

Beware of interplanting so densely that too little light is available for crops on the ground level. It's easy to get carried away when you're setting out 12-inch-tall tomato plants. But once those seedlings take off, you can end up with wall-to-wall greenery, squeezing out the tiny lettuce seedlings you've carefully set between the tomatoes. Keep in mind the mature crop's size and shape, and select and space companions accordingly.

As a general rule, root crops with compact leaf and stem growth do well with leafy greens or relatively shallow-rooted fruiting crops such as cucumbers, eggplants, peppers and summer squash. Make sure the lower level plants aren't being cut off from the sun completely. You may need to prune or train upper level plants in order to maintain enough light for lower crops. That means staking or caging tomatoes and pinching off suckers. Consider growing indeterminate cucumbers and some of the smaller melons upright by training them to fences or stakes. That way you can squeeze in bush beans, radishes, carrots or other compact companion crops below. All sorts of plant supports from ordinary stakes to fancy three-dimensional A-frames and cages

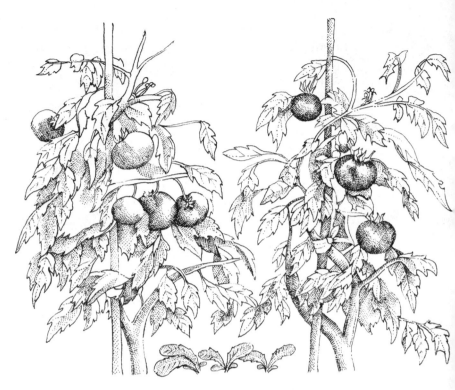

Overzealous Interplanting: *Beware of planting companions too closely. Lettuce seedlings can be cut off from the light by rangy tomato plants; scallions can be shoved aside by*

are sold through garden catalogs, and even more can be made at home. With vertical support, vine crops hardly take up any ground space at all. Or, you can keep vine crops on ground level and treat them as low growers in interplanting schemes with corn, pole beans or various tree crops.

Keep Growing All Season Long

Some plants complement one another in the ways they use

expanding cabbage heads; and carrot tops can become tangled with pea vines unless you allow enough space right from the start to accommodate mature plant shapes.

the season's time. Well-timed companion planting can assure that every inch of the garden is being used every minute of the growing year. Farmers call this relay planting—sowing one crop in between another that's almost finished. Traditionally they've planted cotton in a cereal crop, sorghum in among beans, and beans between corn. Shade provided by the older crop keeps the soil moist so newly planted seeds can germinate.

In most gardens, relay or succession planting is a matter of course. No gardener likes to see a row or section of bed lying idle.

(continued on page 90)

87

Relay and Succession Plantings

For gardeners who are on the ball, short-season crops such as radishes, beets, snap beans and various greens expand planting options tremendously. These relatively rapid growers can be succession planted before or after main season crops, such as tomatoes, are set out so that garden space is in constant use.

For even better use of space and even more crops each season, you can allow some of these plants to grow along-side the main crop until they're crowded out. For instance, an early spinach crop can still be growing when you inter-plant tomato seedlings. By the time the tomatoes overrun the bed, you'll have harvested the spinach. Where weather and soil conditions permit, you might squeeze three or even four relay crops into a single season. Plastic mulches, cloches and hot caps expand the growing season on both ends, allowing you to plant even earlier in the spring and later in the fall. These season-extending aids make double and triple relay plantings practical for almost all regions.

Below you'll find a few relay combinations. Southern gardeners whose frost-free growing season practically spans from Valentine's Day to New Year's Day hardly need such a list. For other growers, however, a few suggestions may encourage more elaborate, creative planting schemes that make productive use of the garden space for as long as possible. Be sure to choose fast-maturing varieties wher-ever possible.

Two-Way Relays

Early peas	followed by	Carrots
		Chard
		Corn
		Cucumbers

Early peas	followed by	Leeks
		Melons
		Onions
		Potatoes
		Squash
		Tomatoes
Lettuce or spinach	followed by	Carrots
		Eggplants
		Peanuts
		Peppers
		Pole beans
		Potatoes
		Tomatoes
Bunching onions	followed by	Chard
		Eggplants
		Peppers
		Pole beans
		Potatoes
		Tomatoes
Chinese cabbage	followed by	Carrots
		Eggplants
		Peppers
		Pole beans
		Squash
		Tomatoes
		Turnips

Three-Way Relays

Early peas–Broccoli–Summer squash
Early peas–Tomatoes–Cress
Broccoli–Bush beans–Lettuce
Chinese cabbage–Bush beans–Kohlrabi
Spinach–Cucumbers–Radishes
Lettuce–Onions–Bush beans

Four-Way Relays
Early peas–Broccoli–Bush beans–Beets
Early peas–Spinach–Melons–Turnips
Chinese cabbage–Bush beans–Lettuce–Onions
Spinach–Radishes–Bush beans–Chinese cabbage
Early peas–Onions–Chard–Broccoli

Anticipate when one crop will be harvested, and plan to have another ready to take its place. For instance, set late cabbage seedlings between bean rows. By the time the cabbage really takes off, the bean plants will be finished. Another common scheme is to set tomato plants among early spinach. Where growing seasons are long, all sorts of relays are possible. Louisiana agriculturalist William Poillion recommends setting tomatoes out in late March, followed by an interplant of cucumbers or cantaloupes in April.

Nineteenth-century French market gardeners developed similar planting schemes and made up for their cooler temperatures by using cloches, mulches and hot beds. Twentieth-century gardeners have at their disposal lots of handy new accessories, many made of durable, lightweight plastic, which can help protect plants and make relay companion planting stretch over a longer period of the year.

Learning from Nature

Perhaps the ideal of agricultural ecology has been achieved in Japan by Masanobu Fukuoka, as described in his book, *The One-Straw Revolution* (Rodale Press, 1978). Fukuoka's farming techniques are at once simple and complex. He believes in interfering with natural processes as little as possible. Therefore, he does no plowing or weeding. He uses no chemical fertilizers, herbicides or pesticides. A continuous ground cover of white clover, along with a mulch of rice and barley straw, keeps the ground rich, loose and free of most weeds. Seeds of many grain crops are broadcast during the season in which they would naturally fall. Some vegetable seeds are planted in the same way; less aggressive crops are started in a nursery bed before being moved to the clover-covered gardens.

The farm-garden Fukuoka describes is semiwild, a hodge-podge of fruit trees, grains and vegetable plants all growing in a seeming chaos of lushness. And yet, chaos it isn't. This most natural method of raising crops is, in fact, a system. A microbiologist by training, Fukuoka developed his methods from clues offered directly by nature. With fresh, open eyes, he observed natural cycles, the interactions of plants and animals, and the ways of the crop plants he grew. He then applied these ideas to farming.

Most of the particulars of Fukuoka's system can't be applied to our North American fields or gardens. Our climatic conditions are different, and our needs may be as well. And yet, it's the philosophy behind his system that's most important. If we can put aside our textbook notions of what a garden or farm is and take time to observe nature and understand her cycles, then we may be well on the way to developing a meaningful garden ecology.

Chapter 4

Nasty Neighbors in the Garden

The Roman historian Pliny warned that barley and chick-peas "scorch up" cornland. He also noted that black walnut trees injure "anything planted in [their] vicinity" and that radishes are harmful to grapevines. In the 1900 years since Pliny's time, herbals, farm records and other garden writings have echoed his observations. While certain plants develop "friendships" with other species, others seem to have "hit lists." Cabbage is said to suffer when grapes grow nearby. Thistles injure oats, basil hurts rue, rue hurts cabbage, barberry hurts wheat, and some pine trees hurt all sorts of crops.

Biochemists have confirmed that extracts or exudates from all these plants contain poisons. Hundreds of other crops, herbs and weeds have also been tested to the point that it now appears

certain members of almost every plant family possess some plant-killing compounds. This toxin-producing characteristic has even been given a tongue-twisting name—allelopathy.

In the past 50 years, and most importantly in the last decade, allelopathy has been the focus of extensive research and quite a lot of controversy in several areas of biology. Biochemists are looking at the specific chemicals involved and their potential as replacements for man-made herbicides. Ecologists are interested in allelopathy as an explanation for the natural succession of plants in forests and fields and the distribution and dominance of some particular species. Plants that are able to impair the growth of their neighbors must gain a competitive advantage and establish themselves more easily. Plant pathologists find links between allelopathic chemicals and disease resistance or susceptibility in some plants. Root rot in beans, tobacco and lettuce appears to be related to an allelopathic reaction from certain crop residues. In field experiments, agricultural researchers are studying the allelopathic effects of various interplants, cover crops, mulches and green manures. They believe some cropping combinations, rotation patterns and other programs that are commonly used by farmers may be actually reducing yields because of allelopathy. They also see all kinds of promise for practical applications in the future—weed-killing cover crops, better companion plant selections, even new breeds of grain and vegetable crops able to keep weeds at bay.

Not all scientists are as enthusiastic. Some remain unconvinced that allelopathy exists out in the real world, beyond the controlled conditions of the laboratory. Skeptics argue that even where the toxic chemicals can be identified, their effects are inconsequential. They say that allelopathy is a scientific curiosity, nothing more. Merely because a plant contains poisons doesn't mean that it poisons surrounding vegetation. A vast array of secondary chemicals is found in the plant kingdom, and most of these are never released. (Secondary chemicals are those produced by a plant that aren't necessary for growth; instead, they give a plant its distinctive flavor, repel or attract pests and so on.) Those chemicals that do escape in toxic forms may be diluted by the air or filtered through soil containing neutralizing chemicals and microorganisms. By the time these toxins are finally absorbed by other plants, they may be entirely harmless. What looks like allelopathy is really, according to some scientists, only competition for nutrients, water, light and air.

Researchers working on the other side of the fence are quick to point out that plant-produced chemicals are just one of the factors that influence plant growth. Allelopathy occurs in tandem with competition. In the best experiments, scientists attempt to reduce competition by providing more than adequate resources for the test plants. Still, poor germination and growth rates, wilting, reduced nutrient uptake and other negative effects occur. Interplant competition alone can't explain them, so allelopathy must be the culprit. While it's true that such studies don't prove allelopathy's existence beyond a shadow of a doubt, it's also true that there is a lot of incriminating evidence. Indeed, given the number and variety of chemicals produced by plants, it would be surprising if some of these *didn't* influence other plants. As Alan Putnam, a pioneer in the field, cautiously puts it, "The phenomenon of allelopathy is now more widely accepted than not accepted."

The Most Notorious Nasty Neighbor

The most striking, and by now hackneyed, example of allelopathy in action is the effect the black walnut tree has on a variety of other plants. Gardeners since Roman times have known that this tree stunts, wilts and eventually kills tomatoes, potatoes and other vegetable crops grown in its presence. It wasn't until the 1920s that scientists identified the walnut's toxic compound as juglone. This toxin is found in the tree's roots, leaves and bark and in the hulls of the nuts. By allowing the extracted toxin to be absorbed by roots of tomato and alfalfa plants, researchers were able to demonstrate that juglone, and not simply competition, was indeed the cause of the tree's harmful effects. Today we know that juglone spells trouble for azaleas, blackberries, blueberries, magnolias, potatoes, peas, peppers, tomatoes, alfalfa, lilacs, peonies, mountain laurel, rhododendrons, apples and sugar maples.

The walnut is by no means the only example of allelopathy. There are other plants, as well, that can produce harmful chemicals. In this chapter we'll see the various effects these plant-produced toxins can have.

Herbicides in Plants

Juglone is just one of many plant-made herbicides. Like most others, juglone also functions as a pest-deterrent. And like other plant-produced chemicals, it has a lot to do with the flavor and odor of the plant but seems to be of little importance to the basic functions of the plant.

Only a limited number of secondary chemicals have been identified as allelopathic, but these are found in scores of wild and cultivated plants. Vanillic acid is found in many plants including barley, rye, oats, corn and various weeds. Cinnamic acid, one of the aromatic compounds in various herbs, rye, sunflowers and other plants is a fairly widespread toxin. Several aldehydes in beets, tomatoes, sweet potatoes, radishes and carrots harm many different plants. Tannin is the poison found in pine trees.

How They Work

Nature, in her wisdom, has put some checks on these toxins. First, most allelopathic plants seem to seriously harm only a limited number of other plants. They're not as specific as some man-made herbicides, but neither are they very broad in the spectrum of plants they affect. Obviously juglone doesn't harm every species of plant. If it did, walnut trees would be surrounded by barren circles of soil. In fact, Kentucky bluegrass tolerates the presence of juglone quite well. Most often, a plant will release toxins against a completely different type of plant. For instance, a tree or shrub is more likely to use chemical defenses against a grass or herb than against another tree. However, competing plants of the same type might also fall prey to their neighbors' toxins.

Nature has provided other safeguards, as well. The production and concentration of plant herbicides are greatly influenced by environmental stress, light quality and intensity, and other factors. During times of nutrient deficiency, drought or chilling, plants tend to produce the most of their harmful chemicals. Sometimes, plants store their toxin in a nontoxic form and only convert it when they're damaged. Often the toxin is present during a very limited time in the plant's life cycle—during seedling stage or at maturity.

Even if the allelopathic chemical is present in the plant, it may not reach its target in a toxic form. Toxins can occur almost anywhere in the allelopathic plant, with leaves, stems, roots and seeds being the most frequent sources. A rather long, involved journey is required to get the chemical from its source to neighboring vegetation. In a few cases, volatile excretions from leaves and stems waft through the air. More often, rainwater leaches the chemicals from living plant parts or from plant residues such as stubble, green manure or mulch. Gases and organisms in the air, water or soil may break down or dilute the poison on its travels, rendering it harmless by the time it reaches its destination. Soil texture has a lot to do with how often plant-related poisoning occurs—some toxins are able to concentrate in fine, clay soils but cause fewer problems in coarse, sandy soils where they leach out. In a few instances, as with rye, the reverse is true. In almost all cases, the effects of plant-produced chemicals are short lived when compared with those of man-made chemical herbicides.

The Gardener's Black List

(Compiled from various
historical garden references.)

Basil: "Something is the matter; this herb and rue will never grow together, nor near one another." (Seventeenth century, Nicholas Culpeper)

Beech: There's a "noxious quality communicated to the rain-water which drips from the beech foliage." (Nineteenth century, anonymous)

Black Walnut: Shade of the walnut "even causes headache in man and injury to anything planted in its vicinity." (First century, Pliny)

Cabbage: "There is a naturall enmitie betweene cabbage and the vine (grape): which if such as it growe neere unto it, foorthwith the vine perisheth and withereth away." (Sixteenth century, John Gerard)

Grass: "You must not expect to raise trees and grass off the same ground. The grass will destroy the trees." (Nineteenth century, anonymous)

Sage: "Sage likes to grow not, as might be supposed, with onions ..." (Culpeper)

Thyme: "Thyme impoverishes the ground much for nothing will succeed where thyme has grown the preceding year." (Eighteenth century, anonymous)

Underground Bridges

There is the possibility that some plants are able to send their poisons almost directly into other plant roots without leaching through the soil. Various plant species are connected by a complex network of underground bridges. While the plants in our gardens appear to be distinct individuals, deep in the soil, they are really one large organism. Many link roots with their neighbors, forming natural grafts. Mycorrhizal fungi (the good guys that help roots gather nutrients and water) join other plants together. Disease spores (such as those carrying viral diseases that afflict elm, cherry and apple trees) are transported along these connections, and according to Elroy Rice in his book *Pest Control with Nature's Chemicals* (University of Oklahoma Press, 1983), there's little doubt that chemical compounds are transported as well. So far little research work has been done with root grafts and fungal bridges in crop plants to confirm this.

Symptoms

Once they reach their destination, allelopathic chemicals can cause all kinds of problems for the target plant. For starters, they might inhibit seed germination. If the seed has sprouted, the chemicals may slow the seedling's growth by interfering with its hormones or by interrupting cell division. The poisons may also inhibit photosynthesis (the energy-catching process), slow or speed respiration (the energy-making process) or reduce the plant's ability to absorb certain nutrients. Obviously, some pretty sick plants could result from all this. In most instances, affected plants are smaller than normal and don't yield as well as usual. More dramatic signs include severe stunting, wilting and nutrient deficiency symptoms. Do these symptoms sound just like the ones usually given for competition or stress? Allelopathic symptoms are identical. The only difference is that supplying all the light, water and fertilizer in the world doesn't relieve the symptoms.

It's important to remember that research in allelopathy is still in its infancy. Agroecologists are only beginning to determine the role allelopathy plays. In the interplanted garden or field and where green manures or organic mulches are applied, the combined factors of allelopathy and competition could be particularly critical in determining how well your plants do and how much you harvest. Even at this early stage in the science, you'll find it worth your while to keep up with the latest findings. The current research suggests a few practical techniques for raising crops and provides plenty of material for backyard experiments. See the Appendix, Making Your Own Discoveries, for the names of some garden publications and agricultural journals that can keep you informed of the work that's being done.

Weeds Fighting Crops

Time was when weeds were considered thieves, stealing water, light, food and space from our crops. Now we suspect that some, particularly broadleaf weeds, are murderers, slowly poisoning their cultivated cousins. Seeds, roots, stems, leaves and the decaying debris of some weeds produce allelopathic chemicals capable of harming crops.

This could have important ramifications for organic gardeners and farmers. When you recognize the overall value of weeds as havens for beneficial insects and as deterrents to pests, you must also be aware of the harm some weeds cause when they're associated with certain plants. Yellow nutsedge, leafy spurge, giant foxtail and quack grass are the most notorious. They release potent herbicides that rival many man-made substances.

Yellow nutsedge (*Cyperus esculentus*) is an invasive weed found throughout the country. Tests by Jerry Doll and Dirk Drost of the University of Wisconsin showed that only a small amount of the toxins leached from its leaves and tubers just below the soil surface can have serious effects. Nutsedge foliage concentrations of just one-half of one percent reduced corn yields by 20 percent. Soil containing 1 percent nutsedge root matter lowered corn yields 42 percent. Soybeans were also sensitive to the toxins, showing reductions in their yields of up to 35 percent. M. G. Voltz at the University of Connecticut found that nutsedge also hindered tomato growth. He suggested that the weed assists the "bad" soil bacteria in their denitrification—that is, changing soil nitrogen into forms plants can't use. Since nutsedge is a perennial weed, you should be sure to completely eradicate it, corms, vines and all, so it can't infiltrate your garden.

Giant foxtail (*Setaria faberii*) is a common weed in corn

Weeds to Watch Out For

The common weeds listed here have shown *some* signs of being allelopathic to crops. This listing is given as a matter of interest, not to suggest that it is the final word. Much more research is needed before we can be sure how to handle these plants.

Weed	Harmful Parts
Barnyard grass (*Echinochloa crus-galli*)	Decaying debris
Broomsedge (*Andropogon virginicus*)	Decaying debris
Canadian thistle (*Cirsium arvense*)	Root leachates, decaying debris
Crabgrass (*Digitaria sanguinalis*)	Root leachates, decaying debris
Eucalyptus (*Eucalyptus* spp.)	Leaf leachates
Johnson grass (*Sorghum halepense*)	Root leachates, decaying debris
Lamb's-quarters (*Chenopodium album*)	Decaying debris
Leafy spurge (*Euphorbia* spp.)	Decaying debris
Milkweed (*Asclepias syriaca*)	Leaf leachates
Mustard (*Brassica nigra*)	Decaying debris
Redroot pigweed (*Amaranthus retroflexus*)	Decaying debris
Sunflower (*Helianthus annuus*)	Root leachates, decaying debris

Weed	Harmful Parts
Velvetleaf (*Abutilon theophrasti*)	Decaying debris, seeds
Wild rye (*Elymus* spp.)	Root leachates

country. In laboratory studies, when corn plants were watered with solutions containing root exudates from the foxtail, corn growth was reduced by 35 percent. Even chemicals leached from dead foxtail plants hindered growth. The combined effects of competition and allelopathy can reduce corn growth some 90 percent in a foxtail-infested field.

The ubiquitous weed quack grass, or couch grass (*Agropyron repens*), has been closely studied in the field as well as in the laboratory. It, too, influences the nutrition of surrounding crops such as wheat and corn. Researchers aren't sure exactly what the allelopathic effect is, but the toxins in quack grass may hinder the food crop's ability to absorb nitrogen, phosphorus and potassium. In tests, even when fertilizers and water were supplied in liberal amounts, crop growth couldn't be improved. Other findings support the idea that quack grass doesn't make a good neighbor. Alfalfa planted in soil that had previously supported quack grass yielded only half as much as alfalfa grown in uninfested soil. In greenhouse studies, crops grown in soil containing ground quack grass rhizomes were stunted and pale.

Dozens of other weeds are suspected of harboring toxins harmful to plants. Protect your crops from the possible ill-effects of these weeds by learning to identify them and clearing them from the garden patch. The chart, Weeds to Watch Out For, can help you.

Using Crops to Control Weeds

Many crops release their own poisons as defense against warring weeds. Rye, wheat, buckwheat, barley, beets, oats, sorghum, cucumbers, peas, corn, fescue and hybrid sunflowers all possess some allelopathic properties. Research is sparse, but what studies have been done suggest that some of these plants could be a real boon to farmers and gardeners. As herbicides become more and more expensive to buy and the dangers of 2-4D and other chemicals become more evident, farmers may be turning to these plants for weed control.

Michigan State University's Alan Putnam is looking at the potential of allelopathic cover crops and green manures as weed killers. If they are effective, these crops could reduce the amounts of chemical herbicides needed to control weeds. Cover crops are legumes or grasses planted to cover bare soil and protect it from erosion and runoff. They become green manures when they are tilled under, adding organic matter to the soil. By selecting cover crops with weed-killing potential, Putnam is making these crops still more advantageous. In his experiments with vegetable crops, he plants a cover crop of rye and wheat in the fall and cuts it down in the spring when it is about a foot high. Putnam uses a short-term artificial herbicide, but mowing can be used instead. He then transplants vegetable seedlings directly into the rye cover crop. You can follow his lead by planting seedlings in tilled strips or individual holes within the living rye sod.

The leached chemicals from the mowed debris keep down most small-seeded broadleaf weeds such as purslane, pigweed and lamb's-quarters. Depending on when the rye is cut, weed control can last for most of the season—40 to 60 days. Young, living rye plants produce the most toxins, but the best weed control comes from the debris of older plants. However, if you wait too long before cutting, that can mean greater competition with the main crop. So far, the best results are achieved by knocking down the rye 30 to 50 days after it has sprouted. Under these conditions, vegetable transplants or even large-seeded legumes tolerate any competition or allelopathy quite well.

This method of weed control is especially appealing for several reasons. The rye is cheaper and more effective than the artificial herbicides most farmers must repeatedly spray to eliminate these weeds. As an added bonus, it offers the benefit of erosion control and acts as an organic fertilizer.

In the orchard, Putnam is finding that sorghum makes a good allelopathic cover crop. You might want to plant it in early summer, allow the crop to mature, then mow it in strips. The loose plant debris that accumulates under the trees acts as a weed-killing mulch. It might also be possible to plant sorghum later in the season so it can become established before hard frosts hit. The stress of winter's cold builds up chemicals in sorghum plants, making for more potent residues for the following year.

All sorts of factors complicate this sort of weed control. The cover crops aren't as selective as some herbicides, and they often aren't as thorough, either. Still, Putnam is convinced that within the next few years, many growers will begin using some forms of allelopathic plantings to reduce their dependence on weed-killing chemicals.

Other Weed-Hating Plants

Several workers have studied various grain, fruit and vegetable varieties with the hope that breeding could somehow increase a crop's weed-killing abilities. The research has been limited, but in addition to rye, wheat and sorghum, a number of other grain and vegetable crops have been identified as allelopathic to some weeds. Putnam and others looked at many wild and cultivated cucumbers and found that the wild types were able to inhibit the growth of the weed white mustard (*Brassica hirta*) up to 87 percent. Although cultivated cucumbers didn't have the allelopathic "punch," the researchers felt that such qualities could be bred into crops.

Gerald Leather of Maryland's Agricultural Research Service studied sunflower and Jerusalem artichoke cultivars to see whether or not selective breeding had erased the strong allelopathic quality of their wild forefather, the native sunflower. He found that they not only retained this characteristic, but that some sunflower varieties actually had more weed-killing potential than their native relative. In the greenhouse, chemicals from the stems and leaves of certain cultivars inhibited weed seedling growth some 50 to 75 percent. In field trials, the combined effects of competition and allelopathy kept broadleaf weeds in check.

Other examples of crops fighting back against weeds include corn and lupine against lamb's-quarters and pigweed, barley against a variety of weeds, oats against wild mustard, and beet seeds against corn cockle. At this point, it doesn't appear that native plants are necessarily more potent weed killers than highly bred ones. Indeed, perhaps like sunflowers, many cultivars are more effective natural herbicides than native varieties. As Elroy Rice and other scientists have explained, breeding for disease control often leads to an increase in some of the same plant chemicals responsible for allelopathy. Additional research will surely identify more crops that might be bred as weed killers.

Crops against Crops

Crops releasing allelopathic chemicals are bound to affect not just weeds but other cultivated plants as well. From the plant's perspective, whatever is growing nearby is a worthwhile target—even if it's your prize crop of romaine lettuce. Those knowledgeable in the field recognize that certain crops do, as Pliny and all those early farmers believed, indeed release toxins capable of injuring their neighbors.

Much of the research in this area is limited to studies of plant extracts. It remains to be seen whether results from such laboratory and greenhouse studies really tell us anything about allelopathic activity in the field or garden. To date, researchers have found that under controlled conditions alfalfa extracts delay germination of corn, soybeans, peas, oats and timothy hay; barley, oats, rye and wheat extracts inhibit the root growth of wheat plants; beet seeds contain a powerful growth inhibitor; and *Chrysanthemum* × *morifolium* leaves leach a powerful toxin that prevents lettuce seed from germinating.

Now that mainstream scientists are showing interest in mixed cropping and interplanting, field studies should be forthcoming. A few researchers have already recorded some allelopathic interactions between crops outside of the laboratory. In his experiments with various pest repellent plantings, Virginia State University's M. A. Latheef noted that French marigolds (*Tagetes patula*) had a strong allelopathic effect on bean plants. He noticed that beans grown near marigolds were severely stunted. Latheef also observed that tansy had an allelopathic effect on collards. A Russian study of potatoes planted between rows of apple seedlings showed that the apple trees suffered nitrogen loss and reduced photosynthesis because of toxins produced by the potatoes.

In another study, apple trees also were inhibited by toxins released from certain grasses. University of Rhode Island researchers found that turf grass reduces the growth of dogwood trees and forsythia bushes. In subsequent laboratory studies, chemicals from various species of grass were applied to potted forsythias. Since the same stunting and reduced growth rate resulted, allelopathy must be partially to blame.

Beware of Crop Residues

Considerably more work has been done on toxins released from decaying crop residues. Because so many farmers are stubble cropping (planting in the stubble left from the previous year's corn or other crop), many workers are looking at plant relations to see if there are any "bad neighbors" that might cause problems in such a system. Dozens of grain, vegetable and fruit crops produce allelopathic chemicals as they decompose. This means that subsequent plantings stand a good chance of being harmed.

Work in the 1940s showed that when pulverized leaves of wormwood were added to the soil, pea, bean and other seeds were slow to germinate. In a more recent study, decaying corn, timothy hay and rye all produced allelopathic chemicals that harmed tobacco seedlings. According to Rice, decaying leaves of sycamore and hackberry trees inhibit grasses and other plants. Poor germination and reduced growth rate are typical problems, but sometimes decaying crop residues also promote root diseases.

In the Salinas Valley of California, an elaborate study done by Patrick and others, showed that field debris of barley, broad beans, broccoli, rye, Sudan grass and vetch caused stunting and root injury to subsequent crops. Toxins weren't found throughout the fields but instead were concentrated in small pockets of soil right around each piece of the residue. Wherever lettuce or spinach roots grew near some of this decaying debris, they developed lesions and browning. Somehow the allelopathic chemicals encouraged disease organisms to attack the lettuce roots.

Findings from these and other studies could be of real value in determining the best crop rotation schemes and the best methods for handling residues. Just as poor fertility or lack of water can reduce yields, so allelopathic interactions may be responsible for problems that could be avoided. As we learn more about this complex science, we may find that we need to completely clean up the field or garden after growing certain crops, or change a rotation pattern to accommodate particularly sensitive crops. Many more experiments will have to be done before researchers are ready to give us concrete recommendations.

Rice farmers have already gained some practical tips from current research in allelopathy. Farmers are eager to rotate rice with soybeans or other nitrogen-fixing legumes in order to reduce the tremendous need for nitrogen fertilization. However, experiments show that soybeans don't do well if rice stubble is left in the paddies. The residue has an allelopathic effect on the legume crop; it inhibits nitrogen fixing and even interferes with the development of nodules on the bean roots. By removing the rice straw, the farmers can boost their soybean yields by hundreds of pounds per acre.

Crops against Themselves

Ironically, in what might be termed species suicide, plants often turn their chemical toxins and inhibitors against their own kind. In a vague way, farmers and gardeners have recognized this problem for two thousand years. After several years in one location, most crops begin to lag; yields fall while pest and disease problems rise. The soil seems "sick" or, as an early Greek writer put it, "exhausted." Soil sickness stunts alfalfa after it has been raised in the same field for more than a couple of years. The same is true of wheat, oats and other crops. Apple trees do poorly on land previously occupied by apples. The same is true of citrus trees and stone fruits such as peaches and cherries.

Rotation to the Rescue

In the eighteenth century, growers began rotating crops in order to get around this problem. Rotation helps rebuild soil nutrients and controls many diseases and pests—as long as the scheme includes a wide variety of crops from very different families with different pest problems and nutrient needs. When you alternate plants from different families in the same spot, pathogens and pests eventually die out because they have nothing to feed on. Following a crop that's a heavy potassium feeder with one that's greedy for phosphorus assures that there's not a heavy drain on the same soil nutrient. Following a heavy nitrogen feeding crop with legumes is a simple way to keep soil nutrient reserves in balance.

The herbicides, pesticides, fungicides and fertilizers of the twentieth century have made it seem possible to solve these problems without rotation. It came as something of a surprise when researchers began to discover that even when chemicals supplied the missing nutrients and prevented disease and pest infestations, crops grown over and over in one field *still* lagged. Although several earlier botanists and ecologists had suggested that plant toxins were at least partly to blame for soil sickness, the idea has only been well received in the past 30 years. Now research in this area of autotoxicity or autoallelopathy is well underway. Results show that all kinds of plants produce chemicals capable of harming their own species and that these toxins may accumulate in the soil.

Alfalfa is the focus of many autoallelopathy studies. Canadian agronomist G. R. Webster and others studied areas of Alberta that once supported fine alfalfa but now produce short, spindly, yellowish plants with few root nodules. Adding fertilizers doesn't help the plants. Neither does irrigation, since water is already plentiful. Pathologists can find no trace of disease. To add another element to this puzzling phenomenon, researchers know that clovers perform just fine in these same soils.

At the University of Illinois, comparative studies of single-cropped alfalfa fields and fields rotated with corn or corn and soybeans support the theory that alfalfa slowly poisons itself. The researchers made sure that competitive problems such as nutrient deficiency and disease were all but eliminated. Still, after six years, almost twice as much alfalfa was harvested from fields that had been rotated as from those that had remained in continuous alfalfa.

This is pretty convincing, if circumstantial, evidence for autoallelopathy. Once the toxin is isolated and the exact mechanisms understood, scientists will be better able to recommend rotation patterns for alfalfa or perhaps begin breeding new strains that would not be as self-toxic.

Fruit Replant Problems

Orchardists are confronted with autoallelopathy when they try to replace old trees with seedlings of the same species. Apples, apricots, cherries, citrus, grapevines, peaches and plums all have pretty poor replant records, although sometimes new seedlings can be started with no problems. Many, many factors are involved, including the carry-over of diseases and pests. Autoallelopathy is only part of the replant problem, but according to some researchers, it's often the main part. With peaches, decomposing roots are the source of toxins that are particularly concentrated the first year or two after the old tree has been removed. With citrus trees, their roots seem to inhibit beneficial fungi that usually break down toxins. Without the fungi, poisons build up, and subsequent plantings are dwarfed and sickly.

What the Future Holds

It's easy to argue that allelopathy need not concern gardeners. Aside from the really dramatic toxic effects of black walnut trees or the replant problems associated with some fruit trees, plant-produced toxins don't seem to be seriously harming garden crops. However, as scientists learn more and more about these chemicals, we will surely see exciting applications that could revolutionize agriculture and horticulture. As always, the challenge will be to use this new knowledge wisely and responsibly with an understanding of how it affects the entire agroecosystem.

There are several areas where exciting new developments are likely to occur. Geneticists are beginning to look at alfalfa, cucumbers, sunflowers, rye and many allelopathic weeds in hopes of breeding self-weeding cultivars. Besides this work on developing new varieties, researchers are also looking for natural herbicides. As allelopathic compounds are identified and isolated in plants, this work should turn up some interesting results. Much thought and foresight will be needed to assure that we don't repeat our past mistakes with these new materials.

Mulches and green manures are also coming under scientific scrutiny. Work with rye, sorghum, alfalfa and other plants shows that allelopathic plant debris can be used to keep down weeds during critical stages of crop growth. New rotation patterns may emerge as research yields evidence of the allelopathic effects of certain crop residues. Developments in this area might lead to changes in planting times, crop selection and the order in which crops are grown.

Given all of these areas where breakthroughs are possible, allelopathy and the entire field of phytochemicals might just be the new frontier of agriculture.

Chapter 5

Designing the Companion Garden

Science can teach us plenty about the ways plants and animals influence one another. From research, we can learn which species attract beneficial insects, repel pests or harm or help their neighbors. Yet, ultimately, when we set about actually orchestrating all this information into a growing garden, art and intuition must take over.

So far, science has come up with very few guidelines for designing the interplanted field or garden. We know some crops perform well together, but we don't know in which combinations they perform *best*. When should each companion crop be planted and at what spacing? How close must repellent plants be for their effects to be felt? If, as researchers now suspect, legumes can help "feed" neighboring nonlegumes, what crop to crop ratio

is needed?

Dozens of questions like these have yet to be answered, and indeed, some may never be answered to everyone's satisfaction. Every field or garden is a unique situation, and every farmer or gardener has different goals. Different weather and soil conditions, surrounding vegetation, and cropping history can create very different growing conditions. Depending on the circumstances, crops respond differently to a given planting pattern or spacing. Add to this each grower's needs and sense of purpose, and it becomes very clear that what works well in one place for one grower may not be suitable in another spot or for a different grower.

It's up to each of us to answer these questions ourselves. To the extent that we know the lay of our own piece of land and the sorts of cultural practices that tend to work in our gardens, we are in the best position to do this. By observing plants and animals, by constantly trying new companion planting schemes and even by doing a bit of backyard research, we can discover the best crop spacings and designs for our particular situations. (For some guidance on how to conduct your own research, see the Appendix, Making Your Own Discoveries.)

There are all sorts of interesting possibilities for interplanting in the standard vegetable patch, raised bed or border. You can even apply the basic theory of companion planting (combining different crops to make the best use of available resources and to create the healthiest, highest yields) to the yard itself. Hedges, weeds, surrounding lawn and trees are all part of the garden ecosystem and should be included in your overall interplanting design.

Quiet Revolution in Garden Design

A quiet revolution is underway in the world of gardening— one that has a great deal to do with companion planting. Landscape gardeners are beginning to include lowly vegetables, herbs, so-called weeds and native fruit trees in their planting arrangements. For example, we now hear asparagus recommended as a summer backdrop for bright annual or perennial flowers. Rhubarb is suggested as a bold accent in foundation plantings or wide borders. Thyme is mentioned as a partner with white alyssum for a delicate low border along a front walkway.

Advances in plant breeding have made it much more enticing for gardeners to move vegetables out of the backyard plot and into beds traditionally reserved only for "ornamentals." Breeders have created vegetables that are as compact and colorful as many flowers. Flip through current seed catalogs to take a look at purple podded bush beans and golden-orange peppers, to name only two examples. With a little planning, these edibles can breathe life into your perennial flower bed during those midsummer months when so little blooms. Ahead in this chapter there are lots of suggestions for planning in and around the interplanted garden. Some of these plans have been designed by gardeners,

(continued on page 115)

112

Using Color in the Garden Plan

The recent interest in edible landscaping has made all of us more aware of the beauty to be found in *all* plants, not just ornamentals. If you've ever tried to paint a basket of garden vegetables, you've realized how subtle and beautiful are their hues. There must be twenty shades of green, not to mention the blues, reds, purples, pinks and yellows in our ordinary vegetable flowers, fruits and foliage. When you add the vegetable varieties specially bred for their ornamental appeal, the possibilities for using edible crops to brighten up the landscape seem endless.

Every season exciting new colored vegetables appear in the catalogs. To list them all would be of little use since their availability changes from year to year and according to where you garden. Here, however, are a few general ideas to help you find something different to enhance your garden's color scheme.

Color	Vegetable	Remarks
WHITE		
	Gracillus Ornamental Corn	Grows just 2 to 3 feet tall with white and light green striped foliage; looks like the common garden crop, but ears are not edible.
	White Beauty Tomato	Mild, sweet tomato that turns white as it ripens.
	White Italian Eggplant	Produces small, mild-flavored white fruits.
	White Kohlrabi	Interplants nicely with beets or onions.
	White Scallop Squash	Some varieties start out pale green, then mature to white.
	White Sprouting Broccoli	Produces small white heads that taste and look like tiny cauliflowers.

113

Color	Vegetable	Remarks
YELLOW		
	Banana Pepper	Sweet, long and slender light yellow pepper.
	Golden Acorn Squash	Small, bright yellow squash grows on fairly compact bush plants.
	Golden Yellow Eggplant	Produces tiny fruits that start out white and turn a bright yellow as they mature.
	Honey Gold Canteloupe	Not a compact bush variety, but excellent for trellising; melons are quite small, sweet and tender.
	Yellow Tomatoes	Several varieties produce yellow fruits, but some of the most interesting are yellow plum and pear.
PINK-RED		
	Red Cabbage	Choose small, early maturing varieties for companion planting.
	Red Chicory	Small, reddish-green heads appear in spring, with reddish foliage throughout the summer.
	Red Lettuce	Color ranges from bronze to deep red, depending on variety; rich soil and good growing conditions produce the richest shades.
	Red Okra	Produces deep red pods on reddish-green plants.
	Ruby Chard	Deep red leaf stems and veins with dark green foliage.
	Scarlet Runner Bean	Forms a beautiful screen with its red flowers, but beans aren't particularly tasty.
	Tomatoes	Choose small, determinate varieties for companion planting.

Color	Vegetable	Remarks
PURPLE		
	Flowering Kale	Low-growing plants have white or pink center leaves rimmed by green; choose miniature varieties for companion planting; edible.
	Opal Basil	Deep purple foliage.
	Oriental Eggplant	Compact, yet prolific plants; eggplants are slender and elongated, with a milder flavor than standard eggplants.
	Purple Beans	Purple beans look striking against green bushes; beans turn green when cooked.
	Purple Broccoli	Deep purple heads turn green when cooked.
	Purple Kohlrabi	Lavender and whitish coloring.

landscapers or agricultural researchers purely for improving yields, others for providing continuous harvests and still others for mainly decorative purposes. All are guaranteed to fuel your imagination for designing other planting schemes that work well and appeal to your own sense of order and garden beauty.

Design in the Garden

Whether you're a traditionalist with a rectangular vegetable patch laid out in rows or a new-style gardener with raised beds or circular plots, there are plenty of different companion planting arrangements to try within your garden.

Rows

Although there are lots of other more imaginative options, rows are still the standard in most gardens. In the old-fashioned vegetable patch, crops are lined up like batallions of soldiers with ample pathways for the gardener between the rows. In intensive raised beds where soil is very rich and pathways unnecessary, the

(continued on page 118)

115

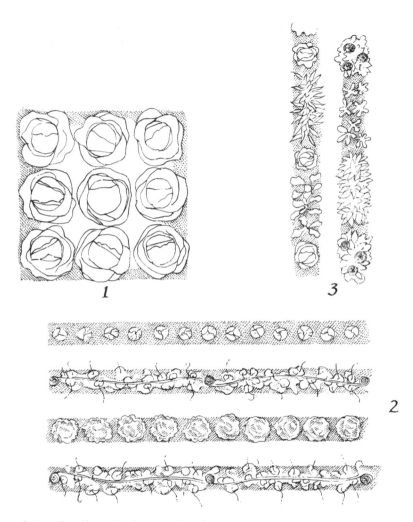

Interplanting Designs: *View 1 shows square center spacing, where the rows are spaced the same distance apart as plants are within the row. In view 2 there's an example of alternate row intercropping. With this design, each row contains a different crop. View 3 shows interplanting within rows, where each row contains a combination of two or more companion*

4

5

crops. Block planting is shown in view 4; each square-foot block is planted with a single crop, and adjacent blocks contain compatible companions. View 5 shows one variation of circle planting; cabbage forms the center, while tansy and onions create a protective ring.

rows can be more closely spaced. To save space in either situation, most of us have by now adopted equidistant spacing. Using this method, you space the rows the same distance apart as plants within the row. The result is a grid pattern of rows in which leaves and rooting zones overlap very little.

As long as you're just dealing with one crop, it's relatively easy to lay out the rows. When companion plants are introduced into the scheme, spacing and arrangement become a bit more complex. It may even be necessary to stake or trellis one or more of the crops in order to make room for the companion and to maximize light.

You have two basic options when it comes to introducing companions into the row garden: You can interplant between rows or interplant within rows. In the first plan, each row contains a different crop. In the second plan, each row contains the same combination of two or more companion crops.

Which is better? Researchers aren't sure. For several years now, they have been debating this question, and it seems clear that much depends on the specific crops involved and on the growing conditions created by the surrounding vegetation, prevailing wind direction and the like.

Interplanting between Rows

It seems that this technique, also called alternate-row intercropping, is particularly productive when one of the companions tends to shade the other. For example, on a large scale, tomatoes and cabbage are best intercropped in alternate rows, so that the tomatoes have less chance of shading the cabbage. Some researchers have concluded that bean yields are highest if single rows of corn are alternated with snap, fava or soybeans. Corn and rice, peanuts or bush squash also do well in alternate single rows. You might want to try intercropping rows of peas with shade-tolerant, low-growing crops like spinach, lettuce or Chinese cabbage. You can allow dwarf pea varieties such as Lacy Lady to trail on the ground, but most of the vining varieties will require trellising. Other interesting alternate-row combinations are trellised cucumbers or oriental melons with lettuce, celery or Chinese cabbage.

You can use alternate rows, of course, for just about any companion crop, not just tall ones. Cabbage with eggplants, potatoes with Brussels sprouts, snap beans with endive, or just about any other combination you can think of is possible. Perennials such as asparagus, strawberries, rhubarb or horseradish also interplant well in alternate rows with annual vegetable crops such as tomatoes, potatoes or cabbage. (Just be sure to keep the strawberry runners and spreading horseradish plants under control.) Your cropping combinations should be based on the criteria discussed throughout the book–complementary nutrient and light needs, insect control and so on. Arrange rows so they run across, not down slopes to avoid erosion problems. Where possible run them north-south so that shading is less of a problem.

How closely you plant companion crops depends on which ones you've chosen and on the condition of your soil. Rich, moist soil is better able to support intensive plantings. As a general rule, follow the between-plant spacing you'd normally use for each crop, but determine the between-row spacing by averaging the distances recommended for the two crops.

Although single rows give the two companions the most contact, some growers prefer to alternate double rows of one or both crops. If a large intercrop such as potatoes forces rows of corn too far apart, pollination might not be as complete, and your corn harvest would suffer. Instead of alternating every row of corn with potatoes, it might be better to plant two rows of corn for every two of potatoes.

Interplanting within Rows

This arrangement is better for crops of similar size and shape or for compact companions that you can easily squeeze in between crops. It's also a good choice for relay companion plants that aren't going to be in the ground the entire time a main crop is growing. An early crop of radishes, onions or beets does nicely between lettuce, beans, cabbage or tomatoes since it only occupies space for about 30 days. You might also tuck an early crop of lettuce or spinach in between large, late-maturing vegetables such as winter squash or cucumbers. Try sneaking a few carrots within rows of your main crops. Keep in mind that the spacing must be a little more generous since this root crop requires most of the season to mature. Another suggestion is to interplant crops with complementary growth patterns within rows. Set garlic in among rows of roses, or anise between heads of cabbage. I've found that kohlrabi-lettuce-radish, spinach-carrot, bush bean-Mexican marigold and cabbage-garlic combinations all perform well in shared rows.

It's possible to interplant two or even more crops of similar size and shape and similar nutrient needs for an entire season, but to do so, soil nutrition must be top notch. As long as you work in plenty of compost, rotted manure or other nitrogen-rich organic matter, and water well, various salad greens will complement one another within the row. A line-up of erect romaine, ruffled red and green leaf lettuce, elegant butterhead and curly endive will provide a lovely assortment of greens for salads. Their contrasting textures and shades of green will also make a lovely swath while they're in the garden.

Some gardeners successfully interplant corn with beans, cucumbers, melons or squash within the row. Researchers have suggested that within-row intercropping of these plants may reduce yields of one or both crops, but those growers who've tried it don't necessarily agree. As an interesting garden experiment, you might try comparing within-row and alternate-row arrangements of these crops. You might plant a hill of vining (not bush) squash after every two or three hills of corn. Then you could compare that arrangement with a bush type squash planted in alternate rows with the corn.

In the within-row design, you might be able to use the same spacing distance between plants and between rows, as long as the soil is quite rich and moist. Determine planting distances by averaging the spacings of all the crops in the row. Using the earlier example of a row of salad greens, you'd take the average of the following in-row distances: 12 inches (romaine), 9 inches (leaf), 12 inches (butterhead) and 18 inches (endive). In your interplanted row, you'd allow roughly 13 inches between plants. Use a bit of common sense along with mathematics. Know the growth patterns of the crops you're dealing with, and where possible, stick to compact varieties.

Strips

Strip intercropping is widely used with forage crops on large farms, but it can also be scaled down to size for good use in home vegetable gardens. It's similar to alternate-row intercropping, but it involves alternating bands of varying width, rather than single or double rows.

Diane Matthews, staff entomologist at the Rodale Research Center, is experimenting with strip intercropping using rye. Lawn-mower-width strips of annual rye lie between plantings of peas, Chinese cabbage or other crops that have been planted in tilled strips at least 1 foot wide. The sod strips are mowed periodically. Matthews finds that these strips help control weeds, conserve moisture and perhaps even discourage flea beetles or other pests from locating their favorite food crop. The rye also keeps the garden area neat and protects the path from too much compaction. In the fall, or even early the next spring, the strips can be tilled under as a green manure crop.

In similar studies at the Rodale Research Center and elsewhere, legumes are used in strip-cropping systems. Main crops of corn or beans are planted within or between strips of clover, alfalfa or other sod that is already established. In addition to moisture conservation and erosion and weed control, legumes boost soil nitrogen levels, particularly once they're tilled under.

If you live in a windy area, you might consider growing sunflowers, asparagus, corn or other tall, fairly sturdy crops in strips to help reduce wind damage in wide open spaces. Strips of these tall crops placed throughout the garden will protect tender low-growing vegetables in adjacent rows. Even bamboo or Jerusalem artichokes can serve the same purpose, although you wouldn't want these invasive plants in a small vegetable garden. Confine them to outlying areas or strip plantings in large plots or fields.

Strip interplanting is also a good way to include repellent crops, trap crops or insectary weeds or wildflowers in the garden. You might plant a band of onions, basil, marigolds or other aromatic herbs between every few rows of a main crop. As a haven for beneficial insects, you might allow a strip of weeds to grow in a bed of cole crops or beans. Perennials such as catnip, chamomile, eucalyptus, mint or tansy can be treated as perma-nent strip plantings in the garden, as long as you take measures to control their rampant growth. Adjacent strips are free for annual tilling and planting of a companion vegetable crop.

Strip interplanting isn't confined only to the vegetable garden.

Controlling Invasive Companions

Tansy and wormwood are highly recommended as companion plants, but anyone who has ever grown them knows how rampantly they spread. Even a little mint can go a long way toward over-running an herb garden. Imagine what it might do as an interplant in the vegetable plot! Invasive companions like these require particular attention and care when you grow them among annual vegetable plants.

As a general rule, such perennials are best confined to a limited area in the main vegetable beds. In order to gain their benefits without their problems, keep hardy perennial herbs, weeds and flowers in strips within the garden. Ecologist Miguel Altieri recommends alternating such strips with every ten rows. A very effective way to keep rambling plants in line is to sink flue tiles or large plastic pots with their bottoms cut out into the soil up to their rims. Fill the insides with soil and plant as usual. You can also control invasive growth by encircling the plant's root area with metal edging.

Flowering annual weeds and herbs can also be handled in strips or blocks. You can control those that reseed themselves by practicing shallow, not deep, cultivation as you work the garden soil. Deep cultivation brings up a great many weed seeds; if you turn only the top 6 inches of soil, fewer seeds will sprout, and you'll have fewer weeds to contend with. Permanent paths between established garden beds make deep digging unnecessary after the first few years.

Watch crops closely for signs of competition and stress. Stunting, yellowing, wilting or a lopsided shape can all indicate that surrounding companions are getting the better of the main crop. Many weeds and herbs will require frequent pruning throughout the season. Clip them back before they shade neighboring crops. Since cuttings often have the same pest repellent or other effect carried by the living plants, you can use them as a mulch.

Among the most ornery weeds and herbs that may require special care are chickweed, goldenrod, goosefoot, mints, mustard, peppergrass, pigweed, quack grass, spurge, tansy, wormwood and yarrow.

In the orchard or vineyard, you can use it to introduce not only insectary weeds but also companion main crops such as strawberries or potatoes. In the wide rows between trees, strips of companion crops are easy to plant, with plenty of room remaining to care for the trees.

Under most circumstances, interplant strips consist of rows placed as close together as plants allow. Use equidistant spacing wherever possible. You can try broadcasting small seeds of grains, grasses, leafy greens and some wildflowers instead of sowing them in rows, but be sure to thin plants to the appropriate density once they sprout.

Blocks

Mel Bartholomew popularized this garden design in his book *Square Foot Gardening* (Rodale Press, 1981). Although he doesn't advocate the square foot plan as a companion planting design per se, the end result is inevitably an interplanted garden bed.

With this system, growing beds are carefully divided into 1-foot-square blocks. Each block may be planted with a single tomato or cabbage plant, or perhaps six beets, or nine bush beans, depending on the size and growth habit of the particular crop. Interplanting is accomplished by planning adjacent blocks so that they contain compatible plants.

Gardeners who, like me, would prefer not to approach gardening as an engineering enterprise, may prefer to use a variation on the theme of square foot gardening. Simply reserve sections of your growing beds for block plantings. I plant compact, low-growing crops such as salad greens or bush beans in blocks. I also block off the shady ends of one or two beds as nurseries for starting seeds. Lettuce, cole crops and summer herbs and flowers like basil, zinnias, cosmos, bachelor's buttons and seed onions along with others get their start in a nursery block before being moved to their permanent garden spots. Spacing can be quite dense, as it's only a temporary arrangement. I've found it's much easier to give that tender loving care seedlings require when they're in this special space. If frost threatens, I can easily pop a cloche over the entire section. Extra watering or dosing with manure or chamomile tea is a snap, too.

Circles

The circle is an almost universal symbol of harmony and completeness, so its role in agriculture should not surprise us. In some native cultures of North and South America and in ancient Greece, circle plantings were as widely used as rows. Throughout the Americas, corn was typically grown in hills, each surrounded by larger concentric circles of beans and sunflowers or squash. Such an arrangement enhances corn pollination and cuts down on weeds and erosion. It's also likely that the beans help "feed" the corn with the nitrogen fixed in their root nodules.

In today's gardens, we can adopt a similar design for all sorts of crops in order to save space and add visual interest. Circles are particularly good strategies for companion planting. Surround susceptible plants with barriers of aromatic herbs or other repellent companions. A trio of cabbage might be enclosed with tansy, onion or any other plant you feel may keep pests at bay. Plant radishes in a circle around each bush squash or cucumber plant with the hope of fending off borers and other pests. Try protecting one or more tomato plants supported by stakes or cages with a circular planting of purple and green basil.

Designs like these offer limitless decorative appeal. Take advantage of the special varieties of low-growing herbs or annual flowers for neatly enclosing all sorts of vegetables. Low-growing marigolds, dwarf or semidwarf zinnias, ageratum, alyssum, pinks, lobelia and veronica all conform well to a circle design.

One fun variation on this circle theme is the wagon wheel herb or kitchen garden. Prepare a garden bed just large enough to accommodate the circumference of an old wooden wagon or buggy wheel. With the wheel in place, plant a different low-growing herb, salad green or other compact crop in each section. Even if you don't have a wheel, you can lay out a circle garden in the same way, and plant in wedge-shaped sections to form an attractive focal point of a patio planting or yard.

Unless pathways are part of your circle garden, keep plantings 4 feet wide or less. If you let plantings get much bigger than this, you'll have trouble reaching in to weed and cultivate.

Around and About the Garden

What grows around our gardens is every bit as important to their ecological well-being as what grows in them. Surrounding plants host insects and diseases, create shade, influence wind patterns and temperatures, and alter the chemical makeup of the soil. Therefore, the decisions we make about where and what we plant or dig up could have a lot to do with the success of our gardens.

In order to make these decisions, we must first understand the specific growing conditions present in each part of our yard or homestead. We also need to begin thinking of which plants can fill these niches and what they will contribute to the total environment. Ideally, every plant we grow ought to serve two or more needs by providing food, hosting beneficial insects or protecting against wind, even as it contributes to the overall design of the landscape.

Borders

What a lot of space is wasted around the edges of our garden beds and vegetable patches! Many of the smaller vegetables can so easily be slipped into the garden perimeter that it's a shame to devote an entire row, block or strip to these plants. Grow onions, garlic, radishes, beets, parsley and the low-growing herbs and salad greens in borders, saving main areas for bigger crops.

With a little extra thought, these border plantings can be a decorative way to unify the entire garden. Although we tend to

125

Plants for Borders

Low Borders (less than 1 foot in height)
Dwarf or compact vegetables form nice borders for a short time, but they leave gaps when they're harvested. Therefore, it's a good idea to combine these with a fast-growing delicate flower or herb such as alyssum or cress, which can fill in as the vegetables are removed.

Some good choices for low borders include: alpine strawberries, chard, dwarf cabbage, dwarf sage and thyme, endive, garlic, kale and flowering kale, lettuce, onions and parsley.

Medium Borders (1 to 2 feet in height)
Herbs such as basil, dill, lavender, thyme and wormwood are best in this category. Some other suggestions are anise, carrots, chamomile, chicory and fennel.

Hedges (over 2 feet in height)
Some of these plants are tall enough to block out sun and air, so don't plant them in too close a border around the garden. They work best as distant borders or natural fences, enclosing fairly large areas. Asparagus and comfrey will die back entirely over the winter and require several months to fill in come spring. The bramble fruits will look rather untidy in winter months, and they'll require careful training and pruning in order to be maintained as a hedge. Asparagus, blueberries, cherries, comfrey and hawthorn are probably the neatest and easiest to maintain. Other suitable plants include currants, gooseberries, grapes and Nanking cherries.

---

think in terms of flowers and herbs as borders for the flower bed, there's no reason why the lovelier vegetables can't be included as well. If you give all garden beds—flower as well as vegetable—the same border treatment, a pleasing harmony results.

Select crops that are attractive throughout their entire lives and resilient enough to withstand all the knocking about they get in this busy garden area. Tender plants like beans, eggplants or even leeks bruise readily and don't perform well in garden edgings. Choose tougher specimens like beets, lettuce, spinach, chard and New Zealand spinach.

The most interesting borders include two or more plants with different textures or colors. Alternate white-veined chard with a crimson-veined variety; intersperse red leaf lettuce among the green; contrast curly mounds of emerald parsley with mounds of silvery white dusty miller. Interplanting within the border also helps keep bare spots from developing. Interplant varieties that mature successively, and keep relay planting to fill gaps in the border throughout the season. Full, ground-hugging plants like alyssum, parsley or lobelia are good candidates for a border since they fill in so easily. Try interplanting perennials like creeping thyme, prostrate rosemary, dwarf sage, oregano and other herbs with annual greens. Cut-and-come-again plants such as leaf lettuce, chard and garland chrysanthemums are valuable border plants since they remain attractive for most of the season. The garland chrysanthemum is an especially nice choice, for come midsummer when you tire of gathering the fresh greens, the plant puts forth loads of bright daisylike flowers. (You can use the dried petals in soups or stir-fries.)

In less formal settings, you can devote borders to wildflowers and weeds such as goldenrod and stinging nettle that attract insect pollinators and predators. Many beneficial insects will travel quite a distance, so it's not necessary to give them shelter right in the garden. A weedy border just outside the garden fence will do very nicely.

You might also want to limit the more pesky perennial companions like mints, Jerusalem artichokes, eucalyptus, tansy and horseradish to these borders. To ensure their permanent confinement, use metal edging or another soil barrier, as described earlier in the box, Controlling Invasive Companions.

Natural Fences

Good fences make good neighbors, and they also make happy gardeners. Unless you have a well-trained dog who can scare away deer, groundhogs and those darling but destructive rabbits without simultaneously trampling through your garden beds, a good fence is a necessity. Wire fences do the trick, but they're hardly an aesthetic asset to your yard. The right shrubbery, either alone or with the fence, is much nicer. Europeans have long relied on boxwood or privet to enclose their formal gardens, but these overly manicured shrubs are far too fussy for today's gardening style. Besides, shrubs with edible fruits or pretty flowers can be a lot more pleasing. In England, I have seen both gooseberry and quince serve as visually stunning fences. In this country, blueberries are another possibility. Espaliered fruit trees are another option, if you have the patience to train and care for these.

As a barrier to people and dogs, dense plantings of bramble fruits can practically replace the garden fence. Even a perennial herb hedge made from southernwood, lovage, sage or tansy can be something of a deterrent. Leeks, beets, lettuce, spinach, onions or Chinese greens make excellent companions in the shade of any of these bramble or herb barriers.

Edible Border Plantings: *Ring the garden with attractive, low-growing plants that serve a dual purpose. The leaf lettuce, beets, oregano and chives in this border can show up on the*

128

Food on Several Stories

In Asia and parts of Africa, the need to raise a variety of crops in the smallest area has led to intensive interplanting schemes that include not only annual vegetables but all sorts of perennial shrubs and trees as well. This is multistory cropping at its finest.

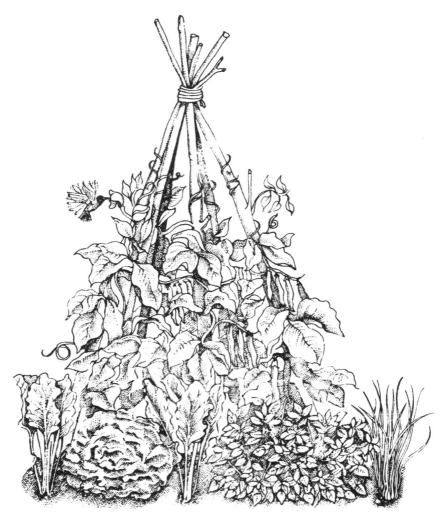

dinner table. Delicate flowering alyssum (shown on the left) is a good border plant since it will fill in the empty spaces left when you harvest the edibles.

It makes use of vertical as well as horizontal growing space. Tropical gardeners interplant coconuts with hedges of cocoa, which they also intersperse with lower growing pineapples. The arrangement often appears, at first glance, haphazard, even chaotic. Very often there may be no rows or pathways and no overall geometric pattern.

Those researchers who have studied such systems find that they are, in fact, quite efficient and complex arrangements, which satisfy many needs. Planting patterns take advantage of the area's hills, valleys and other topographic features. Individual crops are grouped according to their complementary shapes and their needs for light or shade. Some are chosen for planting around the house, to provide shade and privacy, and perhaps to take advantage of the nutrients supplied by human and animal wastes. With these multistory systems, an effort is made to plant as much as possible, leaving adequate room between plants so that their leaves don't overlap.

Certainly growing conditions in the tropics are especially conducive to these very intensive, mostly permanent interplantings. Yet, according to Australian Bill Mollison, the basic principle of these plantings can be applied almost everywhere. Mollison has come up with a concept of permaculture—self-sustaining interplantings that make the best use of available resources with the least harm to the environment. His is a philosophy of companion planting applied to the entire homestead. It's based on the theory that the more complex and diverse a system is, the more stable it is.

Following Mollison's lead, we can start by observing the natural ecosystem of our yards. We can then design crop plantings that fill not only our needs but satisfy nature's needs as well. Once we begin to think of growing area in terms of vertical as well as horizontal space, opportunities for raising fruits and vegetables begin to seem boundless. Imagine the harmonious plantings you can make in your yard to take advantage of this multistory interplanting scheme. Fruit, nut and lumber trees can fill the upper story. Grapes trained along surrounding fences, beds of asparagus, or hedgerows of various brambles, blueberries or other fruits can make up the middle story. Depending on the light levels, the lowest cropping level might support legumes and

Edible Accent Plants

Many of our lowliest vegetables and weedy herbs have such interesting shapes or textures that they can be very successfully used in a variety of garden schemes. In planning your flower beds, rock gardens and foundation plantings, consider including a few of these. You can squeeze the smaller ones in anywhere, but those over 2 feet tall belong in beds large enough to resist being dominated by such magnificent vegetables. Plan carefully before establishing perennials like artichokes, asparagus and rhubarb.

Small Accent Plants (less than 2 feet in height)
Alpine strawberries, basil (green or purple), cabbage (consider a crinkly leaved or red variety), chives, dwarf sage, Egyptian onions, garlic chives, oriental eggplants, parsley (flat or curly leaved), perennial bunching onions, rosemary, thyme, Welsh onions.

Large Accent Plants (over 2 feet in height)
Asparagus, cardoon, globe artichokes, rhubarb, sage, yarrow.

---

grasses, or annual vegetables. Use strip cropping to interplant this lowest level, allowing several feet between it and middle-story plantings.

Landscaping with Fruits and Vegetables

Mollison's permaculture, like traditional Asian homestead plantings, is a special sort of design. The purpose behind it is to combine food production with the home into a system that reflects nature's own system, with all its stability and diversity.

131

Everything that is grown or raised fulfills several functions, and every function is fulfilled by several plants.

You don't need a farm in order to practice this method. A sort of permaculture can be set up in even the tiniest of yards. It's merely a matter of thinking about each plant in terms of what it does and trying to take advantage of as many of those functions as you can. For example, where a windbreak is required, you might combine native fruit trees with a few shrubs such as rugosa rose, honeysuckle, heather or serviceberry. If your soil is poor, you can use nitrogen-fixing species such as locust or Russian olive. Many of these host beneficial insects in addition to building up the soil. Where wind speeds are particularly high and you need very dense plantings, try growing trees in double rows with strips of corn, sunflowers or perennial shrubs between.

Double-Duty Trees

Fruit or nut trees deserve a place in the front yard, as well as in the back. Their shade is just as refreshing as an oak or ash tree's, with the possibility of fresh fruit as a bonus. Some of the native fruit trees such as crab apples or wild plums, or the old-fashioned standard apricot and pear varieties are the best choices since they are hardy sorts requiring little special disease or insect control.

Winter pear varieties, apricots and cherries are especially valuable in the yard because they retain their leaves a fairly long time for a stunning autumn display. Cherry and apricot trees do require some attention as the season winds down because their fruit attracts wasps and bees as it ripens and falls. You must attend to harvesting and clean-up chores promptly, otherwise you risk attracting every wasp and bee from miles around.

Some nineteenth-century farmers planted grapes beneath their fruit trees, but the additional wasps and bees this would attract could really create a problem near the house. A better choice of companions for maturing fruit trees are some of the perennial herbs able to tolerate some shade. Sweet cicely, sweet woodruff and the smaller mints are good choices. Among the annuals, legumes such as peanuts, alfalfa or beans also do well under trees. I've even seen a cucumber vine doing quite nicely as it climbed the trunk of a flowering plum tree.

Double-Duty Trees and Companions: *Trees like this apricot and cherry beautify the yard, give shade and shower you with a delicious harvest. Companions at the base of the trees take advantage of what is often idle space. Peanuts grow beneath the apricot tree shown at top, and mint fills in the area below the cherry tree shown at bottom.*

Encyclopedia
of Companions

In the pages that follow, you'll find vegetables, flowers, herbs, weeds and fruit and nut trees, as well as some common pests, listed alphabetically. Each entry gives you a brief summary of companion planting information. I've made an effort to clearly separate what we *know* from what we *believe* about each plant concerning its relationship with other plants and with insects. You'll find garden lore and the firsthand, but untested, experiences of gardeners presented as "tradition," to be distinguished from those findings that result from formal "research." Since this listing is meant for gardeners, I have omitted many experiments designed for large-scale mechanical cultivation of forage and grain crops. Instead, I've emphasized research involving the most common garden vegetables and fruits. The findings are summa-

rized in very general terms, in order to give you a sense of the
research that has been done. The numbers you see cited after
each research listing refer to specific articles that appear in the
Bibliography at the end of this book. Refer to these sources if you
want to know the particular details of a certain experiment.

As you refer to this section, keep in mind that both tradition
and scientific research are valuable sources of gardening
information. The traditions provide suggestions for research and
home experimentation. Some of the data already gathered support these claims, and some disprove them. In many instances,
scientists have found that a certain planting tradition is indeed
beneficial, but they can't determine exactly why. For the most
part, experimentation has left us with some tantalizing facts but

no clear-cut final planting guides.

Our knowledge in these new sciences is constantly expanding and changing. Every year, gardeners make new discoveries, and researchers produce new results that challenge or enhance old ones. Don't make the mistake of using this encyclopedia of companions as a planting bible. Few of those scientists investigating allelopathy or interplanting are ready to draw conclusions about how to grow fruits and vegetables. Be as leery of embracing the latest results from a single scientific study as you are about adhering to an unfounded tradition. Just because a certain weed hosts a predator of a certain insect pest doesn't necessarily mean that you should allow that weed to grow rampantly in and around the garden. There are lots of other factors you must consider. Similarly, the allelopathic properties of a certain crop don't automatically condemn it to growing all alone. Most of these effects are very, very small and still poorly documented in the field. The real value in this sort of summary is the total picture it gives us of garden ecology. As we look at these facts, we can begin to appreciate the web of life that makes the garden what it is.

Alfalfa

Medicago sativa
Leguminosae
Perennial legume grown for forage

Alfalfa has been recognized as a soil-improving crop since ancient times. It also helps reduce erosion and acts as a host for predator insects.

Companion Role with Plants

Tradition: A companion crop of mustard is said to stimulate the growth of alfalfa plants.

Research: There's no evidence to back up the idea that mustard enhances alfalfa growth. In laboratory work, extracts of alfalfa hay reduced the seed germination and subsequent growth of crops such as corn, soybeans, peas, oats and timothy hay. We don't know whether alfalfa has the same effect on crops when it grows in a field or garden. (91)

Remarks: As a nitrogen-fixing legume, alfalfa is an excellent cover crop or green manure. Since it's slow to take hold, it is often planted with a quick-growing companion crop such as timothy, winter wheat or oats. Alfalfa's long taproot helps break up heavy soil and bring up nutrients. In order to gain the most benefits from an alfalfa cover or green manure crop, take several cuttings before turning it under. In experiments at the Rodale Research Center, freshly cut alfalfa has proved to be an excellent mulch for both tilled and untilled gardens. The alfalfa contains a compound, triacontanol, that promotes plant growth. (94)

Researchers have long suspected that alfalfa slowly poisons itself. When many crops of alfalfa are grown on the same soil, the plants eventually become short, spindly and yellowish and produce few root nodules. The toxin alfalfa releases hasn't been isolated yet. (92)

Companion Role with Insects

Research: Alfalfa is a preferred host of the lygus bug. In California, planting a few strips in among cotton plants significantly reduced the pest. For best results, the alfalfa must be periodically mowed. (102, 44)

Alfalfa cover crops planted in the same spot for several years gradually lower wireworm populations. (3)

Amaranth or Pigweed

Amaranthus spp.
Amaranthaceae
Annual weedy perennial with some forms grown as grain or vegetable

Some species have ornamental potential, with crimson, scarlet and gold leaves. Most types of amaranth tolerate drought, weeds and generally poor growing conditions rather well.

Companion Role with Plants

Tradition: Many strains of amaranth are traditionally grown as grain and vegetable crops. Wild forms are among the most troublesome weeds known to gardeners. Some people say pigweed is a worthwhile garden plant because its long taproot brings up nutrients and prepares the soil for carrots.

Research: The decaying plant matter of various amaranth species may be allelopathic. In field studies, redroot pigweed (*A. retroflexus*) residues reduced soybean yields. (22)

Companion Role with Insects

Research: Pigweed is attacked by cabbage loopers, various aphids, beet armyworms and other common pests. It also hosts over 30 beneficial insect species, including predatory wasps and beetles. One Arizona researcher concluded that the risk of attracting pests was greater than the opportunities for attracting predators, and recommended against letting pigweed remain around cotton fields. (40)

However, in another study, cotton, tomatoes, soybeans and cowpeas that were sprayed with an extract of pigweed suffered less corn earworm damage. The water extract of pigweed encouraged parasitization by a Trichogramma wasp. (2)

Spiny amaranth (*A. spinosus*) is the preferred host of black cutworms. The larvae will eat this weed before they'll turn to beans, cucumbers or tomatoes. (118)

Several common amaranth species are hosts to ground beetles. (53) Since ground beetles are predators for harmful garden pests, providing the beetles with a hospitable environment can indirectly help control insect populations.

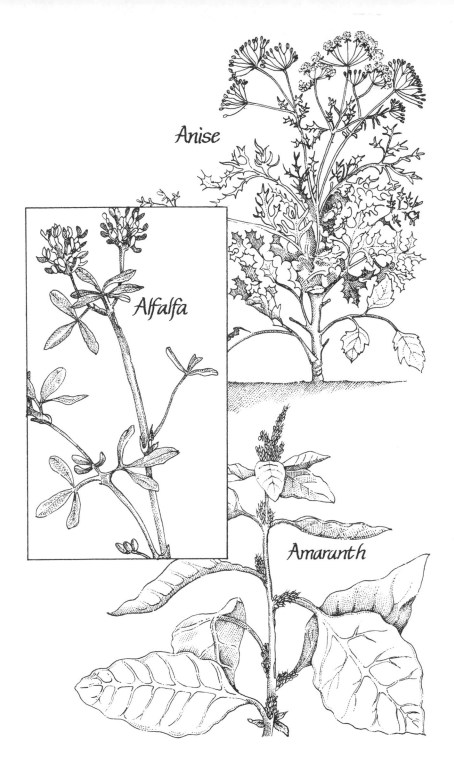

Anise

Alfalfa

Amaranth

139

Anise

Pimpinella anisum
Umbelliferae
Annual herb

Anise is an excellent host of beneficial wasps. In the summer, flowers appear in lacy white clusters. This herb makes an attractive medium-height border plant. You can also plant it in strips within the garden. Since anise reseeds itself, you probably won't have to plant more than once.

Companion Role with Plants

Tradition: Garden lore has counseled to keep anise away from carrots and to plant it near coriander.

Research: No studies have been done that prove or disprove the garden lore.

Companion Role with Insects

Tradition: Some growers have said that anise repels aphids and fleas in their gardens.

Research: In companion plantings with beans, anise had no effect on whiteflies. With cabbage, it did seem to reduce eggs and larvae of cabbageworms, but it also reduced the cabbage yield. (52) Anise oil is an effective insect repellent. (92)

Aphid

Various species of Aphididae

This large family of insects includes many different species, all with different food preferences and habits. Most are pests, sucking out plant fluids and often infecting their hosts with disease.

Tradition: Companion plantings or sprays of chives, garlic, nasturtiums, larkspur, mint and many other aromatic herbs have long been recommended against aphids.

Research: Interplanting with nonhost species seems to discourage many types of aphids. Hedgerows help, too, by forming a barrier that thwarts the entry of wind-borne aphids. When you ring the garden with some sort of dense border, the wind will deposit most airborne aphids along the barrier, where they'll have a hard time gaining access to the garden.

Less is known about the specific effects of companion plants on aphids. Researchers aren't sure whether a reduction of the pests is due to the repellent properties of the companion or to the increase of predators and the camouflaging effect that occurs whenever two different crops are grown together.

Whatever the cause, there are certain planting combinations that have reduced some species of aphids to some extent. Catnip, coriander, tansy, marigolds, onions and nasturtiums have helped peppers. (66, 68) Cole crops have been aided by wild mustard, fava beans, snap beans and a variety of native weeds. (44, 101)

Apple

Malus pumila
Rosaceae
Fruit tree

Because apples aren't self-fertile, you must plant at least two and sometimes three varieties for cross-pollination.

Companion Role with Plants

Tradition: Growers have noted that potatoes tend to develop diseases when they're grown near apple trees.

Research: No specific evidence has been found for potato disease associated with apple trees. However, early studies showed that ripe fruits of some kinds of apples produce a substance that inhibits the normal growth of potato plants. (92) Potatoes themselves produce toxins that interfere with photosynthesis, protein production and nitrogen absorption in apple trees. (91)

Strong evidence suggests that apples are autoallelopathic. The roots exude a poisonous substance, particularly in waterlogged soil. (91) This means that you shouldn't plant apple seedlings in a place just vacated by the same species.

Planting Tips: Some apple viruses can be spread when the roots of an infected tree grow into those of a healthy one. Interplanting with apple varieties resistant to the problem virus or with other resistant fruit trees may prevent this.

Allow 6 feet between dwarf apple trees or up to 15 feet for semidwarfs. Some standard varieties may need as much as 40 feet of growing space. For best cross-pollination, trees should be no more than 50 feet apart. During the first few years, while the trees are small, interplant with annual vegetables or flowers.

Companion Role with Insects

Tradition: For stinkbugs on apples, an age-old remedy is to plant a trap crop of mullein beneath each tree. For apple scab, plant a ring of chives, or spray trees with an infusion of chives. For aphids, plant a border of nasturtiums.

Research: No data confirms these garden traditions. Weeds in the carrot family growing in the orchard attract parasites that control codling moths and tent caterpillars. (61)

You avoid problems with fireblight by replacing susceptible pollinators, such as Jonathan, with resistant types. (76) Chemicals that leach from some hardwood bark reduce spores that cause apple collar rot. A bark mulch may be helpful. (35)

Apricot

Prunus armeniaca
Rosaceae
Fruit tree

Apricots are technically self-fertile, needing no cross-pollination to set fruit. The harvest will be bigger, however, if there are two or more varieties growing together.

Companion Role with Plants

Remarks: Keep apricot trees away from plum trees in areas where yellows (a virus disease) is a problem. Also, don't plant apricots near solanaceous plants (such as tomatoes and potatoes) that harbor verticillium wilt.

Apricots are good middle-story plants when you grow them with taller, mature pecan trees.

Planting Tips: Mature standard varieties need 25 to 30 feet of growing room, but semidwarf trees need just 15 feet, and dwarfs a mere 8 feet.

Asparagus

Asparagus officinalis
Liliaceae
Perennial vegetable

Asparagus interplants nicely with all sorts of ornamentals, where its fernlike foliage creates a pleasing backdrop for bright flowers. As a noninvasive perennial it does well in alternate rows with annual vegetables.

Companion Role with Plants

Tradition: Both tomatoes and parsley are said to enhance the growth of asparagus. Early American farmers interplanted carrots in asparagus beds and trained grapes to grow in the areas between the beds.

Research: No data is available on whether or not these companions are growth enhancers for asparagus.

Planting Tips: Asparagus rows should be 3 to 4 feet apart. When you first set out crowns, there is plenty of room for almost any companion crop between the rows. In subsequent years, lettuce, spinach, beets or other small, early or shade-tolerant crops are good companion choices in close quarters. If you wish to interplant mature asparagus plantings with tomatoes or similar large crops, allow 5 feet between rows.

Companion Role with Insects

Tradition: Companion plantings or sprays of parsley, tomatoes and basil are often recommended for control of asparagus beetles.

Research: There is no scientific data available on asparagus beetle repellent plantings. What researchers do know is that asparagus contains a toxin in its roots, which is effective against some parasitic nematodes. (92)

Barberry

Berberis spp.
Berberidaceae
Perennial shrub

This thorny shrub produces quite colorful blue, black, red or yellow fruit. Most species make good ornamental hedges.

Companion Role with Plants

Tradition: As early as the eighteenth century, barberry was said to be an enemy of wheat, and in at least two states, farmers were forced to eradicate the shrubs.

Research: By the late nineteenth century, scientists had confirmed growers' suspicions. Barberry was found to host black stem rust fungus and to induce blight in rye or wheat. (107)

Barley

Hordeum vulgare
Gramineae
Annual grain

Barley makes a good winter cover crop in central and northern areas.

Companion Role with Plants

Tradition: Since Roman times, farmers have warned against planting barley among other grains because it competes so fiercely. Barley is also said to smother weeds.

Research: Studies show that decaying residues of barley release a toxic substance. In field tests, lettuce seeds failed to germinate, and seedlings developed slowly and had root lesions. For damage to occur, growing roots must be in direct contact with barley debris. (77)

Planting Tips: If you sow barley in late summer or fall, seeds will germinate and form a good cover by winter. In spring, plow under the plants as a green manure or leave them alone until early summer when you can harvest them.

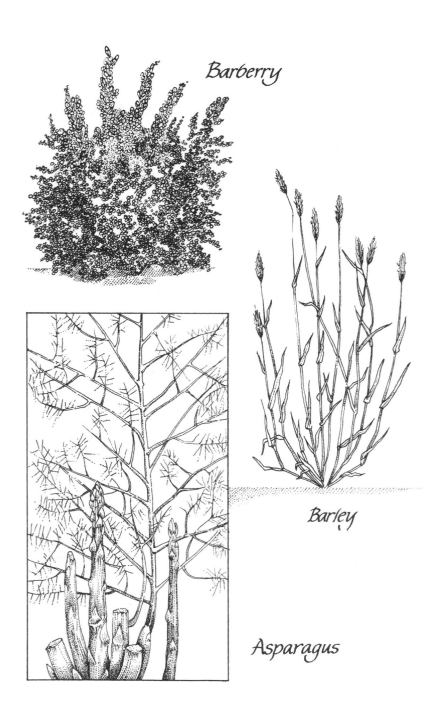

Barberry

Barley

Asparagus

Basil

Ocimum basilicum
Labiatae
Annual herb

Basil's ornamental qualities make it an excellent companion for the vegetable and flower garden, even if its chemical advantages remain a mystery. There are several popular cultivars ranging from large-leaved upright forms to compact ground covers. There's even a variety called Opal basil that has striking deep purple foilage.

Companion Role with Plants

Tradition: Basil is often recommended as a companion for tomato plants. It has gained the reputation of enhancing the tomato's flavor and overall growth. For centuries, gardeners have felt that rue and basil are enemies.

Research: There's no available evidence to confirm the effects of these pairings.

Companion Role with Insects

Tradition: Some gardeners recommend planting this herb to control various bean, cabbage and tomato pests.

Research: Most studies to date show no positive effects from basil interplants or sprays.

In one experiment, basil planted with cabbage or beans controlled neither cabbage pests nor Mexican bean beetles. (52) In another experiment, basil sprays did not control Colorado potato beetles. (69) On the positive side, an emulsion of essential oils from the plant did kill one species of aphid. (1)

Bean

Phaseolus vulgaris, Vicia faba
Leguminosae
Annual vegetable

You may be tempted to squeeze a few bush beans into the border of a garden or flower bed since their growth is fairly compact. Keep in mind that these plants are too tender to take much jostling, so it's best to keep them away from areas of heavy activity.

Companion Role with Plants

Tradition: Gardeners claim beans enhance the growth of corn, cabbage and squash. Beets, borage, carrots and strawberries are said to help beans.

Research: The nitrogen-fixing capabilities of beans and other legume interplants have been well documented. (117) In one study, collards interplanted with beans kept weed growth down and increased the yields of both crops. (44)

This doesn't necessarily mean that the presence of beans will improve yields of the companion crop. One researcher found that interplanting fava beans (*V. faba*) with potatoes had no beneficial effects on either crop. (54)

In research done in the field, a computer-designed hexagonal planting design for beans and tomatoes has led to top yields for each crop per unit space. (89) A tomato plant serves as the center point, and six bean plants surround it in a hexagonal pattern. In the experiment, each bean was located roughly 1½ feet from the tomato bush. You might want to try some experiments in your garden using different spacings.

Planting Tips: Bush beans are good legume companions for corn as long as you time plantings so that the beans aren't flowering at the same time the corn is tasseling. If these two stages coincide, the plants will be competing for water. Plant beans either one to two weeks after corn emerges in the early summer or in the late summer just before it's time to harvest the corn.

Snap beans do well in blocks or strip plantings with spacings as close as 4 inches between plants. You can plant companions around the blocks or between the strips. Pole beans are best left to outer areas of the garden where corn or other large crops are grown. Trained to a fence, they can be companioned with a low-growing, shade-tolerant green, such as spinach or lettuce, or if space allows, cabbage.

Companion Role with Insects

Tradition: For Mexican bean beetles, gardeners recommend companion plantings of marigolds, potatoes, rosemary or winter or summer savory.

Research: Several studies show Mexican bean beetle populations were reduced by the presence of marigolds. Border plantings of French marigolds (*Tagetes patula*) repelled beetles but had a detrimental (possibly allelopathic) effect on the bean plants. (56)

Other companion plants have also proved successful in controlling Mexican bean beetles. Potato interplants do help to some extent, but it may not really matter what the interplant is, as long as it doesn't host the beetle. (3) Even the presence of weeds reduces beetle damage, possibly by encouraging predators. This benefit all but vanishes if weed growth goes uncontrolled and begins to compete with the beans. (9)

In the tropics, grassy weeds helped control certain leafhoppers in bean fields. Borders of goosegrass (*Eleusine indica*) and sprangletop (*Leptochloa filiformis*) repressed or masked the stimuli, which in a monocultured bean plot, would draw the pests. The weeds also supported a variety of predators and parasites. Again, the weeds must be kept in check, either by allowing them to grow only in borders or strips within the plot or by frequently trimming those within the garden. (6)

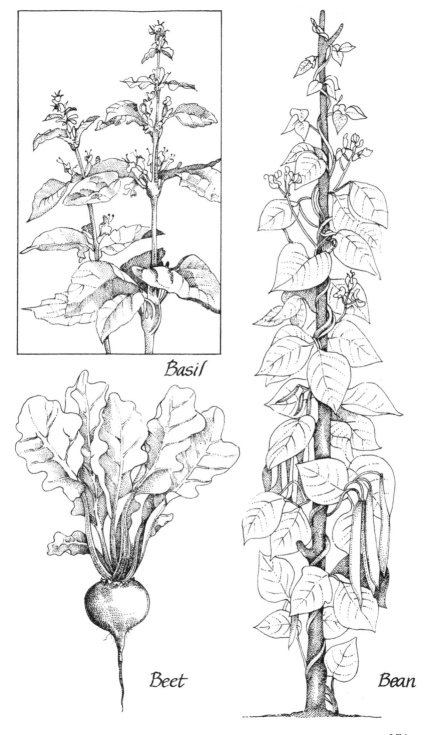

Basil

Beet

Bean

A preliminary study suggested that intercropping beans with corn and/or squash produces no significant reduction in Mexican bean beetle populations. (59) However, another study showed that the corn and bean combination reduces cutworms, fall armyworms and leafhoppers. The key to success lies in planting dates. In Columbia, beans planted 20 to 30 days before corn reduced fall armyworms; corn planted 20 to 40 days before beans reduced leafhoppers. (4) You may wish to study this relationship in your own garden.

Cutworm problems with beans (and other plants) may be helped by the presence of a weed, spiny amaranth (*Amaranthus spinosus*), which serves as a decoy or trap. (119)

As for beans "protecting" other plants, experimental data is scarce. In one study, collards interplanted with beans suffered less flea beetle and cabbage aphid damage. Pest populations were reduced, partly because fewer pests made their way into the field and partly because there were more predators. Yet, this effect can't really be attributed to the beans themselves. In the same study, weeds were even more effective deterrents to flea beetles and cabbage aphids. The researchers suggest that at least part of interplanting success depends on creating a complex canopy of plant leaves that keeps many pests from finding the crop. (44) Similar conclusions may be drawn from a study of beans as a deterrent to Colorado potato beetles. (27)

Bean Leafhopper

Empoasca spp.
See BEAN

Beet

Beta vulgaris
Chenopodiaceae
Annual vegetable

With their red-veined leaves, beets make attractive accents in low borders. Because they have shallow taproots, they won't interfere with the underground growth of neighboring crops. However, if nearby food-traffic is heavy, don't expect them to form nice round beets.

Companion Role with Plants

Tradition: Beets are said to grow best with cabbage or leafy greens and to perform poorly near pole beans.

Research: There's no evidence to support the garden lore. Beet seeds have been found to suppress the growth of some weeds. (91)

Planting Tips: It makes sense to grow beets as a short-season, intensively planted crop. In fertile, moist soil, they can stand 2 inches apart. Harvest when the beets are just an inch in diameter. Within-row intercropping with kohlrabi or onions works well. Alternate-row intercropping is good with just about any crop since beets can tolerate a good amount of shade.

Companion Role with Insects

Research: A substance in the beet plant attracts the adult beet moth and causes it to lay eggs. If plants are sprayed with a water extract of chestnut leaves, the attractive chemical is masked, and the moth ignores the plants. (92)

Birds

Gardeners who have waited patiently for strawberries, blueberries or other fruit to ripen, only to find that they've been beaten to the harvest by the birds, know how voracious these creatures can be. Birds seem to have an innate sense of when ripening fruit is approaching its peak.

Tradition: Eighteenth-century advice to repel birds from newly planted corn was to soak seeds in skunk cabbage brine. Other suggestions using plants to ward off these creatures include planting prickly hedges such as barberry or hawthorn around the garden or planting decoys of their favorite foods.

Research: Researchers echo these suggestions. To keep birds away from peaches and cherries, plant borders of chokecherries, dogwood, mulberries, mountain ash or other very aromatic fruits. Many birds apparently prefer these pungent ones over the sweeter, cultivated fruit we enjoy.

A variety of wild plants around the garden area should generally help reduce birds' inclination to eat seeds and fruits from the garden. (107)

Remarks: Remember, too, that some birds are on the gardener's side, for they prey on caterpillars and other pests. While blackbirds, crows, grackles, sparrows, starlings and quail are pests, swallows, bluebirds, cardinals, catbirds, chickadees, purple martins and dozens of other birds are good to have around. A variety of wild fruiting and flowering trees, shrubs and weeds around and about the yard will provide food and shelter for these garden friends. Autumn olive, bittersweet, crab apple, dogwood, elderberry, firethorn, hawthorn, highbush cranberry, holly, honeysuckle, sunflower and Virginia creeper are particularly good bird plants.

Bird Decoy: *To divert birds from ripe peaches and cherries, plant a mulberry, chokecherry, dogwood or mountain ash tree.*

155

Blackberry

Rubus spp.
Rosaceae
Fruiting shrub

This prickly shrub makes a good substitute for a garden fence. Several plants will act as an effective barrier around the plot and will give you a bonus of luscious berries.

Companion Role with Insects

Research: The blackberry (particularly the wild type) provides an alternate food source and breeding ground for an insect beneficial to grapes. This insect is a leafhopper parasite (*Anagrus epos*) that controls the grape leafhopper *Erythroneura elegantula*. (34, 20) It makes sense to grow blackberries along with grapes. For more information on this beneficial relationship, see GRAPE.

Planting Tips: Like all brambles, blackberries can get out of hand unless you keep them pruned and thinned. Fruit is set on wood produced the previous season, so you should remove fruiting canes in the fall. In spring, cut away any weak canes.

Margin of Safety: *To keep susceptible crops out of reach of the black walnut's toxins, plant them at a distance of at least one and a half times the distance from the trunk to the outermost branches.*

Black Walnut

Juglans nigra
Juglandaceae
Nut tree

This tree has undoubtedly gained the most notoriety as a harmful companion best kept at a distance from the vegetable garden.

Companion Role with Plants

Tradition: For over 2,000 years, growers have recognized that few plants grow near the black walnut.

Research: Research indicates that most parts of the plant contain a powerful toxin, juglone. Where walnut roots come in contact with those of alfalfa, apples, azaleas, blackberries, blueberries, lilacs, magnolias, mountain laurel, peas, peonies, peppers, potatoes, rhododendrons, sugar maples or tomatoes, stunting, wilting or even death result. However, beans, beets, forsythia, grapes, Kentucky bluegrass, onions, raspberries, sweet corn and other plants are relatively tolerant of the toxin. (91, 92)

Planting Tips: Plant crops susceptible to black walnut's toxins well outside the tree's canopy. Allelopathic reactions occur within a circle measuring 1½ times the distance from the trunk to the outermost branches.

Borage

Borago officinalis
Boraginaceae
Annual herb

This lovely herb makes a delightful addition to vegetable beds and ornamental borders alike, where it easily reseeds itself every year. Borage stands 2 to 3 feet tall and in midsummer is covered with nodding star-shaped flowers in shades of pink or blue.

Companion Role with Plants

Tradition: Borage is said to improve the flavor and growth of many crops, particularly strawberries and tomatoes.

Research: No data is available to confirm or refute the companionable effects of borage.

Companion Role with Insects

Tradition: Borage is recognized as a good honey plant since its colorful flowers attract bees. Some growers claim that it makes a good trap plant for Japanese beetles on potatoes.

Research: No evidence is available to support the claims made by gardeners concerning Japanese beetles.

Broccoli

Brassica oleracea, Botrytis Group
Annual vegetable
See CABBAGE

Brussels Sprouts

Brassica oleracea, Gemmifera Group
Annual vegetable
See CABBAGE

Cabbage

Brassica oleracea, Capitata Group
Cruciferae
Annual vegetable

Included in the ranks of cabbage and the other cole crops are some of our most decorative plants. Low-growing, frilly edged, bicolored kales and some of the Chinese cabbages make fine border plants and interplant nicely with delicate summer flowers. The huge collards and Brussels sprouts are dramatic accent plants. Red or green cabbages can be easily landscaped into most any garden.

Companion Role with Plants

Tradition: All cole crops are said to be improved by the presence of aromatic herbs, particularly dill, mint, sage and rosemary. Beans, potatoes, onions and celery are also good companions for cabbage. Some gardeners say cabbage plants abhor strawberries, while others swear that this combination improves both crops. The same controversy exists over tomatoes with cabbage. Most growers agree that cabbage has a detrimental affect on grapes.

Research: There's no research to verify that certain companions enhance cole crops, and no evidence to date supports the claim that any of the cole crops help the growth of companion crops. However, cabbage and its relatives may harm nearby crops by competition. Since they are heavy feeders, they may steal necessary nutrients away from their neighbors.

It is also possible that some cole crops exude chemicals toxic to other plants. For example, decaying residue from broccoli was found to deter the germination of lettuce seed and generally hinder lettuce growth. (77)

In other research, experiments with cabbage-tomato intercroppings showed no adverse effects on cabbage yields. (25)

Planting Tips: Cabbage, broccoli, collards, cauliflowers and other large cole crops interplant well within rows. Cabbage are gorgeous in circle plantings surrounded by low-growing herbs such as thyme and dwarf purple basil. Most of these plants can tolerate partial shade but prefer full sun to achieve the best growth. Allow at least 15 inches between plants.

Take advantage of the fact that most of these are slow-growing crops. While they eventually make heavy demands on space, there is plenty of time to squeeze in companion crops during early growth.

Companion Role with Insects

Tradition: Against cabbage loopers and imported cabbage-worms, gardeners through the ages have recommended companion plantings or sprays of dill, hyssop, mint, nasturtiums, onions, pennyroyal, southernwood, thyme, wormwood and chick-peas. Some growers find that cabbage root flies can be deterred by marigolds or radishes. Radishes were also recommended by eighteenth-century gardeners as a trap for aphids, and mint was extolled as an aphid repellent.

Flea beetles are supposedly controlled by elderberry branches laid beside plants. Several gardeners report that clubroot can be prevented by burying a piece of rhubarb along with each transplant.

Research: Extensive research has been done with cabbage pests, and the results are both fascinating and confusing. We know that cabbage looper larvae are attracted to host plants by

(continued on page 164)

Kale

Cauliflower

Kohlrabi

Collards

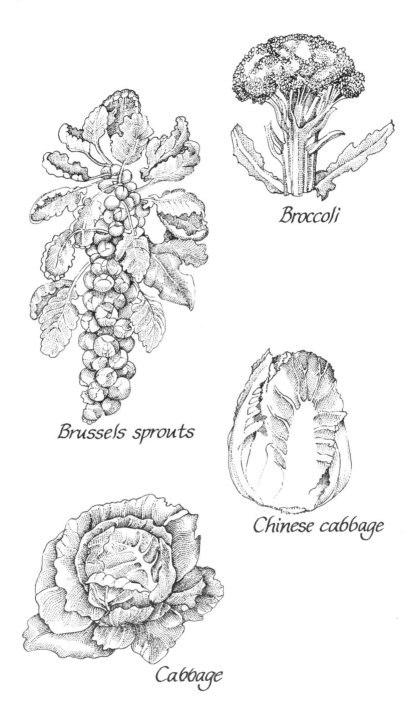

Broccoli

Brussels sprouts

Chinese cabbage

Cabbage

the mustard oils they contain. Other pests also "smell out" their host plants. (91) It seems likely that some interplants could mask this mustard oil odor. In one experiment, tomatoes seemed to have this effect on the familiar cabbage pest, the diamondback moth. Researchers planted two rows of cabbage between every two rows of tomatoes. (26)

Tomato interplants also helped reduce whitefly infestations on cabbage. (80) In another study, interplanting with tomatoes or tobacco plants protected cabbage heads from cabbage flea beetles. The flea beetles seemed to have trouble finding their hosts. (105)

Intercropping was also found to encourage parasite activity. In one study, collards intercropped with beans had more wasp parasites than those grown in a monocropped plot. The intercropped collards had four times fewer aphids and showed less aphid damage. That translated into a greater number of harvestable collard leaves. (44)

The same mustard oils that attract cabbageworms can sicken or even kill, on contact, flies, mosquitoes, spider mites, pea aphids and Mexican bean beetles.

Several researchers have looked at traditional aromatic herb companions for controlling cabbage pests. Southernwood (*Artemisia abrotanum*) does contain a moth repellent, and interplants or sprays may provide some protection against imported cabbage-worms. (3) Some researchers found that when cole crops were repeatedly sprayed with extracts of thyme or sage, cabbage-worms were deterred. (66)

Despite these findings, no researchers are quite ready to recommend repellent plantings for cabbage. Several studies have produced negative results. In one, plantings of marigolds, nasturtiums, pennyroyal, peppermint, sage and thyme produced no significant reduction in cabbageworms or other larval pests, including the diamondback moth. (55) In another experiment, collards were "hidden" between plantings of six different herbs, but cabbageworms still located and destroyed the crop. Many of the herbs even seemed to attract the moths. (58) These findings are supported by Rodale Research Center studies of herbal inter-plants in cabbage. (69, 68)

Some companions are effective because they shelter predators and parasites of cabbage pests. Hawthorn (*Crataegus* spp.) is the winter host of an important parasite of the diamondback moth. (117) Clover interplanted between cole crops provides shelter for ground beetles. (31, 118) Weeds allowed to grow in Brussels sprouts hosted hover flies, which reduced aphid populations. (101)

The weed spurry (*Spergula arvensis*) hosts various predators and parasites that control cabbageworms, cabbage loopers, root flies, aphids and others. As an interplant with Brussels sprouts, it significantly reduced most of these insects, although imported cabbageworms weren't affected. (106) Since spurry is low growing and is easy to mow or remove, it's a fine interplant for cole crops.

Weeds, clover, lettuce or other ground covers within plots also help by camouflaging crops so pests can't find them as easily. This has been demonstrated with cabbage root flies and aphids. (97, 101)

Trap cropping is another potential means of cabbage pest control. Border plantings of kale attract certain bug pests away from cabbage crops preferred by gardeners. (110)

Caraway

Carum carvi
Umbelliferae
Annual or biennial herb

Caraway's family tie to the common carrot is revealed by its flowers and foliage. Biennial forms of caraway will bloom the second year in the garden. Heads of tiny white flowers appear on 2-foot-tall stalks.

Companion Role with Plants

Remarks: Like all carrot family plants, caraway is a good host of tiny predatory wasps. It's a good plant to include in orchard ground covers. However, since it is susceptible to some of the pests and diseases that plague carrots, it's best kept out of the vegetable garden.

Carrot

Daucus carota
Umbelliferae
Biennial vegetable

If you leave a few carrots in the garden to overwinter, come spring they'll send up flower stalks that will attract helpful wasps and other beneficial insects. Try interplanting carrots between tomatoes, cucumbers or some of the compact bush melons.

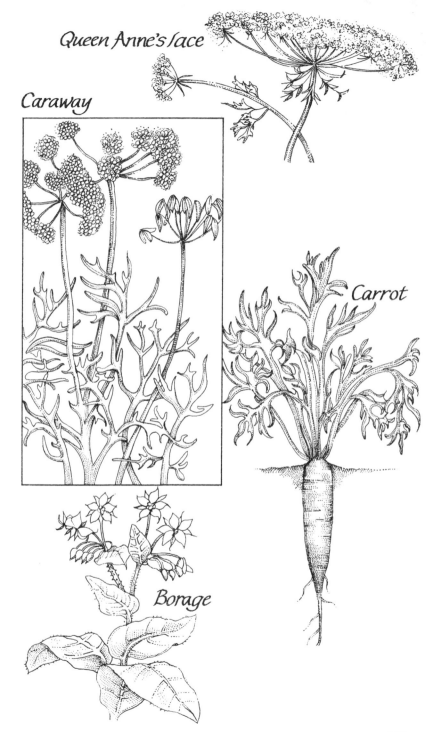

Queen Anne's /ace

Caraway

Carrot

Borage

167

Companion Role with Plants

Tradition: Radishes, peas and sage are supposed to improve the carrot's flavor and growth. Dill is said to be carrot's enemy.

Research: No data is available on the garden lore.

Planting Tips: Carrots tolerate some shade, require little space and are light feeders so they make good long-term companions for many crops. Plant in alternate strips with companion crops or flank a single row of carrots with a companion. Give plants 2 to 4 inches of breathing room.

Companion Role with Insects

Tradition: The Soil Association in England claims that lettuce and onions repel carrot flies. Leeks, according to garden lore, are supposed to do the same thing. Other growers add scorzonera (a root crop), wormwood, rosemary and sage to the list. For their part, carrots are said to combat onion flies.

Research: No evidence is available on these companion pairings. The Henry Doubleday Research Association in England is studying the effects scorzonera companion plants have on carrot root flies. So far there are no conclusive results available.

Castor Bean Barrier: *Some gardeners maintain that a border of castor bean plants will keep moles out of the garden. Others claim that castor beans actually attract moles!*

169

Castor Bean

Ricinus communis
Euphorbiaceae
Perennial ornamental, grown as annual in
temperate regions

Castor bean is a traditional deterrent to moles, rats and other animals. Many growers recommend planting a living fence of castor beans around the garden. Other gardeners say this actually attracts rodents!

Companion Role with Insects

Tradition: This plant has been imbued with the power to kill one of summer's most aggravating pests—the mosquito.

Research: A potent insecticide, ricin, has been isolated, but pest control in the field can't be guaranteed. (98) Young leaves contain the strongest toxins. (39)

In experiments with nematodes, castor beans have proven to be a very effective control. Nematodes enter the castor bean roots but fail to develop well. Most that do manage to mature are males, so the population gradually diminishes. (92)

Catnip

Nepeta cataria
Labiatae
Perennial herb

Not only does catnip tend to take over the garden, but true to its name, it also draws cats. Unless you want the neighborhood toms and tabbies lolling about on your tender seedlings, you'd best confine this plant to fenced gardens or borders or grow a new crop each year in containers.

Companion Role with Insects

Tradition: Catnip plantings are recommended as deterrents against flea beetles, Colorado potato beetles, aphids and other pests as well.

Research: Vapors from catnip plants are a powerful insect repellent that affects 17 species of insects, many of which are common garden pests. (35) This group includes plant hoppers, spiddle bugs, ants, Japanese beetles, flea beetles, darkling beetles and weevils. Unfortunately, some beneficial insects are also repelled.

Just how this translates into effectiveness as a companion plant is another matter. Studies in the field give mixed results. Experiments at the Rodale Research Center suggest that catnip interplantings may significantly reduce green peach aphids on peppers, squash bugs on squash, cucumber beetles on cucumbers and Colorado potato beetle larvae on potatoes. But, at the same time, Rodale researchers found that catnip companion plantings increased imported cabbageworm problems on broccoli. (69, 68) In another experiment, the presence of catnip reduced numbers of cabbageworm larvae and eggs. (52) A catnip border also reduced the number of cabbage flea beetles on collards. (59)

However, in most cases, even where catnip controlled pests, it competed with the main crop so that the harvests were significantly smaller. Clearly, you must frequently clip and trim this invasive plant to the ground in order to minimize competition. (For other pointers, see the box Controlling Invasive Companions in chapter 5.)

As an alternative to interplanting or even border plantings, you might try growing the catnip far from the garden, perhaps even in containers. Then you could use freshly cut branches as a pest-deterrent garden mulch. A catnip and water spray might also be effective. In one experiment, such a spray deterred Colorado potato beetles. (68)

Cattail

Typha latifolia
Typhaceae
Perennial grass

Cattails thrive in boggy, marshy places. Their brown spikes are actually clusters of tiny flowers. If you grow cattails in a bog garden, be prepared to keep the invasive underground rootstalks under control.

Companion Role with Insects

Research: Cattails host insects that predator mites feed on when the Willamette mite, a common grape pest, isn't around. Therefore, this is a good weed to have growing around vineyards. (37)

Cauliflower

Brassica oleracea, Botrytis Group
Annual vegetable
See CABBAGE

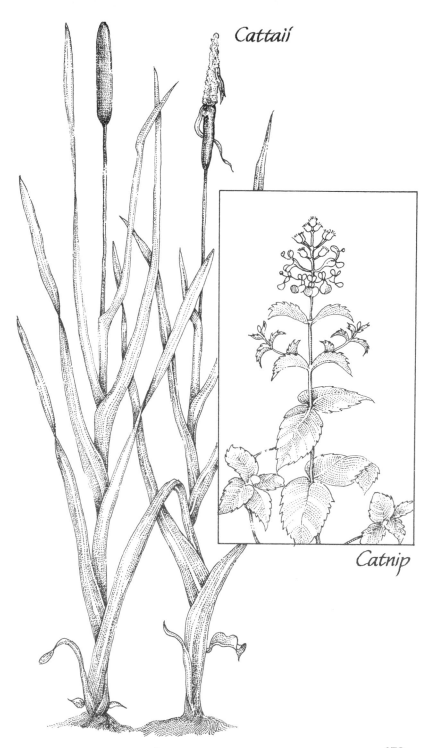

Cattail

Catnip

173

Celery

Apium graveolens
Umbelliferae
Biennial vegetable

Left for two seasons in the garden, a celery plant will send up a flower stalk, which will attract a host of beneficial wasps.

Companion Role with Plants

Tradition: Celery is said to do well with tomatoes, cabbage, onions and beans.

Research: There's no scientific evidence available to confirm the beneficial effects of these companions.

Planting Tips: Celery will grow well in very shady areas and is a fine lower level crop for trees and shrubs. Under these circumstances, it may not form large, heavy stalks but grow rather lanky. Although not "market quality," these plants have a nice strong flavor and are great for soups and stews.

Since it is compact, you can easily interplant celery within rows or in circle plantings with a border of lettuce, beans or almost any other easily managed crop. I find it a nice addition to the flower garden. Its shallow, fibrous roots make celery a well-behaved companion for deeper rooted neighbors.

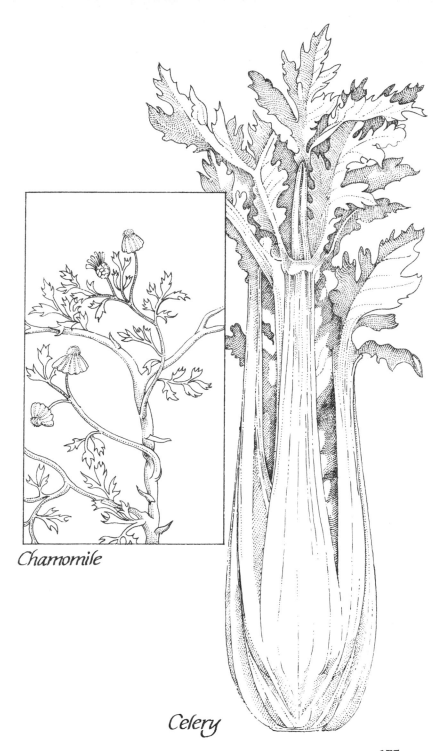

Chamomile

Celery

Chamomile

Chamaemelum nobile
Compositae
Perennial herb

As a member of the composite family, chamomile is a good host of beneficial insects, particularly hover flies and thread-waisted wasps. Keep this plant out of the main part of your vegetable garden, however, as its spreading roots will quickly take over. It performs nicely in perennial flower beds and as a border or mass planting in herb gardens. It also makes an excellent ground cover. Some gardeners claim that it tolerates fairly heavy foot traffic and can even be mowed once it's well established.

Companion Role with Plants

Tradition: Chamomile has a reputation of improving the growth and flavor of onions, cucumbers and aromatic herbs.

Research: No studies have been done to test chamomile's growth-enhancing reputation.

Cherry

Prunus avium (sweet), *P. cerasus* (sour)
Rosaceae
Fruit tree

If you're planning to include a sour cherry in the landscape, you can plant just one tree and still get fruit, for sour cherries are self-fertile. Sweet cherries are another matter. They require a compatible sweet cherry neighbor to provide for cross-pollination.

Companion Role with Plants

Remarks: There is some evidence suggesting that young cherry trees shouldn't be planted in an orchard where old cherry trees were recently removed. However, this autoallelopathy hasn't been studied yet. (92)

Planting Tips: Standard cherry trees require spacings of 20 to 30 feet, depending on the variety, but semidwarfs need just 15 feet.

Chervil

Anthriscus cerefolium
Umbelliferae
Annual herb

Chervil is an excellent ground cover for shady, damp areas. Its lacy, light green leaves make it an attractive addition to border plantings around both vegetable and flower beds. Heads full of tiny white flowers attract all sorts of helpful insect predators and parasites.

Companion Role with Plants

Tradition: Biodynamic gardeners claim chervil and radishes bring out the best in each other.

Research: No formal research has been done with chervil interplantings.

Planting Tips: You can broadcast chervil over entire beds or sow the seeds in strips between rows of companion crops.

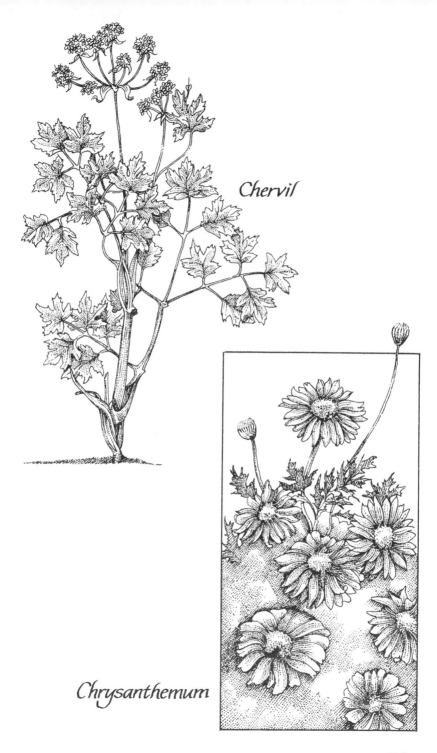

Chervil

Chrysanthemum

Chives

Allium schoenoprasum
Amaryllidaceae
Perennial herb

Chives make an attractive companion for any garden. They form a low-to-medium height, dense green border that breaks forth with pink to lavender pom-pom-shaped flowers in spring. Garlic chives, sometimes called oriental chives (*A. tuberosum*), are particularly compact and attractive plants well suited to the most formal or natural landscapes.

Companion Role with Plants

Tradition: The Soil Association of England recommends chives as a companion for carrots, grapes, roses and tomatoes but warns against planting them with peas or beans.

Research: No research has been done on chives' interactions with other plants.

Planting Tips: When planting chives, remember that they're hardy perennials and will be in the same place for some time. I find that they can be easily managed if planted in clumps here and there in the garden, in the center of circular beds of strawberries or herbs, or in borders along rows of bramble fruits. If clumps get too big, divide them in spring and share some with friends.

Companion Role with Insects

Tradition: Some gardeners claim that chives deter Japanese beetles. They are also said to cure blackspot on roses. Rumor has it that a spray of chives cures apple scab and mildew on cucurbits and gooseberries.

Research: No data is available to support gardeners' claims about the insect-repelling powers of chives.

Chrysanthemum

Chrysanthemum spp.
Compositae
Perennial flower

This is one of the most popular garden plants around, because of its wide range of flower colors and generous blooming habit. The flowers of several chrysanthemum species contain natural pesticides.

Companion Role with Plants

Research: *C.* × *morifolium* contains a toxin that inhibits the growth of lettuce and of the chrysanthemum itself. Rainwater leaches toxins from the plant leaves. These poisons build up in the soil, making it impossible to raise susceptible crops for more than a few years on the same spot. (92)

Companion Role with Insects

Research: *C. cinerariifolium, C. coccineum, C. coronarium* and *C. seticuspe* contain the insecticide pyrethrum. (98, 38) Commercial versions for pyrethrum are widely available, but you can make homemade sprays and dusts from the dried flower heads. (See the chart Recipes for Botanical Pesticides and Repellents in chapter 2.) These natural pesticides contain a strong poison, which quickly paralyzes all sorts of insects–good as well as bad. Fortunately, it breaks down within a week after being applied. Some insects have developed enzymes that allow them to safely digest pyrethrum. At the same time, some pyrethrum plants produce the chemical sesamin, which inhibits these enzymes.

Whether living chrysanthemum plants give off any of these pesticides to protect companion plants is still uncertain. Some species of chrysanthemum (in particular, *C. coccineum*) do reduce harmful nematodes in the soil. (92)

Citrus

Citrus spp.
Rutaceae
Fruit tree

This group of fruit trees includes oranges, grapefruits, limes, lemons and tangerines. If you're lucky enough to live in a climate that's conducive to growing citrus fruit, you'll find that any of these trees make attractive additions to the landscape. They have dark green foliage, fragrant blossoms, and of course, a delectable, vitamin-C rich harvest. There are both full-size and dwarf sizes available, so you can create a multistory interplanting design using various trees.

Companion Role with Plants

Tradition: Tropical farmers often interplant citrus trees with coffee bushes and pepper plants.

Research: Like apples, peaches and other orchard trees, citrus trees have a replant problem. When old citrus trees are replaced by young ones, the new plants grow very slowly and may develop root infections. It seems likely that decaying plants release autoallelopathic chemicals. (91) In waterlogged soils, the problem seems particularly pronounced.

Companion Role with Insects

Research: Studies have turned up some interesting observations. Clean cultivation encourages pests on citrus trees, partly by creating dust on the leaves. Weeds or cover crops encourage parasites of California red scale. (118) Hedgerows may help control brown soft scale. Scale infestations increase according to the distance from the hedgerow. (90)

A chemical in the seeds, juices and rinds of citrus fruits deters fall armyworms and cotton bollworms. Sprays made from this extract discouraged pests from feeding; when they did eat the treated leaves, their growth rate slowed considerably. (10)

Clover

Trifolium spp., *Melilotus* spp.
Leguminosae
Perennial legume

All clovers are helpful companions because they shelter ground beetles and attract pollinators. Sweet white clover, in particular, may very well be one of the best overseeding crops for no-till vegetable cropping. It controls weeds well and helps conserve nutrients. White clover withstands some foot traffic and tolerates some shade, but a combination of these factors may be too much for this plant. To keep competition to a minimum, mow clover plantings frequently.

Companion Role with Plants

Tradition: Growers throughout the world have long recognized the soil building qualities of these legumes and have intercropped them with grasses, vegetables and orchard fruits.

Clover sickness is a well-known problem. For hundreds of years, farmers have realized that clover, particularly red clover (*T. pratense*), grown in the same field year after year gradually fails.

Biodynamic gardeners believe clover is harmed by buttercups (*Ranunculus* spp.).

Research: Studies have revealed that clover sickness is due to toxins released from the plant roots. (92)

Decaying debris from sweet clover (*M. alba*) might reduce germination and growth of wheat seeds. In laboratory experiments, water-soluble extracts from the clover stems reduced wheat growth considerably. Whether or not this same effect holds true in the field isn't certain. (91)

183

Companion Role with Insects

Research: Most clovers are good hosts of beneficial insects. Red or white clovers intersown between cabbage and other cole crops increase the activity of predatory ground beetles. The beetles help control cabbage aphid and cabbageworm populations. (30) White clover (*T. repens*) supports parasites of woolly apple aphids. (53)

As ground covers, clovers make it difficult for certain pests to find their hosts. In one study, a cover crop of clover significantly reduced cabbage root flies on cabbage and simultaneously increased the yield. (97)

Codling Moth

Carpocapsa pomonella
See APPLE

Collards

Brassica oleracea, Acephala Group
Annual vegetable
See CABBAGE

Clover Pathways: *Sweet white clover will tolerate foot traffic and does best when kept clipped short. Red or white clovers will increase the numbers of beneficial insects that help keep crops pest-free.*

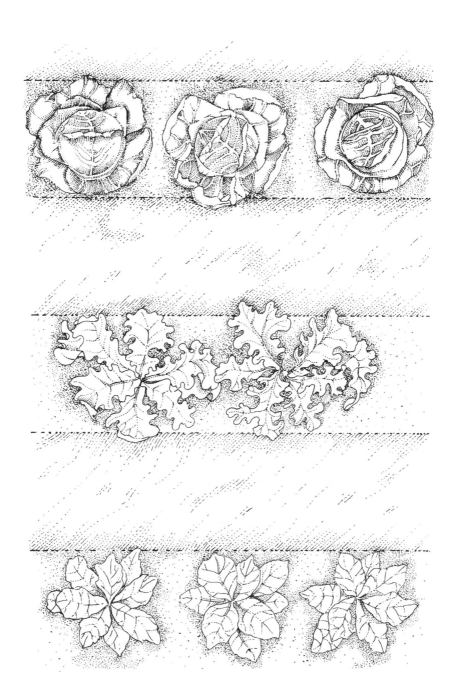

Coriander

Coriandrum sativum
Umbelliferae
Annual herb

This herb makes an especially good host plant for beneficial wasps. It's easy to interplant and blooms readily.

Companion Role with Plants

Tradition: Coriander is said to harm fennel growth but improve the overall performance of anise.

Research: There's no data to support the garden lore.

Companion Role with Insects

Tradition: Coriander spray is sometimes recommended for spider mites and aphids.

Research: No evidence exists concerning coriander's effects on those insects. Coriander interplanted with potatoes did reduce Colorado potato beetle larvae in one study. (68)

Coriander

Corn

Zea mays
Gramineae
Annual grain or vegetable

The shape of corn stalks makes them good upper level companion plants because they won't significantly shade low-growing crops. When you interplant, keep in mind that corn has deep fibrous roots.

Companion Role with Plants

Tradition: In many native cultures, corn is rarely planted alone. Typical intercrops are beans, peanuts, sunflowers and squash or melons. In the eighteenth century, young peach trees were grown among the corn. Growers in the South find that corn and rice intercrop well, particularly if nitrogen fertilizers are added to the soil.

Research: Corn is a heavy feeding crop, so legume companions that can replenish lost nutrients make good sense. It might also be that corn's high demand for nitrogen encourages neighboring legumes to fix even more nitrogen. (117) A few experiments have actually shown higher corn yields when the crop is grown with a companion legume. (117) Strip intercropping of corn and soybeans boosts the yields of both crops. At the same time, it controls wind and water erosion and reduces weed growth. (88)

However, some studies showed no increases in yield from legume interplantings and even suggested that legumes compete with corn. When corn was grown with peas, the ears turned out to be smaller and less mature than the ears on corn grown in a monocultured plot. (54)

Decaying crop residues from corn might be allelopathic. As corn stubble decomposes, it releases toxic substances that may delay germination of seeds. (92) One study has uncovered a notable exception: Corn stubble might actually improve soybean yield. (22)

Researchers found that decaying residues of foxtail and barnyard grass inhibit corn growth. (51)

Planting Tips: For pointers on timing corn and bush bean interplantings see BEAN.

Interplant corn and beans or peas in alternate rows. You can also try planting the two crops in alternate hills within rows. Allow 8 to 12 inches between hills. Per hill, plant three or four beans or four corn plants.

Vining or bush squash, cucumbers, melons or peanuts can be grown between rows or as border plantings, but be sure to provide enough water for both crops, particularly when they are both fruiting.

If you find that corn pollination is being hindered when you plant in alternate rows, try planting two rows of corn for every two rows of companion.

Companion Role with Insects

Tradition: Against corn earworms, gardeners recommend everything from cosmos and marigolds as repellents to borders of sunflowers as trap crops.

Against cinch bugs, beans are sometimes recommended. Wild cucurbits (weeds) are a good trap plant for corn rootworms, as long as you destroy the plants before the pests move on to the corn.

Research: Corn earworms can be controlled if corn is intercropped with soybeans. This encourages the activity of para-

Corn Circle Planting: *This traditional trio of companions makes good use of soil nutrients and available sunlight. Corn stalks in the center are surrounded by bush beans and an outer ring of melons.*

sitic Trichogramma wasps. (5) These beneficials can also be encouraged by spraying corn with water extracts of pigweed (*Amaranthus* spp.). (2, 4)

Intercropping with peanuts or soybeans reduces corn borers, possibly by increasing the number of predators and making it harder for adult borers to locate corn plants for egg laying.

Various bean interplants (*Phaseolus* spp.) help reduce numbers of fall armyworms on corn, while corn can help control leafhopper damage on beans. (4, 5) If you allow a strip of low-growing weeds (such as *Desmodium* spp., *Croton* spp.), soybeans or bush beans to grow in every tenth row of corn, this can also reduce armyworms by encouraging predators and parasites. (4, 118)

Corn wireworms that attack seeds might be deterred by applying extracts from butterfly milkweed (*Asclepias tuberosa*) or possibly English ivy (*Hedera helix*). In some exciting experiments, seeds were soaked for several hours in a solution of blended leaves and flowers plus a solvent. Some compounds (as yet unidentified) in these two plants are very effective against wireworms, deterring their feeding but not killing them. (111)

A cover crop of alfalfa repeated each year will gradually reduce wireworm infestations. (4)

Planting Tips: When planting a bean-corn combination to deter pests, timing can make a difference in how effective the deterrence is. Researchers found that planting corn 20 to 40 days before beans was more effective than simultaneous plantings. Also, beans planted 20 to 30 days before corn had a significant effect on decreasing fall armyworm damage.

Corn Earworm

Heliothis zea
See CORN

Crabgrass

Digitaria sanguinalis
Gramineae
Perennial grass

Many gardeners claim this invasive grass is one of the worst, most persistent "pests" they have to deal with.

Companion Role with Plants

Tradition: Gardeners often recommend oversowing white clover in spring to choke out crabgrass.

Research: Crabgrass not only competes for light, nutrients and water, but evidence suggests that it may be allelopathic to some plants. (92)

Remarks: Crabgrass and other species of *Digitaria* are often infected with viruses, which readily spread to corn, barley and other crops. (107) This is one weed you should be sure to remove from gardens and fields.

Cucumber

Cucumis sativus
Cucurbitaceae
Annual vegetable

Cucumbers make good companions in an interplanted garden when they're trained to grow up trellises. In neighboring rows you can plant lettuce, celery or Chinese cabbage.

Companion Role with Plants

Tradition: Cucumbers have gained the reputation of being compatible with corn, cabbage, tomatoes, beans, radishes and lettuce.

Research: No studies have explored the cucumber's relationship with these plants. Laboratory experiments show that cucumbers produce exudates, which inhibit the germination of many weed seeds. Some genetic strains are more allelopathic than others. (86) In one study, wild cucumbers were found to inhibit the growth of weedy white mustard, while cultivated types failed to have the same effect. (85)

Planting Tips: To save space, train vining cucumbers to vertical supports (fences, poles, tepees, trellises or even shrubs), or select one of the compact bush varieties designed for container growing. Vining cucumber varieties are best grown in hills spaced 3 to 6 feet apart, but the new bush types can be placed as close as 2 feet. Early lettuce, spinach or cabbage do nicely between the hills before cucumber vines fill in.

Like other vine crops, you can also grow cucumbers in rows spaced 12 to 15 inches apart, with alternate double rows of corn or single rows of tomatoes.

Companion Role with Insects

Tradition: Gardeners recommend tomatoes as a pest-fighting companion for cucumbers. Marigolds or radishes are suggested for cucumber beetles, and either radishes or onions for root maggots. Nineteenth-century American farmers relied on an elderberry tea as a spray against cucumber beetles.

Research: There are fewer striped cucumber beetles around when cucumbers are intercropped with corn or broccoli. Interplanting greatly reduces beetle populations, and the disease they carry (bacterial wilt). Not only do beetles seem to have more trouble finding their host plants amongst the companion crop, but they also tend to leave sooner. (21)

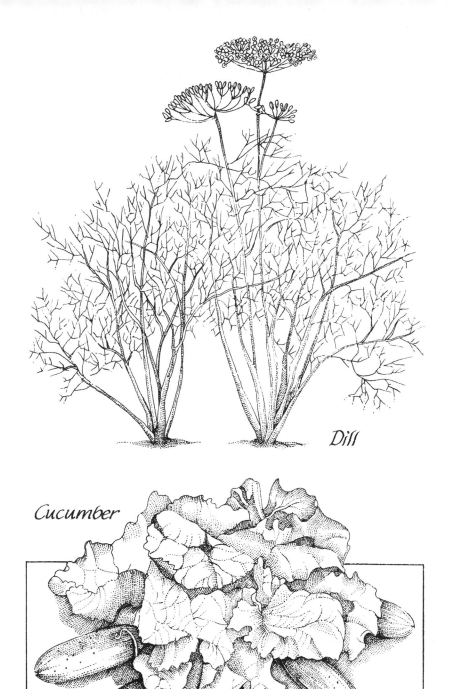

Dill

Cucumber

Radishes sown in each cucumber hill can also help reduce the number of striped cucumber beetles. (4)

For black cutworms, interplant cucumbers with spiny amaranth. (118)

Cucumber peelings have been found to contain some insecticidal compounds. (1)

Cucumber Beetle

Diabrotica spp.
See CUCUMBER

Cutworm

Various species of Noctuidae

Cutworms don't discriminate—they'll attack almost any kind of plant in the garden. Some cutworms climb plants and eat leaves, buds and fruits; others stay at ground level; while still others feast on underground parts. Certain garden denizens make a meal of cutworms. This group includes birds, toads, moles and shrews. Parasitic wasps also prey on cutworms.

Tradition: Traditional remedies for cutworms usually involve putting barriers around the stems of seedlings. There are a few plants that are supposed to repel or discourage them, with onions and garlic the companions mentioned most often.

Research: An oak leaf mulch spread in strips over the garden repels some cutworms. (3)

Black cutworms prefer spiny amaranth over beans, cucumbers or tomatoes, so interplanting with that weed brings good protection. (118)

Dandelion

Taraxacum officinale
Compositae
Weedy perennial

Despite their pesky reputation, dandelions do have some redeeming values. They attract parasitic and predatory wasps and serve as a good pollen source for other beneficials. Young leaves are even relished by some people who view a salad of dandelion greens as a true harbinger of spring.

Companion Role with Plants

Tradition: Dandelions seem to flourish where soil is poorly drained and acidic. Some gardeners believe they are valuable for bringing up nutrients from the subsoil, but few would recommend letting them remain in the garden where they rapidly take over.

Research: Dandelion plants release ethylene, which encourages fruits and flowers to ripen. (114) It's unclear how much of an effect these plants have on fruit trees and flowers out in the garden.

Companion Role with Insects

Research: In laboratory experiments, the dandelion plant's odor repelled Colorado potato beetles. (1)

Deadly Nightshade or Black Nightshade

Solanum nigrum
Solanaceae
Annual weed

This weed is a common sight in fields and along roadsides. It gained the designation "deadly" because the foliage and berries are poisonous.

Companion Role with Insects

Research: Deadly nightshade acts as a decoy plant for Colorado potato beetles. Females are attracted to the weed, where they lay their eggs. The larvae hatch, feed on the poisonous weed and die soon after. (49)

Deer

Deer are creatures of habit. Once they've found your garden and made it one of the stops on their nightly progressive dinner, you'll have trouble getting rid of them. Still, there are lots of controls worth trying. Organic gardeners offer all sorts of recommendations for keeping deer out of the garden—from human hair hung in mesh bags on the branches of susceptible plants, to sprays of oil or plant derivatives. Tall fences and hedges discourage them to some extent, as do dogs and the repellent companions suggested below.

Tradition: There are as many remedies to get rid of marauding deer as there are gardeners who have tried them. Those involving plants include hanging garlic bulbs around the garden,

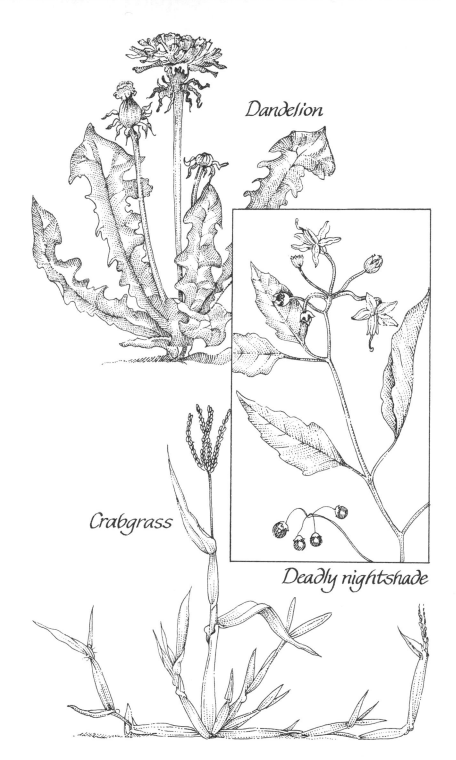

Dandelion

Crabgrass

Deadly nightshade

interplanting corn with bright flowers, spraying with garlic or hot peppers, and dozens of other ingenious measures.

Research: Researchers are developing a garlic pellet to be planted along with saplings. This emits an odor for several years and successfully repels deer. A researcher at the University of Maryland has developed a repellent spray made of Tabasco sauce and water. Spray trees with a mixture of 1 or 2 tablespoons Tabasco sauce plus an antidesiccant in 1 gallon water.

Diamondback Moth

Plutella xylostella
See CABBAGE

Dill

Anethum graveolens
Umbelliferae
Annual herb

Like all carrot family plants, dill supports many kinds of beneficial wasps and other insect predators and parasites. Dill is also useful for its ornamental value. Tuck dwarf varieties in borders or mass plants for a feathery green effect. Taller varieties are suited for background plantings.

Companion Role with Plants

Tradition: Gardeners say dill helps give flavor to cole crops and is good for onions and lettuce, too. Biodynamic growers claim its presence reduces carrot and tomato growth.

Remarks: No data is available to support or disprove the traditional claims. However, since carrots and dill are both susceptible to root diseases, it may make sense to keep the two crops apart.

Companion Role with Insects

Tradition: Dill is recommended as a companion plant to repel aphids and spider mites, to protect cabbage against various caterpillars and to prevent disease on corn.

Research: No data is available concerning these companionable qualities attributed to dill.

Dog

Most dogs seem to lack the understanding that garden paths are made for walking, and they often forge their own ways through gardens plots, mindless of seedlings and other tender plants.

Tradition: A spray of cayenne, garlic, onions and soap may discourage dogs, but a fence is even better.

Dogwood

Cornus spp.
Cornaceae
Flowering tree or shrub

One species, Cornelian cherry (*C. mas*), produces small edible fruits that look a bit like red cherries. It is a large shrub that forms a very effective windbreak. Cornelian cherry performs well in a variety of settings, perhaps with a lower story companion such as asparagus.

Companion Role with Plants

Research: In recent experiments, dogwood was one plant that was inhibited by a turf cover. A combination of competition and allelopathy from the grass reduced the dogwood's growth. This suggests that it may be best to leave an open ring of soil around the base of these and possibly other trees. (11)

Eggplant

Solanum melongena
Solanaceae
Annual vegetable

Eggplants come in all sorts of shapes, sizes and colors. Besides the large, oval-shaped kind, there are the narrow, elongated oriental varieties. There are even some white eggplants. These plants have great ornamental value with their delicate, star-shaped purple flowers and glossy fruit. They're an eye-catching addition to the landscape as long as you keep pests under control. Eggplants are too tender to be placed in a border planting where they're likely to be jostled. Set them in a less-traveled spot and they'll do just fine.

Companion Role with Plants

Tradition: Tarragon and thyme are frequently recommended as companion crops for eggplants.

Research: No data is available on the effects of these recommended eggplant companions.

Special Care for Dogwoods: *Studies have shown that encroaching grass can interfere with a dogwood tree's growth. Protect the tree by leaving a cleared area at its base.*

Planting Tips: Each eggplant requires 18 to 24 inches of space. A particularly nice planting combination is one or two eggplants surrounded by concentric circles of flowering kale, lettuce and a decorative, aromatic herb such as purple basil.

Companion Role with Insects

Tradition: Some gardeners plant eggplants around potato hills, to act as a trap crop for potato beetles. Of course, this sacrifices the eggplants.

To get rid of potato beetles on eggplants themselves, companion crops of beans are often recommended. Some gardeners feel that flea beetles are best controlled by aromatic herbs, particularly wormwood and mint, but I've found these to be of no help whatsoever.

Research: There's no evidence to support or refute these garden traditions.

Eggplant

Elderberry

Sambucus spp.
Caprifoliaceae
Shrub

This shrub grows from 6 to 10 feet tall and is covered with clusters of large, white flowers in spring. The berries of the American or sweet elderberry (*S. canadensis*) are edible, but the fruit of most other species is not safe to eat. Elderberries do best in full sun but can tolerate slight shade.

Companion Role with Insects

Tradition: Throughout Europe and North America, elderberry has long been grown as a house and garden pest repellent. Branches of elderberry were laid around plants to ward off carrot flies and peach tree borers. An infusion of elderberry was recommended against cucumber beetles and various root maggots. Modern gardeners recommend blending elderberry buds and blossoms with water to make an aphid spray.

Research: No data is available to support the traditional insecticidal or repellent properties of elderberry.

English Ivy

Hedera helix
Araliaceae
Perennial vine

This ivy is equally at home indoors as part of a house plant collection or outdoors in the garden in all but the coldest regions. It makes an excellent ground cover since it will thrive in almost any soil and grows quite rapidly.

Companion Role with Insects

Research: In one study, it was found that corn seeds soaked in an extract made from English ivy were less susceptible to wireworm attack. (112) Perhaps as more work is done, the pest-controlling quality of ivy plants can be put to commercial use.

Eucalyptus

Eucalyptus spp.
Myrtaceae
Tree or shrub

Eucalyptus is a good bee plant and is also worth planting as an ornamental, fragrant hedge. Take care to control its vigorous growth with pruning.

Companion Role with Plants

Research: Most eucalyptus are allelopathic to a wide range of plants. For example, *E. globulus* produces substances that inhibit the growth of cucumbers and other plants. (91)

Companion Role with Insects

Tradition: Various species of eucalyptus have long been used as pest repellents and insecticides.

Research: *E. globulus* contains eucalyptol, an insecticide. (100) However, eucalyptus's effectiveness as a companion plant or spray has yet to be conclusively demonstrated. In one experiment, neither interplanting with eucalyptus nor spraying with a eucalyptus emulsion deterred cabbageworms, green peach aphids or Colorado potato beetles. (68)

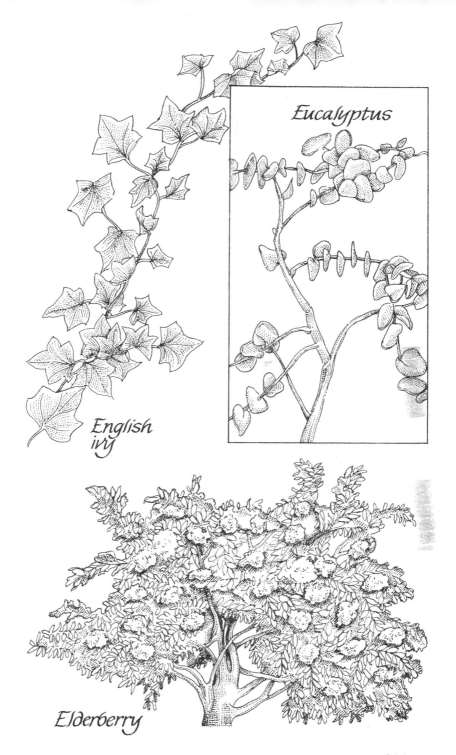

Eucalyptus

English ivy

Elderberry

Euphorbia

Euphorbia spp.
See SPURGE

European Corn Borer

Ostrinia nubilalis
See CORN

Fall Armyworm

Spodoptera frugiperda

This insect pest is found in gardens throughout most of the United States, except in extreme northern areas. You're not likely to catch them in the act of munching on plants, since they tend to feed at night. If you have lots of appealing flowering plants that have attracted Trichogramma wasps, these beneficials can help reduce the armyworm population.

Research: Corn interplanted with beans, soybeans or natural vegetation encourages predators of fall armyworms. (3, 118)

In a tropical study, best results were obtained when beans were planted 20 to 30 days before the corn crop. (6)

False Hellebore

Veratrum album
Liliaceae
Perennial weed

You'll find false hellebore growing in moist meadows and fields. The plant is coarse and leafy and can grow from 3 to 6 feet tall. In mid to late summer it blooms with small, yellowish-green flowers. False hellebore appears throughout North America.

Companion Role with Insects

Tradition: For centuries, various species of *Veratrum* have been widely used as insecticides and rat killers throughout Europe and North America.

Research: Insecticides have been isolated from the rhizomes of false hellebore. (92)

Fennel

Foeniculum vulgare
Umbelliferae
Perennial herb or vegetable grown as an annual

You might easily confuse fennel with dill, since these two related plants have look-alike foliage. Fennel makes a good medium-height border plant. When in bloom, beneficial wasps and other insects like to visit the small delicate yellow flowers.

Companion Role with Plants

Tradition: Some gardeners claim that fennel harms plants growing nearby, particularly beans and tomatoes. Wormwood is said to keep fennel seeds from germinating.

Research: No evidence is available to support or disprove that claim.

Planting Tips: Fennel complements thyme or sage in border plantings. Allow 6 inches between plants.

Companion Role with Insects

Tradition: Some gardeners recommend planting fennel to repel aphids. A mulch of wild fennel is sometimes recommended as a way to thwart snails and slugs.

Research: There's no research to prove or disprove the repellent qualities of fennel.

Fescue

Festuca spp.
Gramineae
Annual or perennial grass

Fescue serves a variety of uses. Some types are sold to sow in meadows or as pasture grasses in areas where the soil is in poor shape. One variety, known as blue fescue, forms attractive tufts of blue foliage, which can be incorporated into ornamental plantings.

Companion Role with Plants

Research: Some strains of fescue are toxic to other plants. Allelopathic chemicals are exuded from the fescue roots, inhibiting the germination and growth of black mustard, trefoil and red clover. The plant also appears to deter crabgrass. Extracts are particularly potent in fall and winter and when nitrogen fertilizers have been added. (16, 92)

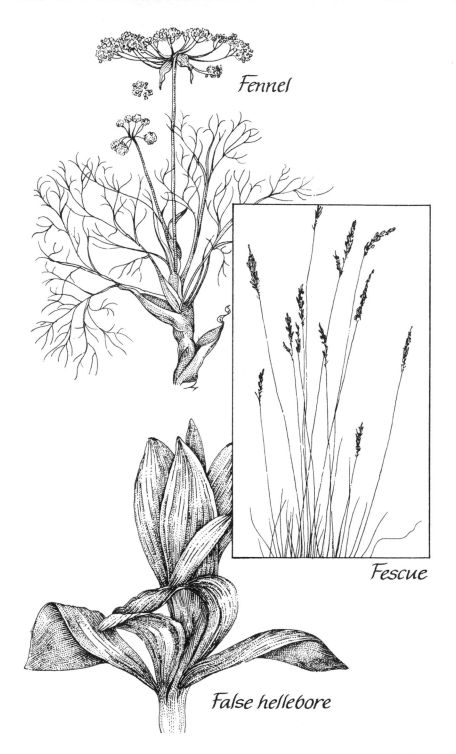

Fennel

Fescue

False hellebore

Fig

Ficus carica
Moraceae
Fruit tree

Although this tree prefers warmer climates, it can be grown in the North in a sheltered area with protection against temperatures that dip below 15°F. The fig is a handsome tree that makes an attractive accent in the landscape. Try interplanting some annual vegetables, herbs or flowers around the base. As the tree matures and the foliage becomes more dense, you'll have to carefully select interplants that can tolerate shade.

Companion Role with Plants

Tradition: Ancient Romans warned against planting rue near figs.

Research: No evidence is available to support the Romans' claims.

Flea Beetle

Various species within several families

When flea beetles visit your garden plants, the leaves look as if they've been shot through with buckshot. As the beetles chew tiny holes in the foliage, they can transmit viral and bacterial diseases.

Tradition: Mint and wormwood are recommended to repel flea beetles from most susceptible crops. An intercrop of lettuce is said to keep these pests away from radishes. Eggplants are a trap for flea beetles on potatoes or tomatoes.

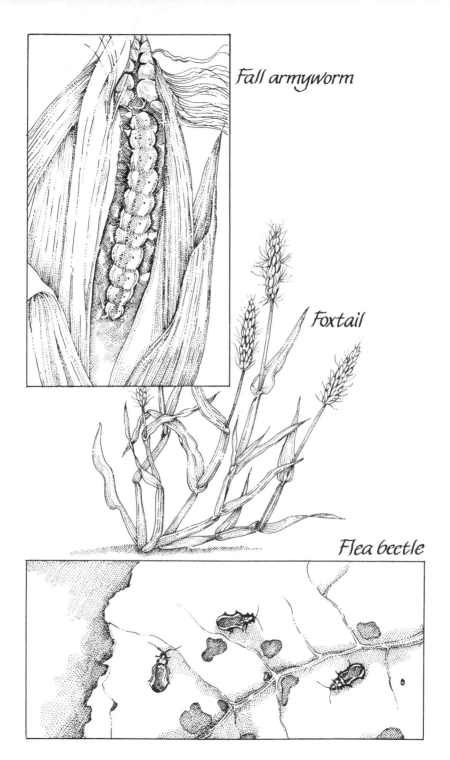

Fall armyworm

Foxtail

Flea beetle

Research: Interplanting with nonhost plants generally seems to reduce damage from flea beetles. Interplanting with tomatoes, tobacco or the weed spurry have all been found to reduce populations of certain flea beetles. (105, 106)

In other experiments, borders of tansy, southernwood, catnip and wormwood all reduced the numbers of flea beetles on cabbage, but they also reduced yields. (59)

Foxtail or Giant Foxtail

Setaria faberii
Gramineae
Annual grass

Foxtail springs up in lawns, gardens and cultivated fields throughout North America. The weed has gained its common name due to the shape of its flower spike. From July to September, yellowish-brown flower spikes appear that look like fox tails in miniature.

Companion Role with Plants

Research: As mature foxtail roots decay they release allelopathic substances, which reduce corn growth dramatically. (92)

In another study, the presence of foxtail actually enhanced soybean growth and yield, but reduced corn yields at the same time. (22)

Garlic

Allium sativum

Amaryllidaceae

Perennial herb grown as an annual

Like onions, garlic fits nicely into just about any planting scheme. Its compact, relatively low growth makes garlic an excellent choice for low borders around flower and vegetable beds.

Companion Role with Plants

Tradition: Garlic is often recommended as a companion to roses to keep aphids away. Some sources say it has a harmful effect on peas and beans.

Research: No evidence is available on any of the garden lore.

Planting Tips: As long as you allow about 3 inches for each bulb, you can grow this vegetable just about anywhere. Enclose garden beds with a garlic barrier. Plant several cloves between tomatoes, eggplants or cabbage plants.

Companion Role with Insects

Tradition: The pungency of garlic has given it a long-standing reputation as a pest repellent. Old farm magazines recommended garlic sprays to ward off all sorts of caterpillars, as well as rodents and snails.

More recently, gardeners suggest garlic sprays or companion plants to deter aphids, borers, codling moths, Japanese beetles, root maggots and various blights and rusts.

Research: Garlic does appear to contain bacteria and fungi-killing substances and some feeding deterrents, but just how effectively these manage pests in the field remains unclear. (91, 14) The Henry Doubleday Research Center in England has been conducting many experiments with garlic emulsion sprays and has had variable success in controlling certain aphids and other pests.

Recent field trials showed that a 3 percent garlic oil emul-

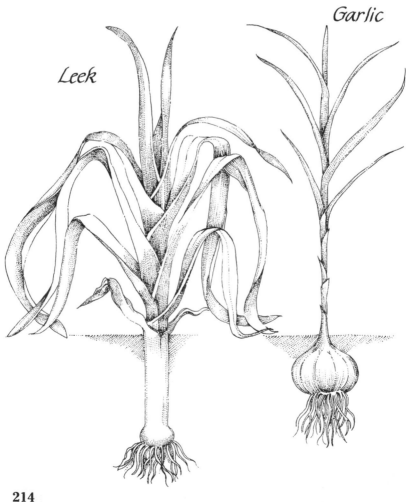

Leek

Garlic

sion spray deterred black pea aphids and other insect pests. What's most encouraging is that the spray remained effective on plants for some 30 days. (38)

Remarks: At the University of Washington, scientists are working on timed-release garlic capsules to protect orchard and forest trees from deer. The capsules, planted with the trees, emit garlic odors for several years, keeping away pests but apparently not slowing growth or harming the trees at all.

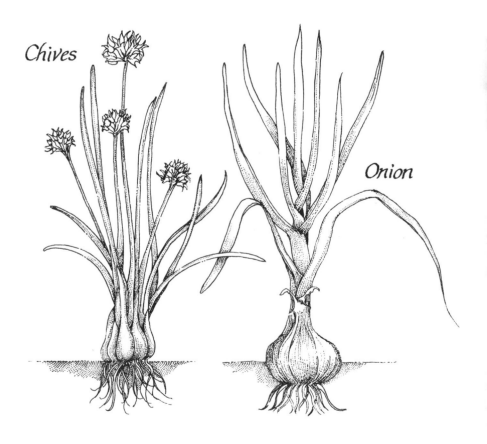

Chives

Onion

Geranium

Pelargonium spp.
Geraniaceae
Annual or perennial flower

Geraniums are garden favorites since they're such showy, continuous bloomers. They come in delectable shades of red, pink, coral and white. Their average height is about 18 inches, but there are some semidwarfs and even miniatures that have a more compact shape. Their size and controlled growth make geraniums excellent plants to intersperse among annual vegetables in a garden plot. If you pot up garden plants in the fall, they will flower off and on all winter, but unless they have adequate light, they will get a little leggy. You may wish to start new plants from spring cuttings.

Companion Role with Insects

Tradition: Gardeners say geraniums repel Japanese beetles, corn earworms and cabbage moths.

Research: No data is available to support these long-standing claims.

Goldenrod

Solidago spp.
Compositae
Perennial weed

Although this weed can be obnoxious and is the bane of many gardeners, resist your urge to completely eradicate it. Let a few plants remain at the garden edge where the golden-

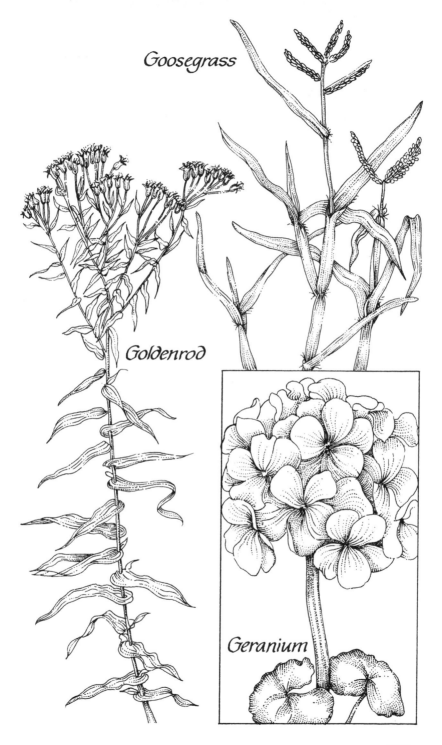

Goosegrass

Goldenrod

Geranium

217

yellow blossoms will serve as a haven for beneficial insects, especially hover flies. Goldenrod grows throughout most of eastern North America.

Companion Role with Plants

Research: Goldenrod may contain allelopathic substances, which inhibit the germination and growth of many different trees, including black locust and sugar maple. (17)

Companion Role with Insects

Tradition: Some gardeners have found that goldenrod growing outside the garden seems to act as a trap for striped cucumber beetles.

Research: No data is available about goldenrod's effect on cucumber beetles.

Goosefoot

Chenopodium spp.
See LAMB'S-QUARTERS

Goosegrass

Eleusine indica
Gramineae
Annual grass

You'll have to look very closely to tell the difference between goosegrass and crabgrass. To the trained eye, there's a subtle difference in the spikelets of each plant, but to most gardeners, these plants are confusingly similar. Goosegrass invades lawns, gardens and roadways.

Companion Role with Insects

Research: In one study, goosegrass growing nearby or surrounding beans reduced colonization and reproduction of a particular leafhopper species. (6) Repeated spray applications of a goosegrass solution on beans also interfered with the leafhopper's life cycle. (6)

Gophers

See MOLES

Grape

Vitis vinifera
Vitaceae
Fruiting vine

Grapes interplant well as a medium-height companion with tall fruit or nut trees. Vines also make good neighbors when trained on garden fences to make use of idle vertical space.

Companion Role with Plants

Tradition: In the past, grapevines were often interplanted with all sorts of trees, shrubs and grasses. Some of the earliest grape growers, the Romans, sowed grains between the vines. In this country, early farmers grew them with asparagus or trained them up fruit trees.

Grapes are said to thrive near hyssop or any legumes. They

supposedly don't do well near radishes, cabbage or most other garden vegetables.

Research: No evidence is available to confirm or deny any of these relationships.

Planting Tips: Grapes don't require as much space as you might expect. Most nurseries recommend 6-foot spacings between vines, but I've known gardeners who grow grapes in much closer quarters by fertilizing and watering well. It's even possible to grow grapes in whiskey barrel planters. Set planters on either side of a gateway, and train the vines up and over an arched trellis.

Companion Role with Insects

Research: Vineyards shouldn't be tilled, for bare ground creates dust, which encourages mite problems. A cover crop seems to help discourage mites. (118)

The presence of Johnson grass or Sudan grass controls the Willamette mite, a common grape pest. These grasses support insects that are alternate food for an important predator of the Willamette mite. (37)

Grape leafhoppers are dramatically reduced where blackberries (*Rubus* spp.) border vineyards. The blackberries provide alternate winter hosts for *Anagrus epos*, a parasite of grape leafhoppers. (33, 2, 20) In early spring, before the grape leafhoppers emerge, *Anagrus epos* can feast on the early-emerging leafhoppers that frequent blackberry vines. Blackberry plants located as much as 4 miles away from grapevines have provided effective control of grape leafhoppers, but closer plantings are even better.

Two Good Companions: *When grapevines, shown on the left, grow near blackberries, the blackberry bushes sustain parasites of grape leafhoppers, thereby helping keep the grapevines free of pests.*

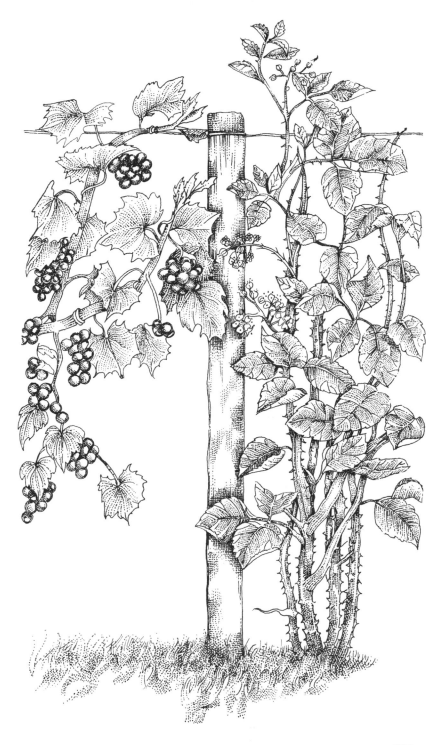

Grass

See LAWN GRASS

Hackberry

Celtis laevigata
Ulmaceae
Tree or shrub

In optimal conditions, a hackberry tree can reach up to 90 feet tall. Hackberries are often grown as street trees throughout the South.

Companion Role with Plants

Research: Hackberry inhibits the growth of many grasses. Substances that leach from decaying leaves and from living branches reduce germination as well as growth of many plant species. (91)

Hawthorn

Crataegus spp.
Rosaceae
Flowering tree

Hawthorns cover themselves with lovely white, pink or red flowers, but beware of the thorns! These prickly features can serve a purpose, though. If you desire an attractive barrier around the orchard or vegetable patch, you can maintain a hedge of hawthorns that will help keep dogs and other creatures out. Note

Hawthorn

Hellebore

Hackberry

that hawthorn trees are susceptible to cedar apple rust, fireblight and other diseases that also attack apple trees.

Companion Role with Insects

Research: A parasite of the diamondback moth overwinters on hawthorn trees. (111)

Hellebore

Helleborus niger
Ranunculaceae
Perennial ornamental

This plant also goes by the name of Christmas rose. Hellebore makes a nice addition to the garden because it blooms in late fall, when most other flowers have faded from the scene. Hellebore flowers are white, tinged with pink.

Companion Role with Insects

Tradition: Various species of hellebore have been widely used as insecticides and repellents.

Research: Today we know that hellebores, like foxglove (*Digitalis* spp.), contain depressants and insecticides. (92, 100)

Horseradish

Armoracia rusticana
Cruciferae
Perennial vegetable

This plant spreads quickly and requires strict control if you grow it in the vegetable or flower garden. As long as you confine it, horseradish can be planted in alternate rows with annuals. (For tips on how to do this, see the box Controlling Invasive Companions in chapter 5.)

Companion Role with Plants

Tradition: Horseradish is frequently recommended as a companion to potatoes, supposedly making plants disease resistant.

Research: No data is available to substantiate the claim.

Remarks: Some growers use horseradish tea as an antifungal spray for fruit trees.

Horsetail

Equisetum spp.
Equisetaceae
Perennial weed

This weed is a common sight in moist fields and meadows and along roadways. It grows throughout the United States and the southernmost parts of Canada. Horsetail doesn't reproduce by seeds; instead it spreads by spores and creeping underground stems. In the past, horsetail was used to scour and polish metal dishes.

Companion Role with Insects

Remarks: Some gardeners dry horsetail plants and crush them to form a powder to use against slugs. This powder contains silicon, which abrades the soft bodies of these pests. Powdered horsetail is most effective when sprinkled in a circle around each plant in the garden.

Hyssop

Hyssopus officinalis
Labiatae
Perennial herb

Hyssop is a good herb to plant in permanent borders. It grows slowly and won't overrun the garden as quickly as some other perennial herbs do. It also attracts beneficial insects.

Companion Role with Insects

Tradition: Hyssop is a widely recommended companion herb. It is said to repel all sorts of insect larvae, flea beetles and flies. Some gardeners say it is a decoy for cabbage butterflies.

Research: So far, hyssop's repellent or trapping qualities haven't been demonstrated in the field. In an experiment with cabbage flea beetles on collards, a hyssop border had no beneficial effect. (58) It also wasn't much help in controlling cabbageworms on collards. (58)

Imported Cabbageworm

Pieris rapae
See CABBAGE

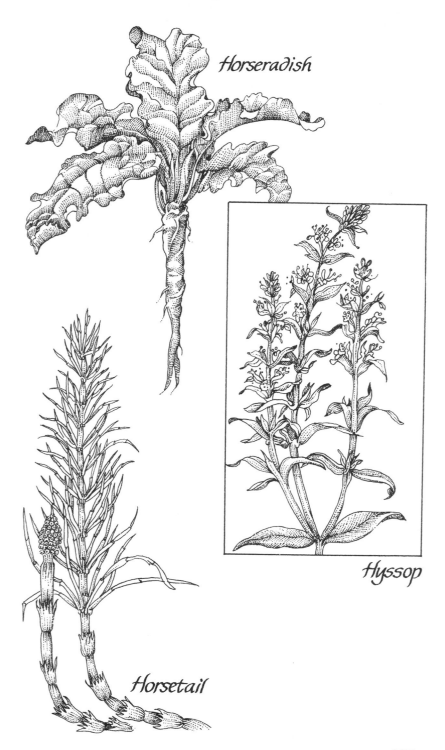

Horseradish

Horsetail

Hyssop

227

Jimsonweed or Apple of Peru

Datura stramonium
Solanaceae
Annual weed

This is a particularly bothersome weed in orchards. Jimsonweed gets quite tall and with its prickles can make fruit picking difficult, if not downright painful. It's best to keep this weed well mowed and under control in both the orchard and garden. Jimsonweed appears throughout North America.

Companion Role with Plants

Tradition: Jimsonweed is traditionally said to give protection to nearby plants.

Research: There's no evidence on the protective powers of this plant. In fact, jimsonweed seeds may be somewhat allelopathic. (91)

Companion Role with Insects

Tradition: Some growers say this weed should be left around the garden as a repellent to Japanese beetles and Colorado potato beetles.

Research: There is some evidence to support the notion that jimsonweed is effective against potato beetles. Jimsonweed growing near potatoes attracts egg-laying females. When the larvae hatch, they feed on the poisonous weed and eventually die. (20)

Sorghum cover crops do a good job of eliminating this and other weeds. (87)

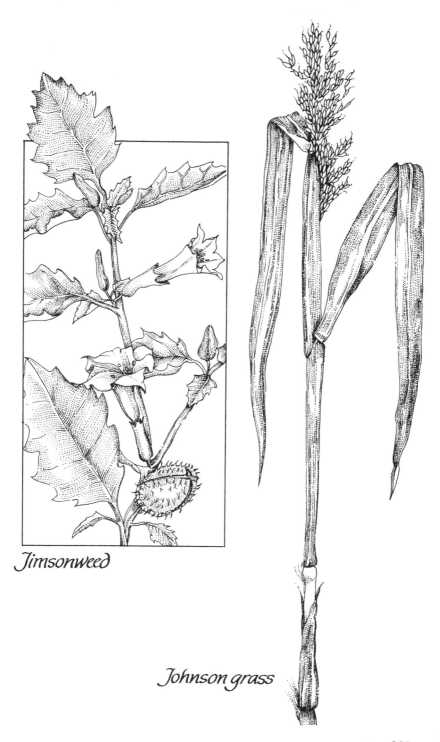

Jimsonweed

Johnson grass

Kale

Brassica oleracea, Acephala Group
Annual vegetable
See CABBAGE

Kohlrabi

Brassica oleracea, Gongylodes Group
Annual vegetable
See CABBAGE

Lacewing

Various species of Neuroptera

This predatory insect has earned the name aphid lion for its voracious appetite. In its larval stage, it eats thrips, mites, caterpillar eggs, scales, leafhoppers, corn earworms and mealybugs in addition to aphids. As an adult, a lacewing will feed mostly on aphids and mealybugs. You can help lacewings be more effective in their control of aphids by keeping down the ant population in the garden. Ants "herd" aphids and, in return for their honeydew secretions, defend the aphids against attack.

Lacewings are available from mail-order suppliers. To help sustain adults in the garden, be sure to grow flowering plants rich in nectar and pollen in and around the garden and orchard. Lacewings like to seek shelter in the tree of heaven and various evergreens.

Lady Beetle

Cycloneda spp.

This familiar predatory beetle, also commonly referred to as the ladybug, is known to eat aphids in record numbers. It's been calculated that a single adult can consume 50 aphids in one day.

Lady beetles are available from mail-order suppliers, but they may not be such a good buy. Since they're collected while still in hibernation, their first response upon being released in your garden may be to fly away and lay their eggs elsewhere. You could be left with no more lady beetles than you started out with.

Your best bet is to maintain a good ecosystem in your yard,

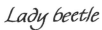

Lady beetle

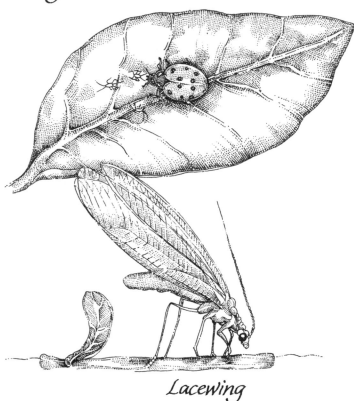

Lacewing

which will allow a natural population of lady beetles to establish itself. To do this, keep strips of flowering plants and native vegetation around the garden and orchard. In particular, grow strips or borders of tansy. Researchers at the Rodale Research Center have noticed that lady beetles seem to show a preference for tansy and seek it out as a place to lay their eggs. They also are drawn to yarrow.

Lamb's-Quarters

Chenopodium album
Chenopodiaceae
Annual weed

This is one of the few edible weeds that, along with the lowly dandelion, is truly delicious. It's probably not worth planting, but you might allow a few volunteers to grow in early spring so you can savor the young leaves and tender stems. They're best when steamed or sautéed lightly. Lamb's-quarters appear in cultivated fields and gardens throughout the East.

Companion Role with Plants

Tradition: Some gardeners say lamb's-quarters help corn grow well.

Research: A water extract of lamb's-quarters inhibited the early growth of corn seedlings and in the field reduced soybean yields. Root exudates of lupine, corn and sunflower, on the other hand, reduced the growth of lamb's-quarters. (92, 60)

Companion Role with Insects

Tradition: Some gardeners maintain that lamb's-quarters may be useful as a trap or decoy crop for leafminers and gophers.

Research: No evidence is available on the garden lore.

Larkspur or Delphinium

Delphinium spp.
Ranunculaceae
Perennial ornamental

These tall and stately flowers are truly breathtaking. Their graceful spikes are full of large blooms that range in color from blue to lavender to white. The tallest varieties can reach 5 to 6 feet and are best as background plantings. Smaller delphiniums grow 2 to 3 feet tall and can be used in lower borders.

Companion Role with Plants

Tradition: Members of this genus are said to harm beets and other root crops but are claimed to grow well with oats, cabbage and beans.

Research: No data is available to support any of the claims made for and against larkspur.

Planting Tips: These flowers are heavy feeders, requiring full sun and 8 to 12 inches of growing space, although larger varieties may need up to 2 feet. Choose garland larkspur (*D. belladonna*) or *D. grandiflorum* cultivars for their compact growth and lovely cut flowers. You can interplant them within or between rows, as well as in borders.

Companion Role with Insects

Tradition: During the Middle Ages, this flower was used in a concoction to kill head lice. It also had widespread uses against other pests.

Research: We know now that *Delphinium* species do contain insecticides, but no one has reported on tests with interplantings or garden sprays for pest control. (100)

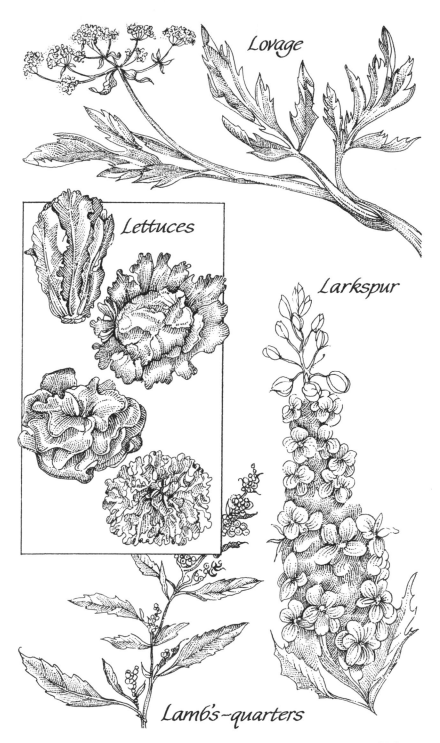

Lovage

Lettuces

Larkspur

Lamb's-quarters

Lawn Grass

Many species
Gramineae
Perennial grass

Even though you may find the sight of a green carpet of grass growing right up to and around a fruit or ornamental tree appealing, researchers have found that such an arrangement may not be the best for the tree's health. Brick, plastic or aluminum edging that you partially sink into the ground can neatly keep grass away from the tree.

Companion Role with Plants

Research: Studies show that turf suppresses the growth of trees and shrubs. In experiments with forsythia and dogwood, researchers found that competition plus allelopathic substances leached from grass roots slowed the development of the test plants. (11)

Lettuce

Lactuca sativa
Compositae
Annual vegetable

Lettuces make delightful border plants since they're compact and available in a lovely range of colors with different foliage shapes. Ruffly leaf lettuce comes in all shades of green, plus ruby red and bronze. Conical heads of romaine lettuce contrast nicely with the full, well-folded shape of butterhead and crisphead lettuce. Wherever they are in the garden, allow a few lettuce plants to bolt and flower. They'll attract beneficial insects and reseed themselves for next season.

Companion Role with Plants

Tradition: Gardeners say that lettuce does best near strawberries, cabbage or beets. Other lore maintains that radishes and lettuce benefit each other.

Research: There's no data to support or refute the garden lore. However, lettuce is sensitive to toxic chemicals found in various plant residues, including broccoli, broad beans, vetch, wheat, rye and barley. Where decomposing plant parts touch developing lettuce roots, lesions and rot occur. (77)

Planting Tips: Lettuce tolerates lots of shade and even prefers filtered light in hot summer months. The leaves are paler, but they're more tender under shady conditions. Upright varieties such as romaine or the compact leaf lettuces interplant particularly well between individual cabbage, bean or other plants. Regular-size leaf lettuces, which tend to require more space, are best interplanted between entire rows of peas, beans and tomatoes. Make frequent plantings in a nursery area for a continuous supply of transplants for the intercropped bed.

Companion Role with Insects

Tradition: To control flies, many growers maintain that you should plant radishes and onions together with the lettuce.

Research: No information is available on the fly-controlling qualities of various lettuce companions. However, as an intercrop with cabbage, lettuce helped reduce cabbage root flies in one study. The beneficial effect of the lettuce plantings could probably be duplicated by any low-growing intercrop that covers the ground. Companion crops of clover and an artificial green covering also reduced root flies on cabbage. (98)

Leek

Allium ampeloprasum, Porrum Group
Biennial vegetable grown as an annual
See ONION

Lovage

Levisticum officinale
Umbelliferae
Perennial herb

This bushy plant gives you plenty of celery-flavored stems, leaves and seeds to use in soups, stews and salads. In full sun, a single lovage plant can spread up to 2 feet in width and measure up to 6 feet tall, from ground level to the tops of the flower stems. Once a plant starts blooming, the leaves will yellow and fade unless you snip the flower heads off. If you have more than one plant, let one bloom and keep the other clipped for a plentiful supply of leaves. If you have only a single plant, collect leaves before the flowers appear and dry the extras, so you'll have some on hand for the soup pot.

Companion Role with Plants

Tradition: Gardeners often recommend growing lovage between beans (both bush and pole types) to enhance the legume's growth.

Research: No companion planting experiments have been done with lovage to confirm or deny its helpful role.

Marigold

Tagetes spp.
Compositae
Annual flower

Many gardeners would consider these perky golden flowers to be the classic companions. Over the years they have certainly been vested with many healthful benefits in the garden. Marigolds are a visual pleasure because they bloom prolifically, all season long. This benefits the hover flies they attract.

Companion Role with Plants

Tradition: Marigolds have a glowing reputation as helpmates for potatoes, tomatoes and roses.

Research: There's not much data that relates to the marigold's ability to help or hinder a neighboring plant's growth. In one study, French marigolds (*T. patula*) seemed to have an allelopathic effect on beans. (56) Studies at the Henry Doubleday Research Association in England did find that the golden marigold (*T. minuta*) suppressed the growth of certain weeds. This group includes ground elder, shepherd's purse, groundsel, tansy, ragwort, ground ivy and quack grass.

Companion Role with Insects

Tradition: The marigold has always had many gardening fans who claim it works wonders against insects. Various species of *Tagetes* have long been used as insecticides and pest repellents. Some Africans hung plants in their huts to keep away flies. In India, certain marigold species were always grown around cotton fields.

Today's gardeners recommend marigold companion plants to ward off everything from Mexican bean beetles to aphids and cabbage loopers.

Research: In one experiment, interplantings of French marigolds repelled Mexican bean beetles but seemed to have an allelopathic effect that stunted the beans' growth. (56)

This same marigold was found to have no effect against the cabbageworm. (58) But in another study, marigolds did reduce cabbage pests significantly. The only catch is that the harvested heads were much smaller than usual. (52)

On other garden crops, marigolds appeared to reduce aphid populations on pepper plants. (68) Marigold interplants also seemed to mask potato odors and save plants from hungry Colorado potato beetles. (27)

Research into the marigold's pest repellent properties began in the 1930s with studies of certain species' ability to suppress nematode (or eelworm) populations. Several species have since been shown to reduce root-knot, meadow, potato root and other kinds of nematodes. Some marigold species are toxic to the nematodes, while others cause nematode larvae to change their life cycle. The most effective are African marigolds (*T. erecta*), French marigolds and golden marigolds. In one study, when any one of these species was grown in infested soil, nematode populations were reduced to low levels within 42 to 70 days. Each of these marigolds will control certain species of nematodes, but no single marigold provides blanket protection against *all* kinds of nematodes.

Planting Tips: In some studies, marigolds were planted very densely well ahead of the main crop, then turned under. In essence, they were treated as a green manure crop. If this treatment doesn't appeal to you, you'll be interested to know that several studies have shown that it isn't always necessary to plant a cover crop of marigolds in order to suppress nematodes. Successful results were had by simply interplanting with the marigolds. As long as marigolds are within 24 inches of one another, they may be effective.

When you interplant marigolds, be sure to pick a size that's compatible with neighboring crops. African marigolds come as semidwarfs (20 inches) or giants (2 to 3 feet). French marigolds are more diminutive—you have your choice of 10-inch dwarfs or 7-inch extra-dwarfs.

French marigold

African marigold

241

Melon

Cucumis melo
Cucurbitaceae
Annual vegetable

Now that breeders have come up with compact melon varieties, these fruits are practical companions in the smallest of gardens. Take advantage of their space-saving size by tucking a hill of melons into the corner of a bed or between hills or rows of corn. Try growing a neighboring crop of early, compact vegetables such as radishes or beets amidst the young melon vines.

I've seen vining forms trained along trellises or other supports. When fruits appear, they're supported by slings made of nylon stockings, mesh or cheesecloth. In my own garden, I've had no luck with this method, but I know it *is* possible, and I keep trying.

Companion Role with Plants

Tradition: In tropical countries, different melon varieties are often intercropped with peanuts, corn, manioc (the tapioca plant), yams and other crops. Closer to home, in North America, gardeners also plant melons with corn or pair them with sunflowers. Melons are supposedly harmed by potatoes.

Early gardeners kept melons far from gourds and cucumbers because they feared those related plants would spoil the taste of the fruit they harvested from melon vines.

A Garden Tradition: *For years, gardeners have been planting melons with nasturtiums and radishes in the belief that cucumber beetles will look elsewhere for their meals.*

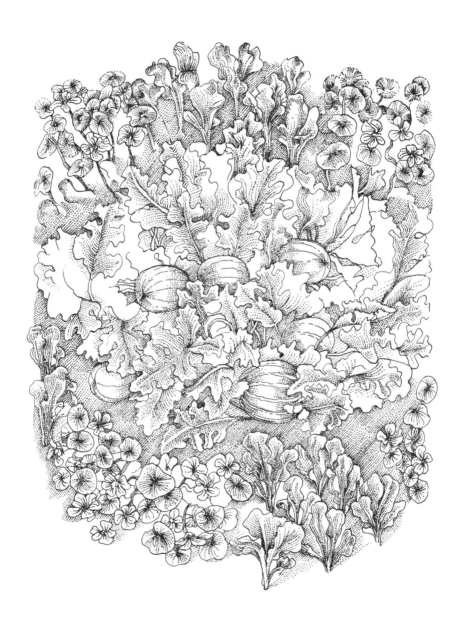

Research: No data is available about the benefits of pairing melons with any particular crop. However, while it seems unlikely that the melon's flavor would be affected by other cucurbits, cross-pollination would prevent seed saving.

Companion Role with Insects

Tradition: Nasturtiums and radishes are supposed to repel cucumber beetles and keep melons safe.

Research: Very little research has been done to study those combinations. However, in at least one study, nasturtiums didn't seem to reduce cucumber beetles on cucumbers. (47)

Mexican Bean Beetle

Epilachna varivestis
See BEAN

Mice

Many a fruit grower has had the unpleasant surprise of brushing away snow from the base of a young fruit tree, only to find that mice have been gnawing away at the tender bark.

Tradition: Wormwood is recommended against most animals, including mice.

Research: Recent work suggests that cluster amaryllis (*Lycoris radiata*) planted around rice paddies keep out mice.

Researchers are studying extracts from jojoba seeds (*Simmondsia chinensis*) as potential rodent repellents in fields and gardens. (92) So far there have been no conclusive results.

Milkweed

Asclepias spp.
Asclepiadaceae
Perennial weed

Milkweed is a common sight in fields and pastures and along roadways. In the fall, the brown pods let loose their seeds, which are carried aloft by the wind, thanks to the fine silken threads attached to the seeds. Although it is a pervasive weed, milkweed does have some redeeming qualities. Its flowers attract parasitic wasps, so this weed is valuable to have in orchards and around vegetable gardens. It also serves as a good host for parasites of cabbageworms, tent caterpillars and codling moths.

Companion Role with Plants

Research: A toxin in the leaves of common milkweed (*A. syriaca*) may harm crops. (92)

Companion Role with Insects

Tradition: For aphids on tomatoes, one gardener suggests letting milkweed grow up each tomato plant. This grower plants a single milkweed seed beside each tomato plant and lets the milkweed twine up the stem.

Research: No data confirms the aphid-fighting ability of a milkweed companion. The colorful butterfly milkweed (*A. tuberosa*) contains a feeding deterrent to corn wireworms. Studies showed that corn seed treated with an emulsion of the weed effectively prevented wireworms from feeding. (112)

Mint

Mentha spp.
Labiatae
Perennial herb

When in flower, mints attract all sorts of beneficial insects. This makes them valuable to have growing around the garden, particularly in hedge borders and perennial beds. When it comes to the main vegetable garden, you're better off keeping them out. Mints are rampant growers with spreading, tenacious roots. They can crowd out annual vegetables in short order. (See the box Controlling Invasive Companions in chapter 5.) Mints are available in a pleasing variety of scents. For a change, consider growing pineapple mint or the petite-leaved, creeping Corsican mint (*M. requienii*). The latter will need some winter protection in northern areas.

Companion Role with Insects

Tradition: Spearmint and peppermint supposedly repel ants, aphids, flea beetles and cabbage butterflies.

Research: No data is available to support these claims. In one study, pennyroyal (*M. pulegium*) had no effect on imported cabbageworms on cabbage and may have even attracted the pests. (55)

However, mint species do contain several fungicides (salicyllic acid, for example) and repellents (menthol, citronella, camphor).

Growing Milkweed and Mint: *When milkweed, shown on left, is trained up tomato stems, it may repel aphids. To confine mint roots, plant in bottomless pots buried in the garden soil, as shown on right.*

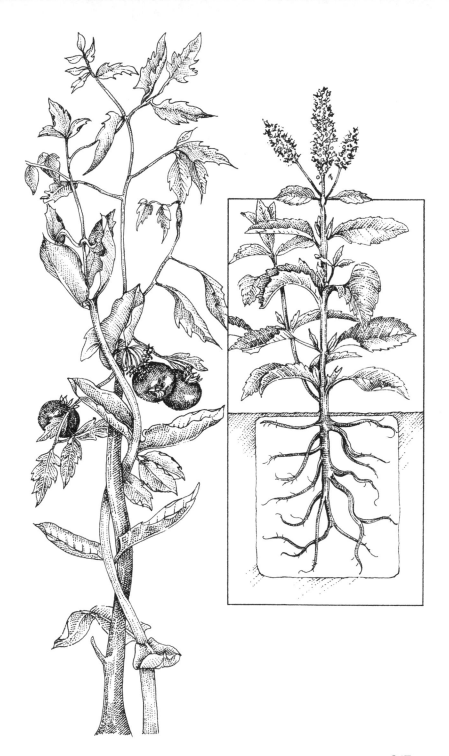

Preliminary studies done with the waste product left after peppermint oils are distilled from the plants have found that this material is effective against Colorado potato beetles. (38)

Mole Plant

Euphorbia spp.
See SPURGE

Moles

Some people mistakenly believe that moles nibble on underground plant parts. In fact, moles are more interested in eating grubs than they are in the carrots or beets growing in your garden. Moles can wreak havoc, though, when their tunneling disrupts root growth.

Tradition: Borders of mole plant or castor bean are said to keep moles away from the garden. A few gardeners report that daffodil bulbs, planted 12 inches deep in double rows are equally effective and prettier, too. Some growers say dandelions are also good deterrents.

Research: No evidence is available to support or refute the garden lore.

Mullein

Verbascum thapsus
Scrophulariaceae
Biennial weed

This weed has earned the nickname flannel mullein because of the woolly, rather coarse surface of its foliage. You'll find mullein growing in fields, pastures and along roadways. It prefers dry, rather gravelly soil. One good reason to have mullein around is that it attracts beneficial hover flies.

Companion Role with Insects

Tradition: A few gardeners recommend common mullein as a trap crop for stink bugs. They let the weed grow around the orchard.

Research: No data confirms the trapping ability of mullein.

Mustard

Brassica spp.
Cruciferae
Annual weed or vegetable

Mustard plants play several roles in the garden. Some mustards (*B. juncea*) are cultivated for their tasty, vitamin-rich leaves. Then there are their weedy cousins that commonly appear, uninvited, in garden plots and fields.

Companion Role with Plants

Tradition: Various mustard species are said to stimulate the growth of grapes, beans, alfalfa and fruit trees. Mustard is supposedly an "enemy" to turnips.

Research: There's no evidence to support or refute the garden lore. In one experiment, material leached from wild mustard (*B. nigra*) roots stimulated the growth and development of buckwheat. (92) Decaying leaves and stalks of wild mustard seem to be allelopathic to some plants, particularly grasses. (91)

Planting Tips: If you let the vegetable form of mustard flower and set seeds, you'll be hard pressed to get rid of it. Unless you're willing to faithfully pull out plants before they reseed, keep this vegetable in border and strip plantings, allowing 6 to 10 inches between plants.

Companion Role with Insects

Research: As an intercrop with collards or Brussels sprouts, wild mustard reduced cabbage aphids significantly. It also helped divert flea beetles away from collards. (44)

Like the cole crops to which they are related, all mustards produce a chemical that is released into the soil during growth and attracts diamondback moths. At the same time, this substance inhibits the emergence of cyst nematodes and prevents pea root rot. (118)

White mustard (*B. hirta*) supports a parasite of various larval pests and of the pea aphid. (53)

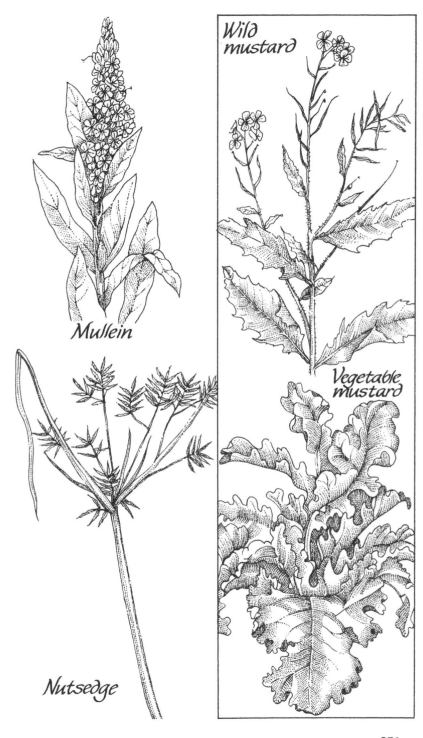

Mullein

Wild mustard

Vegetable mustard

Nutsedge

251

Nasturtium

Tropaeolum spp.
Tropaeolaceae
Annual flower

The old-fashioned trailing forms of nasturtium can be grown on trellises and fences as a stunning colorful screen. Compact dwarf forms interplant nicely within the garden, but if the soil is too rich, they won't flower well.

Companion Role with Insects

Tradition: Gardeners plant nasturtiums to trap aphids or to repel white flies, various cabbage pests and squash bugs.

Research: The results are conflicting. As a companion to peppers, nasturtiums seemed to have a repellent effect on green peach aphids. Planted with potatoes, nasturtiums were less effective in reducing Colorado potato beetles. (69, 68) In another trial, nasturtiums didn't reduce whiteflies on beans. (52)

In one study, nasturtiums had no effect on imported cabbageworms on collards. (57) In another, they did help reduce the number of larvae and eggs on cabbage but didn't significantly reduce the amount of worm injury. In addition, cabbage heads harvested from interplanted plots were much smaller than those taken from monocropped ones. (52)

Nematodes or Eelworms

Various species of Nematoda

If there are nematodes in your garden soil, you aren't likely to see them. These tiny worms, also called roundworms and eelworms, give away their presence by causing symptoms such as malformed flowers, leaves, stems or roots.

Tradition: Marigolds have long been used in India to repel nematodes.

Research: In addition to marigolds (see MARIGOLD), a number of other plants contain feeding deterrents or toxins effective against plant-eating nematodes. Against some species, castor beans, mole plants (*Euphorbia lathyris*) or chrysanthemums are effective as cover crops or intercrops. Rattlebox (*Crotalaria spectabilis*) is effective in peach tree orchards. Asparagus also shows some promise. (92)

Nicotine

See TOBACCO

Nutsedge

Cyperus spp.
Cyperaceae
Annual or perennial grassy weed

Species of this weed appear throughout most of the United States. Nutsedge spreads by means of rhizomes that have tubers on the ends. If you ever want to rid an area of nutsedge once and for all, you must be sure to dig up *all* the roots and tubers. Any small portion you leave behind is enough to start a fresh infestation.

Companion Role with Plants

Research: Nutsedge infesting corn fields decreased the availability of nitrogen to corn roots during the growing season. The cause seems to be some allelopathic substance that's released from the nutsedge roots. (113)

Leaves of nutsedge are also allelopathic. As little as 0.5 percent yellow nutsedge foliage in the soil reduced corn growth and yield by some 20 percent and also greatly reduced soybean yield. (16, 32)

In soil that previously supported purple nutsedge, germination of barley, mustard and cotton was reduced. (23)

Oak

Quercus spp.
Fagaceae
Tree

Native American oak species are particularly attractive in the landscape since most have leaves that turn a rich, burnished red or deep brown in the fall. There are a few exceptions, notably the shingle oak (*Q. imbricaria*), which displays yellowish-bronze autumn leaves.

Companion Role with Insects

Remarks: Oak trees contain tannin, a substance toxic to some insects and mammals. Moreover, at least some kinds of oaks appear able to alter concentrations of this and other toxins, according to the amount of stress they are undergoing. Scientists have found that when the red oak is attacked by gypsy moths, the new leaves it puts forth contain more tannins, which in turn slow larva growth. (70, 78)

A mulch of oak leaves may repel slugs. (3) Be sure the oak leaves are well chopped before you use them to mulch. Otherwise, you'll end up with a wet, cold, impenetrable layer that will require years to decompose.

Oat

Avena sativa
Gramineae
Annual grass

Besides the oat that's grown for human and animal consumption, there are several other interesting species. In particular, there's one that is grown as an ornamental. Known as the animated oat (*A. sterilis*), this annual plant grows about 3 feet tall. You can see the tiny flowers along the flower head start to open when they're suddenly exposed to moisture.

Companion Role with Plants

Tradition: Gardeners have long held that thistles injure the growth of oats.

Research: There's no evidence to support the idea that thistles are enemies of oats.

Some researchers have suggested that oats are allelopathic to certain other crops. Oat straw as well as living plant matter may release toxins. (91)

Onion

Allium cepa
Amaryllidaceae
Biennial vegetable grown as an annual

Since they're a compact crop with shallow, fibrous roots, onions can fit almost anywhere in the garden. Treat them as companions to individual annual or perennial plants or squeeze them into borders and row edgings.

Companion Role with Plants

Tradition: Onions are often recommended as companions to cabbage, beets, strawberries and lettuce. Some gardeners say that onions harm beans, but others say that the two crops are fine companions. Sage and onions have the reputation of not doing well together.

Research: No data is available to confirm or deny the garden traditions.

Planting Tips: Onion sets are the easiest to use for precision plantings. If space gets too tight, harvest the onions before they mature.

Companion Role with Insects

Tradition: Onions planted between potatoes are supposed to keep away Colorado potato beetles. They are also suggested as deterrents to carrot flies.

A spray of onion tea is recommended against thrips and many plant diseases and mildews.

Research: No data from relevant field studies is available. However, it is known that alliums contain sulfur compounds that are fungicidal.

Oregano

Origanum spp.
Labiatae
Perennial or annual herb

Oregano makes an attractive, fragrant companion worth planting in any garden. Use one species, pot marjoram (*O. heracleoticum*), as a lush, low-growing permanent border. This plant grows about 1 foot tall. The more common form, *O. vulgare*, is somewhat taller, growing to 2½ feet. Its gray foliage and tiny, pale purple flowers make this oregano a pleasing accent in perennial beds or rock gardens.

Companion Role with Insects

Tradition: Gardeners sometimes recommend oregano, along with other members of the mint family, as a general pest repellent in the garden.

Research: There is no scientific evidence to support these traditional claims about oregano's pest repellent powers.

Planting Tips: When you direct seed in early summer, oregano will readily establish permanent residency. It's easy to keep under control by simply thinning, pruning and transplanting.

Parasitic Insects

These beneficial insects use another insect's body as a living food source for their young. Parasitic wasps or flies seek out a host to carry their eggs. They lay their eggs in or on the host insect, and as the young develop they feed on the host's organs.

Parasitic insects tend to be highly specialized—only one type of host will do. This sets them apart from predator insects,

257

which often have a broader range of pests they'll attack.

The Trichogramma wasp is one of the most commonly known parasites. This particular wasp is one of the few that doesn't specialize in a certain host; it will attack over 200 insect species, including codling moths, gypsy moths, cabbage loopers and cutworms. Another familiar parasitic wasp is the braconid. If you've ever come across a tomato hornworm with many small white tubes sticking out of its back, you've seen the braconid's handiwork.

You'll seldom actually *see* parasitic wasps. They are very, very tiny, some no larger than mere specks. Their small size prevents them from reaching the nectar in what are relatively cavernous vegetable flowers (the adult wasps need nectar to sustain them as they search for hosts). Carrot family flowers are more to their liking since they are small and the nectar is easily accessible. To encourage the presence of parasitic insects in your garden and orchard, establish strips or borders of enticing flowers such as Queen Anne's lace. Allow herbs like anise, caraway, chervil, dill, fennel, lovage and parsley to bloom. In the garden itself, you might let a few odd carrots, celery or parsnip plants go to flower. Composite family flowers such as black-eyed Susans and daisies are also very appealing to parasitic insects.

Pea

Pisum sativum
Leguminosae
Annual vegetable

Peas are especially good companions since they occupy the ground for just part of the season. Trained to a fence or trellis, peas form a terrific sunfilter and windbreak that protects developing companion crops such as tomatoes, eggplants, lettuce, spinach or peppers.

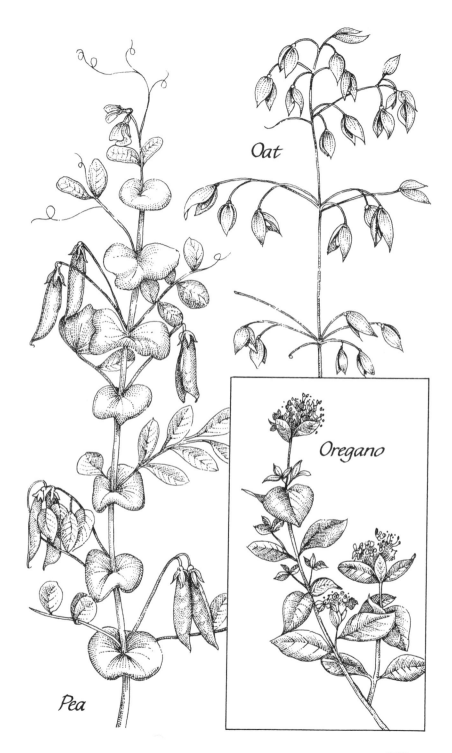

Oat

Oregano

Pea

Companion Role with Plants

Tradition: Gardeners plant peas with corn, cucumbers, radishes, carrots and tomatoes. One gardener has found that both crops benefit when tomatoes are transplanted into cages where peas are already growing up the sides. In the spring, dwarf, early peas are planted around the outside of a 3-foot-wide tomato cage. After danger of frost is past, a single tomato is transplanted into the center of each cage. The peas will be harvested before the tomato needs full sun and support. In the meantime, the pea vines protect the tomato seedling from the drying effects of sun and wind.

Some growers say that onions and garlic inhibit the growth of these legumes.

Research: No data is available on the effects of these companion pairings. In one study, tomatoes intercropped with peas produced higher per row yields for the peas and better fresh market value for the tomatoes. However, when two varieties of peas were intercropped with two sweet corn varieties, neither crop's yields increased. (54)

Planting Tips: Rows of peas do well alternated with shade-tolerant, low growers like spinach, lettuce and Chinese cabbage. You can allow dwarf varieties to trail on the ground, but taller varieties need trellising. If your soil is rich and moist, you can plant seeds thickly in double rows on either side of the support. Allow 2 to 4 inches between plants.

Companion Role with Insects

Research: Weeds growing near a pea patch provide syrphid flies with egg-laying sites. (111) Since syrphids eat aphids and other tiny pests, they're worth attracting.

White mustard (*Brassica hirta*) supports a parasite of pea aphids. (53)

Pea root rot is less likely to occur when cole crops are growing nearby.

Peach

Prunus persica
Rosaceae
Fruit tree

As with any tree crop, you can interplant peach with almost any vegetable or herb during the first several seasons while you're waiting for the trees to reach fruit-bearing size. If necessary, provide additional nutrients and water to make up for any competition that may result. Peaches are self-fertile, but they do bear a better harvest if they receive cross-pollination. Nectarines, apricots and almonds all pollinate with peaches.

Companion Role with Plants

Tradition: In the past, growers set peach trees amongst corn or other grain crops. More recently, grapes, asparagus, perennial onions (also called Egyptian onions) and strips of strawberries are also being intercropped with peaches. To fill in the upper story, tall and open nut trees such as walnuts or chestnuts are being used.

For centuries, farmers have realized that young peach trees don't perform well when planted where old ones grew.

Research: Evidence suggests that peaches are auto-allelopathic. Decaying roots of mature peach trees emit substances that cause damage to the roots of young ones. This makes it possible for nematodes, fungi and insect pests to cause further harm. (91)

Planting Tips: Dwarf peaches and nectarines require 8 to 12 feet between trees, and standard trees need 12 to 20 feet.

To reduce the chances of verticillium wilt, don't plant peach trees in soil that has previously supported susceptible crops such as tomatoes, potatoes, strawberries and raspberries.

To avoid replant problems, don't put a new peach tree in the same spot where one formerly grew.

Companion Role with Insects

Tradition: Garlic is said to prevent borers from harming peach trees.

Research: No data is available to confirm the protective powers of garlic, but certain companion plantings have helped with other pests. For example, strawberries are alternate hosts of a parasite that attacks oriental fruit moths. Where strawberries grow nearby, moth populations are reduced. (118)

A sod cover crop in the orchard was found to reduce oriental fruit moths and various other pests, including nematodes. Weeds around the peach trees in an abandoned orchard hosted parasites and predators that controlled red spider mites. (6, 118) However, grass and weeds growing right around the tree base might actually increase peach tree borers.

Peanut or Groundnut

Arachis hypogaea
Leguminosae
Annual vegetable

Peanuts are traditionally thought of as a southern crop since they need plenty of warmth and a four-month-long growing season. Northern growers can give peanuts a try if they grow the variety Spanish, which takes a little less time than most to mature. Spanish is also a more compact grower, so it can save some space in small gardens.

Companion Role with Plants

Tradition: In the tropical countries where peanuts are a staple food, they are almost always grown with other crops. They are typically intercropped with grains (millet, corn or sorghum, for example); squash or melons; bananas or dozens of other plants.

Research: Some studies have shown that intercropping peanuts with a nonlegume crop increased yields of both crops. (117)

Planting Tips: Testing suggests that peanuts perform best when densely planted. Although most seed packets and planting guides suggest spacings of 12 to 18 inches between plants, some researchers believe that peanuts yield even better when they're planted as close as 3 inches, in rows just 10 inches apart. This dense spacing seems to be a bit extreme, but it's certainly worth a home garden experiment.

Since peanuts produce lots of lush topgrowth and tend to overrun their neighbors, they aren't well suited to intercropping with most of the smaller vegetable crops. They do well with corn and squash, however. Interplant between wide rows or strips of corn, or try alternating hills of peanuts with hills of corn within the row. You may wish to try circle plantings with corn in the center and squash and peanuts interplanted around the outside.

Companion Role with Insects

Research: When peanuts are intercropped with corn, predatory spiders are more abundant, and the pest *Ostrinia furnacalis* is regulated. (4)

Pear

Pyrus communis
Rosaceae
Fruit tree

A few of the old-fashioned winter pear varieties are self-fertile, but most pears require a compatible neighboring pear tree for cross-pollination.

Companion Role with Plants

Tradition: Currants were often planted among pear trees to promote the good health of both crops.

Remarks: There's no evidence to support the idea that currants are growth enhancers, but currants and other bush fruits make good companions for pears in multistory cropping designs.

Sod cover crops such as grass, clover or alfalfa help reduce chances of fireblight and also increase populations of beneficial insects.

Planting Tips: Plant dwarf pears 8 to 12 feet apart, and give standard pears about 15-foot spacings.

Pecan

Carya illinoinensis
Juglandaceae
Nut tree

This handsome tree is long-lived and a hardy, rapid grower. Given the right conditions, a pecan tree can reach 40 to 50 feet. A mature tree shuts out most light at its base, but during a tree's early years you might be able to grow a slightly shade-tolerant crop there. You should plant two or more pecan varieties for cross-pollination.

Companion Role with Insects

Remarks: A cover crop of vetch helps suppress a variety of pests by hosting beneficial insect species. The key seems to lie in mowing the cover crop at just the right time to force predators and parasites up into the trees. (118) This timing varies from place to place, but as a general rule, mow before beneficials lay their eggs.

Pennyroyal

Mentha pulegium
Perennial herb
See MINT

Pepper

Capsicum spp.
Solanaceae
Annual vegetable

Take advantage of the ornamental qualities peppers have to offer. With their glossy foliage and bold, waxy fruits, these plants belong with zinnias, marigolds and other bright flowers. You have your choice of green-, yellow-, orange- or red-fruited varieties.

Companion Role with Plants

Tradition: The herbs marjoram, basil, oregano and lovage are said to promote pepper growth. Peppers also do well with carrots and onions. Kohlrabi and fennel are said to harm peppers.

Research: No data is available to support the garden lore.

Remarks: Both beans and peppers are likely to get anthracnose, a fungus disease, so keep those crops separated in the garden. Mosaic virus is carried by aphids from deadly nightshade and other solanaceous weeds, so keep these plants well away from peppers in the garden.

Companion Role with Insects

Tradition: Some of the hot peppers are traditional insect repellents. Gardeners concoct any number of different brews made from hot peppers to spray on their crops.

Against aphids on peppers, gardeners recommend interplanting or spraying with aromatic herbs, onions or rhubarb.

Research: Peppers contain capsaicin, a toxic compound or irritant. (100) However, little research has been done with this compound or with pepper plants themselves.

In preliminary experiments, interplantings of both catnip

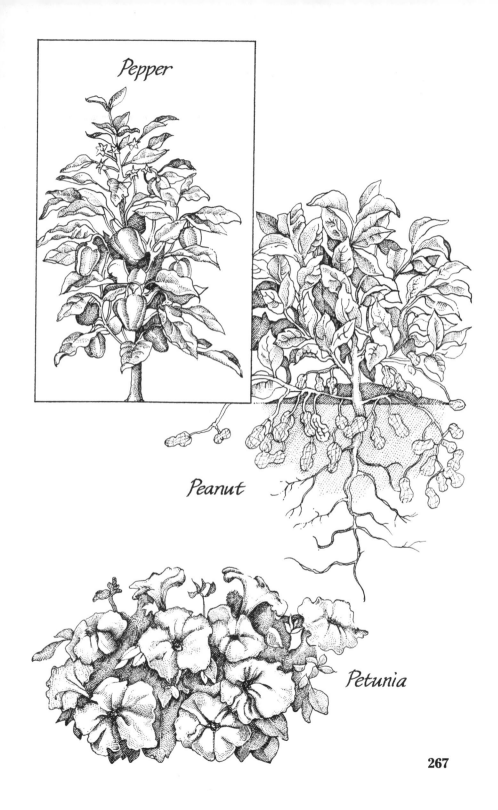

Pepper

Peanut

Petunia

267

and nasturtiums seemed to reduce green peach aphids on peppers. Tansy, marigolds and onions also had some effect. (68)

Peppermint

Mentha × piperita
Perennial herb
See MINT

Petunia

Petunia spp.
Solanaceae
Annual flower

To add bright splashes of color to a border around a vegetable bed, you can't go wrong with petunias. These flowers are available in a rainbow assortment of hues. Most varieties grow about 12 to 15 inches tall, but there are long trailing types available, as well.

Companion Role with Insects

Tradition: Gardeners claim that petunias repel squash bugs, Mexican bean beetles and potato bugs. Some even go so far as to say that pink petunias are more effective than other colors.

Research: There isn't much research to substantiate these claims. In fact, in one experiment, petunias interplanted with snap beans failed to reduce Mexican bean beetles. (56) Another study has shown that some species are toxic to tobacco hornworms. (1)

Pigweed

Amaranthus spp.
Annual
See AMARANTH

Pine

Pinus spp.
Pinaceae
Evergreen tree or shrub

While some pine species can rise to towering heights, there are others that are better suited to small yards or gardens. Where space is at a premium, try the bristlecone pine (*P. aristata*), the Swiss stone pine (*P. cembra*), the Swiss mountain pine (*P. mugo*) and the Balkans pine (*P. peuce*). The white pine (*P. strobus*) needs disciplined pruning to keep it in line in small spaces.

Companion Role with Plants

Tradition: As far back as the eighteenth century, farmers noted that certain crops didn't grow well under pines. In particular, currants and gooseberries are often diseased when pines grow nearby.

Despite these ill effects, pine needles are often recommended as a mulch for strawberries, blueberries and bramble fruits because they slowly increase soil acidity while adding humus.

Research: Experimental data confirms that some pine species produce toxins, which may leach from roots or needles to accumulate in the soil. (91) Since white pines host the fungus that causes rusts on currant and gooseberry bushes, you should keep these plants well apart. In fact, some states prohibit the planting

269

of these fruiting bushes near white pines. Check with the local extension agent to see if any restrictions apply to your area.

Companion Role with Insects

Research: Pines contain a substance known as terpene, which is strongly repellent to some bark beetles. Terpene hasn't been extensively tested on other pests. (92)

Potato

Solanum tuberosum
Solanaceae
Annual vegetable

When you treat potatoes as companion crops, keep in mind their particular root growth pattern. Early in their life, potatoes have shallow roots. Later in the season, the root growth of a maturing potato plant pushes 1 to 2 feet deep.

Companion Role with Plants

Tradition: Onions, radishes and lettuce have gained the reputation of doing well among potatoes. Organic gardeners and farmers recommend planting potatoes with corn or beans. Some growers say they also fare well with cabbage or early peas. Biodynamic gardeners suggest a few horseradish plants near the potato hills will improve the harvest.

Research: There isn't any data to back up these claims.

Potatoes have been mentioned as a possibly allelopathic crop, but the data is inconclusive. (91)

In one study, the ripe fruits of certain apple and pear varieties produced substances that inhibited the normal growth of potatoes. (92) If you have potatoes planted near an apple or pear tree and the potatoes aren't doing well, it may be that the fallen

Pine

Currant

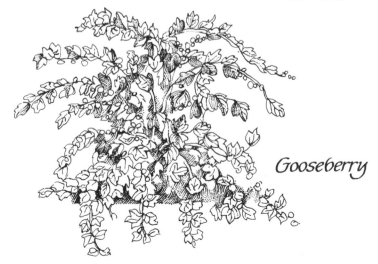

Gooseberry

271

fruit is harming the potato growth. In that case, be sure to clean up all fruit as soon as it falls.

Continuous potato-soybean rotation has been found to increase the occurrence of potato scab. (118)

Planting Tips: Plant seed potatoes 10 to 12 inches apart in hills or rows. Allow at least 10 inches between neighboring hills and rows. You can grow companion crops in these open spaces. Two rows of peas or corn or a single row of bush beans can fit between rows, but you may want to adjust the spacing to allow for wider strip intercropping.

Companion Role with Insects

Tradition: Beans, petunias or marigolds interplanted with potatoes are frequently recommended to repel Colorado potato beetles. Eggplants are often planted around potatoes as a trap crop.

Research: Scientists have determined that potato beetles search out their food by smell, so it seems likely that intercropping with a plant that masks the odor could be an effective deterrent. In the laboratory, odors of dandelion and of meadowgrass kept Colorado potato beetles away from potatoes. (27)

Bean and marigold interplantings also seemed to mask the host plants so that fewer beetles moved into the plots. However, the companion plants didn't seem to affect pests once they found the potatoes. The researcher concluded that almost any nonhost plants would have the same effect. (27)

Jimsonweed and deadly nightshade attract female potato beetles away from potato plants. The beetles lay their eggs on the weeds, but since the plants are toxic, feeding larvae soon die. (20)

Potato Companions: *Researchers have found that plantings of catnip, coriander, nasturtium and tansy may reduce the number of Colorado potato beetle larvae in the potato patch.*

In field tests, catnip, coriander, nasturtium and tansy inter-plantings reduced beetle larvae somewhat. (68)

The wild potato (*S. berthaultii*) is almost pest-free. Researchers have isolated an aphid alarm pheromone produced in glands within tiny hairs on this plant. Gardeners can only hope that, through breeding or the production of a spray, cultivated potatoes can be similarly protected. (42)

Praying Mantid

Various species of Mantidae

This garden predator is a big eater. It devours aphids, beetles, bugs, leafhoppers, flies, bees, caterpillars and butterflies by the score. Sometimes, praying mantids will even turn around and eat other beneficial insects or each other if there aren't enough pests around.

Praying mantid egg cases are available from mail-order suppliers. Each case hatches several hundred mantids. You can also gather egg cases yourself. They're especially easy to spot in the late fall and winter when leaves have fallen and underbrush has died back somewhat. Look for papier-mâché type masses clinging to weed stems or twigs and branches. Goldenrod is a common site for egg cases.

Break off the twig with the egg mass and store it in the refrigerator or put it outside. If you leave the case in a warm house, you'll find yourself sharing your living space with hundreds of newly hatched little invaders. In the spring, place the egg mass in a box with a screen over the top to hatch. Once the young mantids have emerged, move them out to the garden within one to two days, otherwise they'll start feeding on each other. If you place the egg case outside, tie it to a twig or branch, anyplace to keep it off the ground where it could be drowned by spring rains or eaten by field mice.

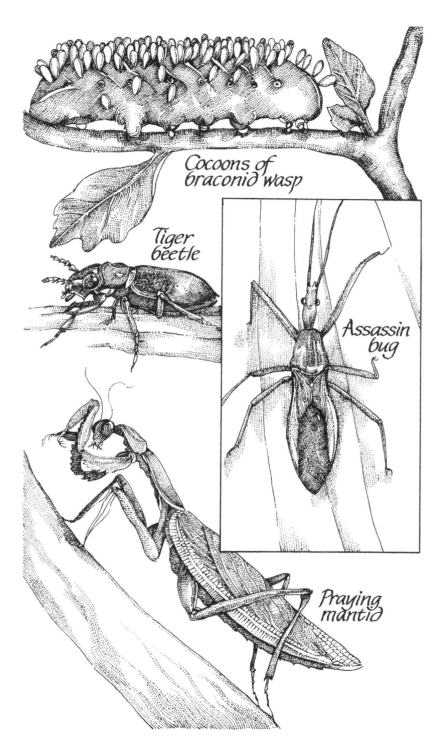

Cocoons of
braconid wasp

Tiger
beetle

Assassin
bug

Praying
mantid

Predatory Insects

Predatory insects do just what their name implies—they prey upon smaller, weaker insects. Fortunately for gardeners, the insects the predators devour are the same ones that are devouring garden crops.

The most well-known predators are lady beetles, praying mantids and lacewings. There are a host of others, including ground beetles, thrips, mites, spiders and bugs with such descriptive names as ant lions, ambush bugs and pirate bugs. Many of these are available from mail-order suppliers to boost the natural garden population.

A single predator insect will eat many pests over the course of its life. To encourage the predators' pest-control activities, provide lots of nectar and pollen-rich flowers and weeds in and around the garden. If at some point during the season, the insect pest population dwindles, the beneficials will be able to turn to the high protein nectar and pollen and won't be forced to flee the garden looking for food. Should the pest numbers increase again, the predators will still be around, ready for a meal.

Goldenrod is a favorite flower of predators. They like other blooming members of the composite family as well, including black-eyed Susans and daisies.

Pyrethrum

Chrysanthemum coccineum, C. cinerariifolium
Perennial flower
See CHRYSANTHEMUM

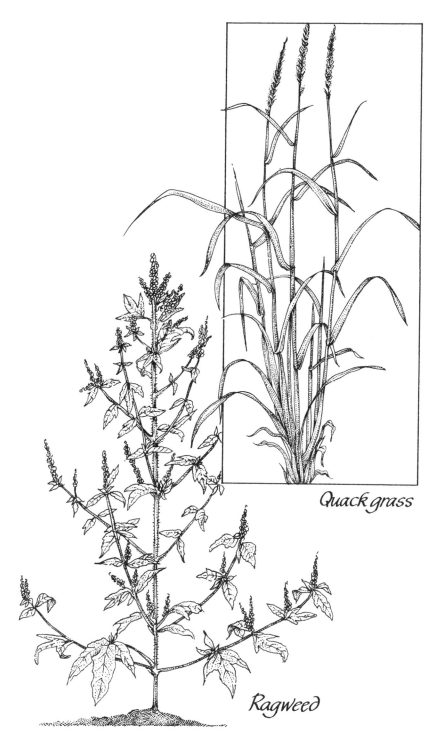

Quack grass

Ragweed

277

Quack Grass or Couch Grass

Agropyron repens
Gramineae
Perennial grass

Once quack grass makes an appearance in your yard, you'll be hard-pressed to eliminate it completely. This is one of the most persistent and invasive of all weeds. To rid it from flower and vegetable beds, you'll have to dig up every bit of underground rootstalk. Any pieces left behind will be enough to start a whole new flush of growth.

Companion Role with Plants

Tradition: Sowing a legume or thick cover of turnips, tomatoes or lupines will choke out this bothersome weed, according to some gardeners.

Research: There's no research to support gardeners' claims about ridding the garden of quack grass with cover crops.

Several important studies suggest that quack grass produces allelopathic effects on a number of crops. Corn growing in areas infested with this weed develop symptoms of nutrient deficiency. Even when adequate water and nutrients are supplied, corn plants are unable to take them up. Somehow the quack grass renders soil nutrients unavailable. (24, 51, 92) In another study, alfalfa planted in fields previously infested with quack grass yielded only half that of crops planted in an uninfested field. (72)

Queen Anne's Lace

Daucus carrota var. *carota*
Biennial weed
See CARROT

Rabbit

These adorable furry creatures can ravage a bean planting in a single night. Among their other favorites are lettuce and squash seedlings—but experience has shown that these garden vegetarians will eat almost anything.

Tradition: Lettuce planted among squash is said to put rabbits to sleep. Marigolds, onions, garlic and most pungent herbs are supposed to repel them.

Research: There's no evidence to support these rabbit-proofing claims.

Raccoon

In many corn patches, as the ears inch their way to maturity, it's a race to the wire to see who will get to eat them first—the gardener or the raccoon. Raccoons seem to know just when the corn is reaching its peak.

Tradition: Where pumpkins, squash or cucumbers thoroughly cover the ground around and between corn stalks, raccoons supposedly won't enter, but I for one have found this ineffective.

Research: No studies have been done to confirm that vining crops are effective corn protectors.

Radish

Raphanus sativus
Cruciferae
Annual vegetable

This compact, fast-growing root crop is the perfect companion to set between lettuce, bean, cabbage and tomato seedlings. Try scattering a few radishes in among a low flower border, too. You might want to consider surrounding a hill of squash with a ring of closely spaced radishes.

Companion Role with Plants

Tradition: Radishes supposedly do well near peas and let-

Traditional Animal Deterrents: *Over the years some gardeners have maintained that lettuce planted among squash will make rabbits drowsy, and a barrier of squash vines will keep raccoons out of the corn.*

tuce (these companions make the radishes tender). Frequently, they are also intercropped with parsnips, onions and carrots. Early farmers believed that radishes were harmful to grapes.

Research: There's no evidence available on the beneficial or harmful effects as described in garden lore. However, radishes were among several crop plants found to contain volatile, toxic compounds. What, if anything, this means in terms of actual allelopathy is still unknown. (91)

Companion Role with Insects

Tradition: As a companion to squash, radishes supposedly prevent borers, particularly if they are allowed to go to seed. Some gardeners claim they also repel cucumber beetles. Sown among cauliflowers, radishes are supposed to trap root flies.

Research: No data is available on any of these companion traditions.

Radish

Ragweed

Ambrosia spp.
Compositae
Perennial weed

Obviously, you'd be crazy to plant this weed in your garden. You probably have more than you want right now! Just be aware of its value, and as you uproot it, pay this lowly plant some small homage. In the orchard, it does only good and should be allowed to remain.

Companion Role with Insects

Research: Ragweed may be valuable around peach orchards and strawberry fields. It's an alternate host for a parasite of oriental fruit moths and for strawberry leaf rollers. (118)

Common ragweed (*A. artemisiifolia*) growing around collard fields interfered with flea beetles' ability to find their hosts and feed on them. The weeds seemed to mask collards' attracting odors so that fewer flea beetles made their way into the plot. (105)

Raspberry

Rubus idaeus (red and yellow), *R. occidentalis* (black)
Rosaceae
Fruiting shrub

This thorny bramble makes an effective barrier around the garden plot. Besides being much more attractive than a length of chicken wire or various other fencing materials, a border of raspberry plants will give you a harvest of delicious berries.

Companion Role with Plants

Tradition: According to many gardeners, raspberries do poorly with blackberries and should be kept away from potatoes.

Research: Wild brambles host several diseases to which cultivated raspberries might succumb, so it's a good idea to clear wild plants away from the raspberry patch. Both potatoes and raspberries are likely to succumb to verticillium wilt, so there's also good reason to separate these plants.

Rhubarb

Rheum rhabarbarum
Polygonaceae
Perennial vegetable

Rhubarb makes a fine ornamental plant that you can use as a dramatic accent or as a massive backdrop. Because it's a large but noninvasive perennial, rhubarb is well behaved when planted in alternate rows with annual vegetables such as cabbage, potatoes and tomatoes. Although we can eat the leaf stalks, the leaves themselves are poisonous and should never be eaten.

Companion Role with Insects

Tradition: Rhubarb's pesticidal properties were recognized by gardeners in the last century. Sticks of rhubarb were buried beside cabbage transplants to prevent clubroot. Rhubarb tea was recommended to eliminate all sorts of insects.

Today's gardeners make a tea from rhubarb soaked or boiled in water. This is used against aphids, leafminers and red spider mites.

Research: We know now that rhubarb contains oxalic acid, but just how much protection the living plant gives its neighbors

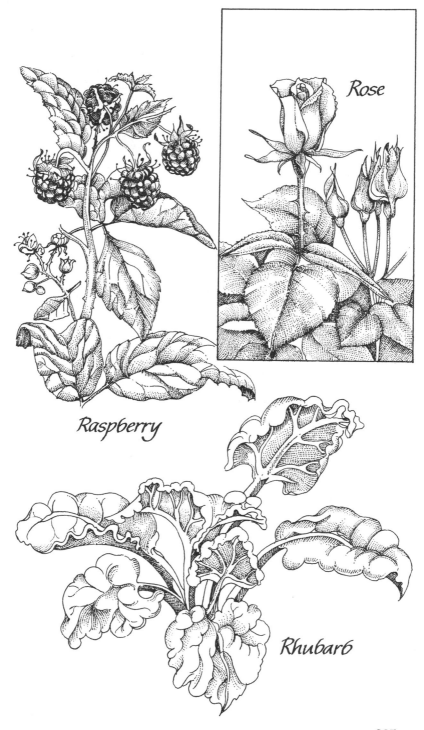

Rose

Raspberry

Rhubarb

or how effective a tea might be remains uncertain.

Planting Tips: Don't be misled by the small size of those shriveled crowns you plant. Mature rhubarb plants can get very large—up to 4 feet in diameter.

Rose

Rosa spp.
Rosaceae
Perennial ornamental

Don't overlook the versatility of miniature roses in the garden. These diminutive plants are as hardy as standard-size roses and require the same basic culture. They grow from 18 to 30 inches tall, which makes them perfect to tuck into low borders around large ornamental beds. You can even feature them in a tranquil corner of a vegetable plot.

Companion Role with Plants

Tradition: Garlic is unanimously praised as a companion to roses. It has a reputation for chasing away aphids and generally improving growth. Parsley and onions are also recommended as good neighborly companions.

Research: No data is available to verify the effects of those crops.

Companion Role with Insects

Tradition: Against Japanese beetles, gardeners recommend planting chives, garlic or geraniums. Garlic spray is also supposed to deter the beetles. Rhubarb sprays are supposed to get rid of aphids and black spot.

Research: There's no data to support gardeners' contentions that those companions are effective.

Rosemary

Rosmarinus officinalis
Labiatae
Perennial herb

In my corner of southeastern Pennsylvania, this perennial is too tender to survive the winter out of doors. I find it performs best if allowed to remain in its pot where it can be easily pampered and moved in and out as the weather requires.

Companion Role with Insects

Tradition: The strong, pleasant scent of this herb has lent it a reputation for pest repellency. The bluish-white flowers are supposed to repel various moths and root flies. Branches laid on the garden soil are alleged to keep away slugs and snails.

In Venezuela and the Philippines, rosemary is used as an insecticide.

Research: No data is available on the power of rosemary as a pest repellent.

Rue

Ruta graveolens
Rutaceae
Perennial herb

Rue grows up to 3 feet high, but you can easily check its growth by frequent pinching back. Plant it in clumps as an accent plant among perennial flowers. Rue also complements thyme in small groupings. There are several different varieties offering variegated or blue-green foliage.

Companion Role with Plants

Tradition: This bitter herb is said to have a bad effect on sage, basil and cabbage. However, Pliny believed it grew well with figs, and today some gardeners recommend pairing it with roses.

Research: No data is available to confirm or refute the garden lore.

Companion Role with Insects

Tradition: Rue supposedly deters various beetles and fleas.

Research: No data is available on rue's ability to deter insects. We do know, however, that rue leaves can cause a painful skin rash in some people.

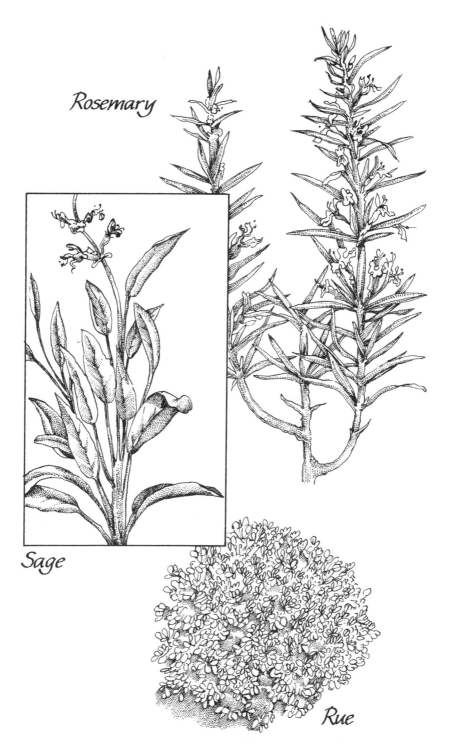

Rosemary

Sage

Rue

289

Rye

Secale spp., *Lolium multiflorum* (ryegrass)
Gramineae
Annual or perennial grass

Ryegrass is the most common form of rye grown in this country, and there are both annual and perennial species available. Rye withstands heavy foot traffic and makes a fine cover crop or green manure for vegetable gardens and orchard areas. A cover of rye will keep down weeds, conserve moisture, and when it's mowed, will help keep the garden neat and provide a cushioned pathway.

Companion Role with Plants

Research: At Michigan State University, ryes are being studied as a weed-controlling, moisture-conserving cover crop. As these plants decompose, they release toxins, which inhibit the growth of various weeds. (74)

Planting Tips: You can plant annual or perennial rye at any time, but most growers sow seeds in late summer or fall for a winter cover crop. In early summer, you can turn under the entire planting as a green manure crop or plow 1-foot-wide strips for planting within the sod. Leave lawn-mower-width strips of rye as paths.

Sometimes rye and clover seed are mixed for an even richer green manure. The rye helps keep down weeds while the more tender clover is getting started.

Rye Cover Crop: *Mowed pathways of rye keep the orchard or garden area free of weeds and help conserve soil moisture. These neat, cushioned pathways withstand heavy foot traffic well.*

Companion Role with Insects

Research: As it decomposes, rye releases substances that may control parasitic nematodes. (92)

Sage

Salvia officinalis
Labiatae
Perennial herb

The blue, white or pink flowers of this herb attract bees and other insects. Sage makes a fine informal hedge plant, since it grows only 2 feet high. There are also dwarf types that do well in lower borders. Its gray-green foliage is attractive in almost any setting, particularly in an informal garden. Warm-climate gardeners might want to try some of the colored-leaved varieties. These come with purple, gold and green, or white, purple and pink streaked foliage.

Companion Role with Plants

Tradition: Sage supposedly helps cabbage, carrots, strawberries and tomatoes but harms cucumbers. Over the years it has gained the reputation of growing well with marjoram but languishing next to rue. Culpeper wrote that sage dislikes growing near onions.

Research: No data is available on any of sage's companion qualities.

Companion Role with Insects

Tradition: Gardeners recommend sage as a repellent for imported cabbageworms and white cabbage moths and as a deterrent to various root maggots. In some countries, smoke from burning *Salvia* is used to drive away pests.

Research: In two studies, sage interplants or borders had no effect on cabbageworms on cabbage. (52, 55) In another study, a sage spray did provide some protection against this pest. (69)

Santolina or Lavender Cotton

Santolina chamaecyparissus
Compositae
Perennial herb

Santolina is a good medium-high edging plant. The compact, grayish foliage makes it useful as an accent in almost any setting. When the flowers bloom, they appear as flat heads of bright yellow. The plant has a lovely fragrance similar to that of lavender.

Companion Role with Insects

Research: In one experiment, santolina didn't deter cabbageworms on nearby cabbage plants. (58)

In preliminary tests, extract of santolina showed some promise as a feeding deterrent to corn wireworms and southern corn rootworms. (112)

Savory

Satureja hortensis (summer), *S. montana* (winter)
Labiatae
Annual (summer) or perennial (winter) herb

Both of these savories share the same flavor although summer savory isn't quite as intense as winter savory. Summer savory grows about 18 inches tall and produces tiny pink to purple flowers. This plant tends to sprawl about, so you may need to give it some support. Winter savory grows a bit smaller, reaching only 12 inches tall. Winter savory flowers are white or purple.

Companion Role with Plants

Tradition: Savories, particularly summer savory, are often planted near beans and onions in order to improve their flavor.

Research: No data confirms the flavor-enhancing properties of savories.

Companion Role with Insects

Tradition: Gardeners claim these herbs repel Mexican bean beetles and other insect pests.

Research: Interplanted with beans, summer savory seemed to attract, not repel, corn earworms. (56) In another study, it had no effect on cabbage pests or whiteflies. (52)

Sedge

Cyperus spp.
Annual or perennial weed
See NUTSEDGE

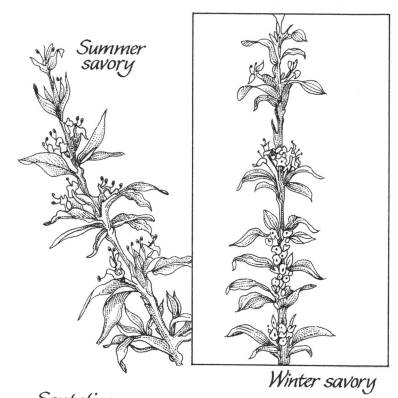

Summer savory

Winter savory

Santolina

Slugs and Snails

Various species within many families

Slugs and snails may not seem to move very fast, but they can certainly do a lot of damage in a single night! These pests both attack garden and orchard crops. The main difference between the two is that snails have a shell and slugs do not.

Tradition: Gardeners claim that wormwood interplantings kill or at least repel slugs. Garlic cloves laid about the garden are also supposed to keep them at bay.

Research: No data is available on either of these garden traditions.

Sorghum

Sorghum bicolor
Gramineae
Annual grass

In India, sorghum is a frequent companion crop. Growers there pair sorghum with soybeans, cucumbers or onions, and sometimes plant it in the midst of a field of sugar cane.

Companion Role with Plants

Research: Decaying leaves of curly dock (*Rumex crispus*) have been found to inhibit sorghum's growth. (92)

Slugs and Snails: *Garden tradition holds that garlic cloves scattered about will keep these destructive pests away from plants.*

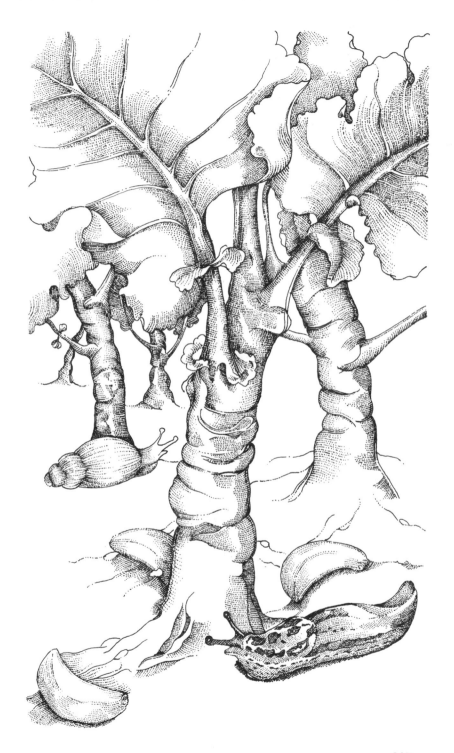

Sorghum is itself allelopathic to many weeds and seems to have practical use as a cover crop. (85, 74, 87)

Planting Tips: You can try using sorghum as a weed-killing cover crop in an orchard or large garden. It grows quickly and produces a tremendous amount of green matter in just two to three months. Sow seed in early summer, let it mature, then mow it in strips. The loose plant debris will serve as a mulch. This practice is best suited to an orchard. In a garden, sow seeds in early summer and plow under just before it's time to plant fall crops. The vegetables will benefit from growing in the weed-killing residue.

Southernwood

Artemisia abrotanum
Perennial herb
See WORMWOOD

Soybean

Glycine max
Leguminosae
Annual vegetable

Soybeans are an easy-to-grow vegetable crop that is all too often overlooked. They generally have few pest or disease problems and can tolerate a variety of soil conditions. In the kitchen, their rich, nutty flavor can be enjoyed fresh or dried.

Companion Role with Plants

Tradition: The soil-building characteristics of soybeans are widely known. They're typically interplanted with grain crops or

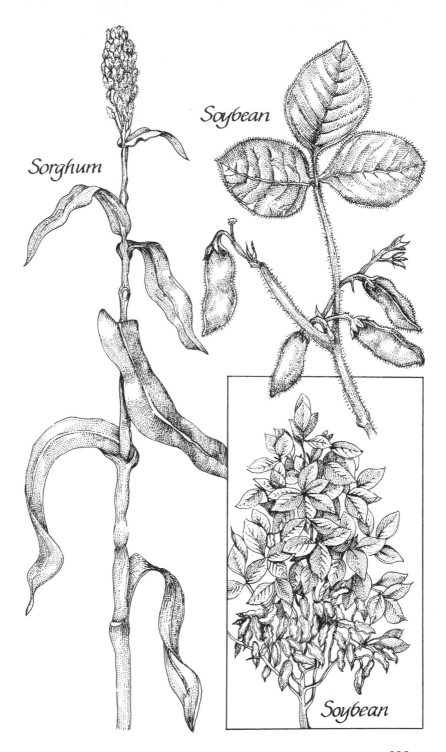

Sorghum

Soybean

Soybean

299

rotated with heavy-feeding vegetables.

Research: Because of their nitrogen-fixing capabilities, soybeans are a valuable intercrop. When they were planted into wheat after that crop had reached boot stage (or flowered), both crops enjoyed greater yields. (88)

Strip intercropping of corn and soybeans also brings increased yields, although not always for the beans. Researchers say this is particularly true if the corn strips are narrow. The growing beans don't interfere with the corn's share of sunlight, and they offer little competition for nutrients and water. In addition, the beans offer excellent erosion control. (89)

Some studies indicate that soybeans growing with corn produce more and larger nitrogen-fixing nodules. Because corn depletes the available nitrogen, soybeans may be stimulated to fix more. (117)

Soybean yields may be affected by weed or crop residues. In one trial, both corn and giant foxtail residues enhanced soybean yields. Other decaying plants seem to have an allelopathic effect on the crop. Residues of lamb's-quarters, redroot pigweed, velvetleaf, sunflowers and soybeans themselves reduced soybean yields. (22)

Other experiments have shown that soybean-rice interplantings don't succeed if rice stubble is left in the paddies. The rice residue seems to have an allelopathic effect on legumes, which inhibits their nitrogen-fixing ability and the development of nodules on bean roots. But once the rice straw was removed, soybean yields were shown to increase by 100 pounds per acre. (92)

Non-nodulated varieties of soybeans may be allelopathic to certain other crops. Grown with white clover and alfalfa, they inhibited the companion crop's growth, but researchers haven't yet isolated the toxin that's responsible. (51)

Multiuse Companion: *Spinach fits in well throughout the garden. Plant slower-to-mature crops like eggplants and tomatoes among an early spinach planting. Or, tuck it between crops of cabbage and celery.*

Planting Tips: Be sure to select a good garden quality soybean, rather than the sort grown for cattle feed or industry. Short-season types that can be harvested as green shell beans are the best choice, particularly if you garden in central or northern regions. Interplant in strips between wide rows of corn, or plant in a circle around each hill of corn. Most soybean varieties require about 4 inches between plants.

Companion Role with Insects

Tradition: Some soybean growers plant a small trap crop of soybeans one to two weeks before they sow the main crop. They locate these traps near areas where bean leaf beetles hibernate. Once the beetles have emerged and started to feed on the soybeans, the growers release a parasite or predator into the infested area.

Research: In one study, soybeans planted with a dense cover of the weeds sicklepod (*Cassia obtusifolia*), wild pea (*Desmodium* spp.) and others, had less damage from velvet bean caterpillars, green stink bugs and corn earworms. The presence of these and other weeds greatly increased insect predators. (5, 2)

Spinach

Spinacia oleracea
Chenopodiaceae
Annual vegetable

Many gardeners recommend compact, quick-growing spinach as a companion to strawberries, celery, eggplants, cabbage, peas and onions.

Companion Role with Plants

Remarks: As a short-season, shade-loving plant, spinach

actually fits in just about anywhere in the garden, often as part of a staggered relay. You can plant beans, tomatoes or any main season crop among early spinach. This leafy green also fits nicely in a low border. Be sure to allow each spinach plant 4 to 6 inches of growing room.

Spurge

Euphorbia spp.
Euphorbiaceae
Perennial weed

Gardeners consistently recommend the mole plant (*E. lathyris*) for borders to keep out those burrowing animals. However, since this is a rangy, rather weedy plant, it may not be the best solution in an orderly bed devoted to annual vegetables.

Companion Role with Plants

Tradition: Some gardeners say cypress spurge (*E. cyparissias*) is harmful to grapes.

Research: Researchers have found that even the smallest amount of plant litter from some species reduces the growth of certain other weeds, wheat and tomatoes. (51, 92) There doesn't seem to be any evidence concerning cypress spurge's effect on grapes.

Companion Role with Insects

Tradition: A number of the 1,600 species of *Euphorbia* are used in native cultures as insecticides.

Research: No data is available to confirm this traditional usage.

Spurry

Spergula arvensis
Caryophyllaceae
Annual weed

You won't find this relative of the familiar flower garden pinks listed in the seed catalogs, but you may find spurry growing in and around your garden. Don't be too quick to eliminate all of it. It can serve as a helpful cover crop. Spurry appears throughout most of North America.

Companion Role with Plants

Research: Spurry seems to be a noncompetitive companion plant that controls soil erosion and improves soil structure. It is low growing and easily mowed or pulled up if it appears in areas that you'd prefer to keep weed free. (106)

Companion Role with Insects

Research: In an important experiment, intercropping Brussels sprouts with spurry gave excellent control of several important pests, including various caterpillars, aphids and root worms. The spurry provided shelter for spiders and ground beetles. By providing a weedy background, it also seemed to discourage various caterpillars and aphids and other pests from entering the plot. (106) We can assume that spurry would be a good companion weed for not only Brussels sprouts but for other cole crops as well.

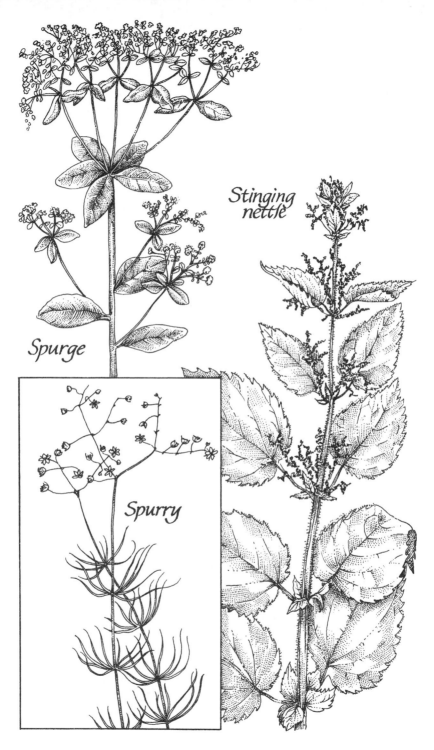

Stinging
nettle

Spurge

Spurry

Squash

Cucurbita spp.
Cucurbitaceae
Annual vegetable

Plant breeders have been hard at work developing bush forms of both summer and winter squashes. This space-saving growth habit makes squash a more well-behaved companion in interplanting schemes.

Companion Role with Plants

Tradition: Pumpkins and winter squashes are traditionally planted with corn, beans and possibly sunflowers or peanuts as well. They are said to harm potatoes.

Research: No data is available on any of the traditional companion pairings.

Planting Tips: Bush forms of squash interplant well with corn or beans, but even the most compact forms require at least 2 to 3 feet between plants. I've found that squash can fit nicely in 2-foot strips between double rows of corn.

Companion Role with Insects

Tradition: Nasturtiums or aromatic herbs such as mint are recommended by many gardeners for getting rid of squash bugs. Radishes planted in each hill and allowed to go to seed are supposed to prevent vine borers.

Companions to Get the Bugs Out:
Studies have shown that catnip and tansy seem to be able to lower the number of squash bugs that visit zucchini squash plantings.

Research: No studies support these traditional plant pairings. But research has shown that catnip and tansy companion plantings seemed to reduce squash bugs on zucchini. (68)

There's also the possibility that wild cucurbits (weedy relatives of the garden squash) may serve as a trap crop for corn rootworms.

Stinging Nettle

Urtica dioica
Urticaceae
Perennial weed

This weed earned its nickname from its covering of stiff hairs, which sting on contact. Nettle appears throughout all of North America. It spreads by means of a creeping rootstock.

Companion Role with Plants

Tradition: Some gardeners, and the Soil Association in England, claim that stinging nettle stimulates the growth of nearby plants and seems to increase the essential oils in aromatic herbs. It is also said to improve the soil's iron content.

Research: There's no data to confirm or refute these claims.

Companion Role with Insects

Research: Stinging nettle is good to have growing in and around beans. It hosts 11 species of beneficial insects, which prey upon Mexican bean beetles, aphids, flea beetles and other bean pests. (79)

Strawberry

Fragaria spp.
Rosaceae
Perennial fruit

There are two basic types of strawberry plant growth–one type produces runners and the other doesn't. You can use runner-producing plants in alternate rows with annual vegetables, as long as you keep the runners out of garden paths and out of the way of neighboring plants. Runnerless strawberries, such as the alpine type, do well scattered around the garden or featured as neat borders for flower and vegetable beds.

Companion Role with Plants

Tradition: Biodynamic gardeners recommend pairing strawberries with lettuce, spinach, beans or borage. Some growers say that cabbage and strawberries are "enemies," but others say they are fine companions.

Research: No data is available to sort through the various claims made about strawberry companions.

Planting Tips: Set crowns of runner-producing plants 20 inches apart in rows spaced 3 feet apart. During the first year while plants are small, you can set companion crops of cabbage or lettuce between these rows, at the usual spacings. If, like me, you prefer the look of a solid bed of strawberries, you can plant the crowns randomly, with companion crops as a border.

Alpine strawberries need 8 to 12 inches of growing room.

Companion Role with Insects

Research: Strawberries are alternate hosts for a parasite that attacks oriental fruit moths in peaches. (118) For this reason they make a good border or strip crop in the orchard.

Sunflower

Helianthus spp.
Compositae
Annual flower

A row of these tall, bright-faced flowers can serve as a colorful garden divider or even shield the compost pile from view. In windy areas, a strip of sunflowers planted in the garden will protect low-growing vegetables.

Companion Role with Plants

Tradition: Throughout the Americas, farmers have long interplanted sunflowers with beans, corn and squash. Today, some gardeners also grow them as support for tomatoes. Sunflowers are said to inhibit the growth of potatoes.

Research: The wild, common sunflower (*H. annuus*) is strongly allelopathic to many plant species. (91, 92) In laboratory and field experiments, cultivars of *H. annuus* were examined for possible allelopathic properties. The cultivated sunflowers had indeed retained this ability to release toxins and were able to reduce the growth of certain weeds up to 75 percent, particularly in drier soils. Leaf and stem tissue were found to be particularly allelopathic. Among the weeds inhibited were jimsonweed, velvetleaf, Johnson grass, curly dock, red sorrel, ragweed, smartweed, wild mustard and lamb's-quarters. (60)

In another field experiment, sunflower residue reduced soybean yields. (22)

Planting Tips: Plant the tallest sunflower varieties along the northern side of the garden where they won't shade other plants. For intercropping, choose species such as *H. annuus* that reach a maximum of 3 feet tall.

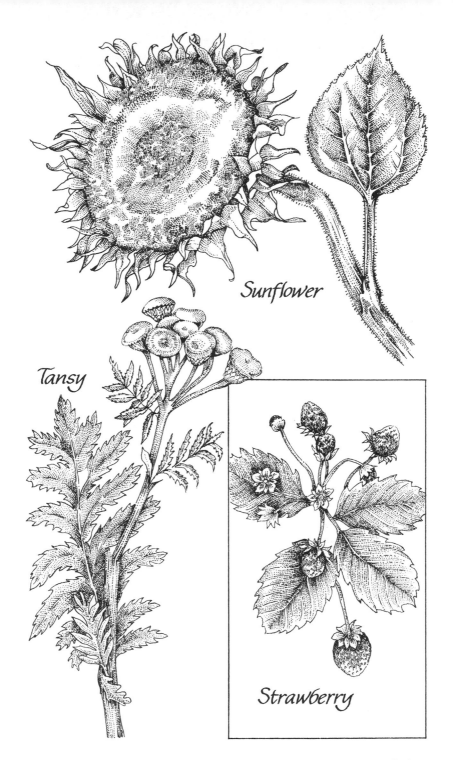

Sunflower

Tansy

Strawberry

Companion Role with Insects

Tradition: Sunflowers are sometimes planted as traps for stinkbugs or corn earworms.

Research: No data is available about the sunflower's abilities as a trap crop. However, lots of beneficial insects, including lacewings and wasps, are found on and around this composite family flower when it's blooming.

Tansy

Tanacetum vulgare
Compositae
Perennial herb

Tansy's fernlike foliage has a pungent, but not unpleasant, odor. Tansy grows about 2½ feet tall and spreads by means of a creeping rootstock. In the summer, it produces flat, buttonlike yellow flowers.

Companion Role with Plants

Tradition: Gardeners recommend planting tansy among the bramble fruits and roses, for it is supposed to promote healthy growth and improve the flavor and aroma of nearby fruits and flowers.

Research: Because it is a very fast-growing, invasive plant, tansy is difficult to manage as a companion. It may even be somewhat allelopathic to collards. (57)

Planting Tips: Tansy is a rampant grower, so unless you're willing to devote a large area to this herb, you need to keep it under control. For tips on how to manage tansy, see the box Controlling Invasive Companions in chapter 5.

Companion Role with Insects

Tradition: Tansy is often listed as a repellent to all sorts of insect pests including flea beetles, squash bugs, ants, aphids, Japanese beetles and cabbageworms.

Research: In preliminary studies, tansy did appear to reduce some pest populations. Interplanted with peppers, tansy did seem to repel aphids. With squash, it provided some relief against squash bugs, and with potatoes, it reduced Colorado potato beetles. Reversing this trend, when tansy was interplanted with broccoli, it actually increased the number of imported cabbageworm larvae. In most cases, vegetable crops were smaller because of the competition from the herb. (68)

Other researchers have found that tansy is not only ineffective against cabbageworms but may actually attract the moths. (56)

Tarragon

Artemisia dracunculus
Compositae
Perennial herb

There are two types of tarragon. The most widely available form, usually labelled "common" or Russian tarragon, is rather weedy and of small value as a culinary herb. It's really too cumbersome for the vegetable garden, because in just a few seasons it develops into a large, rank bush. French tarragon is the preferred form. It is harder to find and a little harder to grow, but well suited to companion planting. This plant reaches 3 feet tall. If you can find French tarragon, grow it. For information on related plants, see WORMWOOD.

Companion Role with Plants

Tradition: Tarragon is sometimes raised with vegetables in order to improve their growth and flavor.

Research: No studies support or refute tarragon's role as a growth enhancer. Other members of this genus are allelopathic, but no data is available on tarragon.

Thistle

Cirsium spp.
Compositae
Annual or perennial weed

These prickly intruders can be tough to clear out of a garden or field. When you dig them out, try to remove *all* of the root growth, otherwise you'll never be rid of these pests. Despite their less-than-endearing traits, these plants do produce attractive pinkish-purple flowers.

Companion Role with Plants

Tradition: Growers in the last century noticed that thistles interfered with the growth of certain crops, among them oats.

Research: Scientists found that roots and shoots of the Canadian thistle reduced the growth of sugar beets, wheat, alfalfa and members of its own species. Corn and beans were slightly less affected. (23)

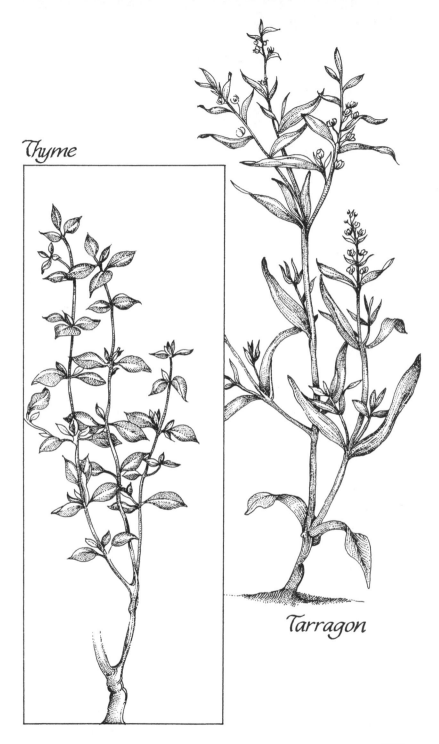

Thyme

Tarragon

Thyme

Thymus vulgaris, T. serpyllum
Labiatae
Perennial herb

Each one of the many varieties of thyme performs well in the companion garden. Most are excellent bee plants and attract other beneficial insects as well. Plant thyme alone or with a delicate flower such as alyssum or lobelia as an edging around garden beds or individual fruit trees. Its coloring and shape also complement spinach, broccoli or red cabbage. Besides the solid green variety, there are also thymes with silver and gold edges. There is even a lemon thyme with a citrusy flavor and odor.

Companion Role with Plants

Tradition: Thyme has a long-standing reputation as a heavy-feeding herb that exhausts the soil. At the same time, many growers say that, like other aromatic herbs, it improves the flavors of surrounding herbs and vegetables.

Research: No evidence is available to support or deny any of the garden lore.

Planting Tips: Divide thyme plants every two or three years, when they begin to get woody. Some growers even recommend replacing plants after several years, but I haven't found this necessary.

Companion Role with Insects

Tradition: Gardeners suggest planting thyme to repel white-flies, cabbage loopers and cabbageworms.

Research: In one study where it was used as a border plant around cabbage, thyme did not repel imported cabbageworms. In

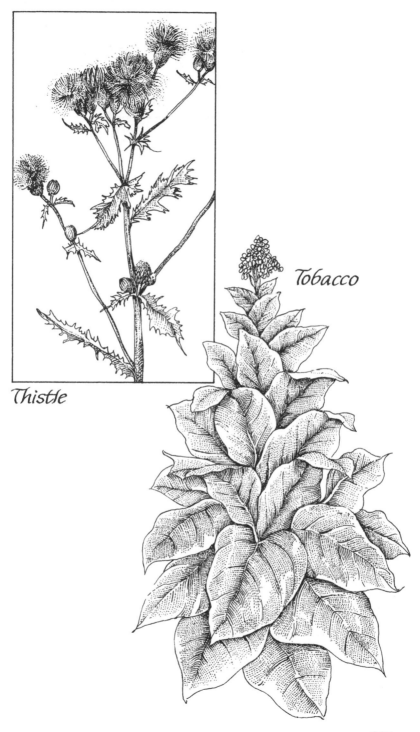

Tobacco

Thistle

fact, the thyme may have actually attracted the pests. (55) However, in a laboratory experiment, an extract of thyme did protect cabbage from egg-laying cabbage butterflies. (66)

Tobacco

Nicotiana tabacum
Solanaceae
Annual ornamental

This tropical plant needs warm temperatures to grow well. In areas outside of the Deep South, seedlings will get off to a good start if they're sown indoors, then moved outside once the weather warms.

Companion Role with Insects

Tradition: Tobacco and other members of this genus have been used as insecticides for centuries. Interplantings, mulches, sprays, dusts and even smoke from burning tobacco plants have been used to kill almost every insect pest from flea beetles to caterpillars.

Research: Nicotine is the toxic substance in tobacco and is found throughout the plant. Cigarette tobacco is about 3 percent nicotine, whereas wild tobacco (*N. rustica*) may contain up to 18 percent. Sprays and dusts made from nicotine are very toxic. They're of limited use since they kill virtually all insects, beneficial as well as pest species.

Remarks: You mustn't apply nicotine sprays to other solanaceous plants such as potatoes, eggplants, tomatoes or peppers. The spray may transmit mosaic virus to them.

Tomato

Lycopersicon lycopersicum
Solanaceae
Perennial vegetable grown as an annual

The ever-popular tomato now comes in a range of colors and different growth habits. Seed catalogs carry the standard red-fruited type as well as yellow, orange and even white varieties. Determinate plants tend to be bushy and more practical for the interplanted garden. They generally grow 12 to 18 inches tall. Indeterminate plants can get quite rangy and really should be staked or caged in the close quarters of an interplanted garden.

Companion Role with Plants

Tradition: For good growth and flavor, tomatoes are typically interplanted with cabbage, asparagus, onions, carrots, sage, basil or parsley. They are said to do poorly near fennel or potatoes.

Research: Although some studies have been done on tomato companions, most of these traditional pairings remain untested. When tomatoes were intercropped with snap beans, peas or cabbage, total tomato yields were less than in a monoculture, but the crops were of better quality. When tomatoes were grown with peas alone, the per row yields of peas were greater than in monocultures.

Tomato root exudates have been found to contain potentially allelopathic compounds. (92)

Planting Tips: Don't underestimate the size of mature indeterminate tomato plants when you're setting out tiny seedlings. Staking or caging can confine them somewhat, but unless you're really ruthless in your pruning of suckers and training, most plants require at least 2 feet of growing room. If you're on the ball, early crops of lettuce, onions, beets, spinach or even a cole crop can be set out before the tomatoes. Arrange them so they grow

319

between the rows or between where the tomato plants will go. You must harvest them before the tomatoes begin to take off in midsummer.

Companion Role with Insects

Tradition: Milkweed plants near tomatoes are supposed to repel aphids. Some gardeners plant dill and borage to repel hornworms. A tea made from boiled tomato leaves is sometimes recommended against aphids on various plants.

Research: A compound found on the hairs of tomato leaves and stems repels some insects. The compound lycopersicon in tomatoes was found to inhibit the growth of some bacteria and fungi and proved toxic to potato bugs. (1)

In interplantings with brassicas, tomatoes appear to be effective pest deterrents. In separate studies, they reduced diamondback moths and flea beetles. (25, 105)

Spiny amaranth protects tomatoes from black cutworms. When growing nearby, the amaranth serves as a decoy for the pest. (118)

Tree of Heaven

Ailanthus altissima
Simaroubaceae
Tree

This tree is a common sight in many American cities. Since it reseeds itself quite easily, it has become something of a pest in

---

Tomato Companions: *Many gardeners swear that basil growing near tomato plants will enhance the tomatoes' flavor. Tomatoes planted among broccoli, cabbage and other brassicas may be good pest deterrents.*

some areas. Small, yellow flowers bloom in June. If you rub these flowers, as well as the bases of leaves, they will give off an extremely unpleasant odor.

Companion Role with Insects

Tradition: Members of this family have been used throughout Africa to make insecticides.

Research: The bark and wood of this tree contain an insecticide. (92)

Tree of heaven is a good insectary plant, as it attracts hover flies, bees, various wasps and lacewings. (53)

Turnip

Brassica rapa, Rapifera Group
Cruciferae
Annual vegetable

Although many people think of turnips as mainly a root crop, they actually give you two harvests in one. Besides the roots, the leafy tops are also edible. Turnips make good companions since they're compact and quick to mature.

Companion Role with Plants

Tradition: Some gardeners often plant turnips with mustard greens, although others say that mustard harms this root crop. Turnips are supposed to benefit peas.

Research: No evidence is available to support or refute the claims made by gardeners.

Planting Tips: Turnips are best grown as a fall crop, so they can benefit from those nippy nights, which seem to make them sweeter and more tender. Allow 4 to 6 inches between plants.

Lettuce, spinach, kohlrabi, beans or other companions do well between rows or as a within-row intercrop. Turnips tolerate some shading, so they perform quite nicely as a lower story plant with tall crops such as peas or pole beans.

Companion Role with Insects

Tradition: Against maggots, early American farmers recommended intercropping turnips with tobacco.

Research: Although there's no evidence relating to maggots, in the fresh peelings of turnips and rutabagas, a pesticide was found that kills flies. (1)

Vetch

Vicia spp.
Leguminosae
Annual, biennial or perennial legume

You can tell that vetch is related to the familiar garden pea when this plant is in bloom. It produces blue, violet or yellow flowers that look just like those on pea vines. Some species are considered pesky weeds, others are grown as forage or green manure crops, and one, the fava bean (*V. faba*), grown as a vegetable crop.

Companion Role with Plants

Tradition: Farmers plant this vigorous legume with grain crops such as oats or rye in order to provide nitrogen and improve soil structure. A legume-vetch mixture might also be grown as a cover crop in orchards. Common vetch (*V. sativa*) is a fine winter cover crop for milder regions. Hairy vetch (*V. villosa*) is the best choice for fall planting in northern climates as it is the hardiest.

Fava beans are typically intercropped with potatoes in Latin America.

Research: No relevant data is available.

Companion Role with Insects

Tradition: The early Roman writer Pliny believed that sowing rape with vetch would repel various caterpillars.

Research: There's no evidence to support Pliny's contention. But as a cover crop in walnut and pecan orchards, vetch reduced pests by increasing lady beetles and other predators. (118)

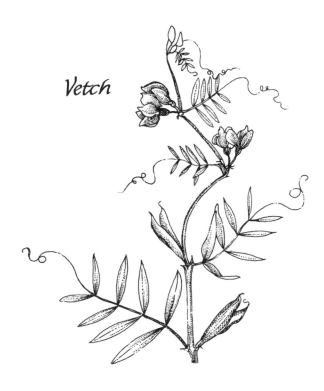

Vetch

Walnut

Juglans spp.
Juglandaceae
Nut tree

Walnut trees and small yards don't make a good match. These trees demand a lot of space and can grow from 90 to 150 feet tall. They tend to be a little messy, too. If you value a neat yard, you may find the catkins, leaves and husks that they drop to be a nuisance. Fortunately, these trees have wonderful redeeming values—their rich-flavored nuts and high-quality wood.

Companion Role with Plants

Tradition: Black walnut (*J. nigra*), Persian walnut (*J. regia*) and to some extent butternut (*J. cinerea*) are well known for their toxicity to other plants. Since ancient times, farmers have realized that few plants grow well beneath these trees.

Research: Members of this family produce juglone, which harms a number of plants including tomatoes, alfalfa, potatoes and apples. Juglone is found in the trees' roots and to a certain extent in the foliage, as well. Rainwater leaches this potent substance into the soil. (91, 92)

Companion Role with Insects

Research: A sod cover crop in walnut orchards reduced walnut aphids by increasing the numbers of lady beetles present. However, in order to be most effective, the sod should be mowed periodically. This forces the beetles up into the trees. (118)

Juglone is a repellent to elm bark beetles (*Scolytus multistriatus*). (92)

Remarks: For more information, see BLACK WALNUT.

Wheat

Triticum aestivum, Aestivum Group
Gramineae
Annual grass

If you want to grow wheat as a grain crop, you'll need at least 500 square feet in order to make your efforts pay off. If you don't have that much room, you still might want to grow wheat but for a different purpose. Plant a strip in the center of a large garden where it will provide cover for beneficial insects and look pretty while growing.

Companion Role with Plants

Tradition: Rye and poppies are supposed to injure wheat. Barberry was recognized by farmers as an enemy to wheat some 200 years ago. Farm lore also has it that corn and wheat do well together. There's an ancient Chinese saying that holds that wheat and legumes are never parted.

Research: The only tradition to have a scientific basis is the relation between barberry and wheat. It's been found that barberry does host black stem rust fungi, which infect wheat.

In one early study, wheat straw mulch reduced corn seed germination. Subsequent research suggests that wheat residues may be allelopathic to a number of crops and to some weeds including lamb's-quarters. (92)

The corn cockle weed (*Agrostemma githago*) growing in wheat seems to stimulate the grain's growth. (92)

Companion Role with Insects

Tradition: Early gardeners reported that elderberry branches brushed over stalks of growing wheat prevented the yellows, a virus disease.

Research: No data is available to support the beneficial effect of elderberry on wheat.

Researchers have found that strips of brome grass in wheat serve as traps for wheat stem sawflies. You can then destroy pests along with the brome grass. (110)

Whitefly

Aleyrodes spp.

These insects tend to flock to the undersides of plant leaves. Very often you won't know they're there unless you move the plant, and then they'll flutter away. Whiteflies cause damage by sucking juices from new growth, making the plant susceptible to disease.

Tradition: Aromatic herbs including peppermint, wormwood and others are recommended against whiteflies. Some gardeners say that nasturtiums also repel these pests.

Research: On cabbage, whiteflies seemed especially abundant when the surrounding soil was bare instead of covered by weeds or an intercrop of peanuts. (101)

Wormwood

Artemisia spp.
Compositae
Perennial herb

There are several kinds of wormwood, and each has a special place in the companion garden. Absinthe wormwood (*A. absinthium*) grows some 3 feet high, but a special cultivar, Nana, is a much lower, creeping form that interplants well as a border plant in the perennial bed. Southernwood (*A. abrotanum*) is best kept in background plantings where it won't shade or overrun other plants.

Companion Role with Plants

Tradition: Gardeners say that almost nothing thrives near absinthe wormwood. Southernwood doesn't have the same reputation, however, and is recommended for interplanting with all kinds of vegetables, flowers and fruits.

Research: Absinthe wormwood contains the growth inhibitor absinthin. According to one researcher, this is secreted by glandular hairs on the leaves. Rainwater leaches the substances onto the soil and neighboring plants. Seedlings growing within roughly 3 feet of a wormwood plant are affected. (92)

Similarly, fresh or ground wormwood leaves added to the soil slowed pea and bean germination and subsequent growth. (92)

Planting Tips: Many wormwood species are ornamental, such as the popular silver mound (*A. schmidtiana*). This particular plant has leaves covered with silvery-white hairs, hence its name. Once established, some species may quickly take over. Prune them vigorously, and pull up unwanted volunteers to keep them under control.

Companion Role with Insects

Tradition: In spite of its reputation as a poor plant companion, wormwood has been widely grown for its insecticidal and repellent powers. Southernwood is said to repel cabbage pests, codling moths and other flying insects. A spray of absinthe wormwood is recommended against fleas and ticks, and the fresh or powdered leaves are said to repel pests from stored grain.

Some gardeners say that wormwood repels slugs and certain rodents. It may be worth growing as a living fence around the garden area for this reason.

Wormwood

Yarrow

Wheat

329

Research: In one study, companion crops of southernwood and wormwood reduced flea beetles on collards. However, overall flea beetle damage to the plants was still great. (59)

Yarrow

Achillea spp.
Compositae
Perennial ornamental or weed

Yarrow performs well in a variety of settings. No matter where you put it, it will attract helpful hover flies. Some low-growing varieties are suitable for borders or "carpets." Woolly yarrow (*A. tomentosa*) interplants well with root vegetables. It forms a gound hugging mat with its fernlike, woolly foliage.

Companion Role with Plants

Tradition: Biodynamic gardeners say the presence of yarrow in the garden increases the oil production of aromatic herbs.

Research: No data is available about yarrow's companionable qualities with other plants.

Planting Tips: If you grow yarrow in the midst of an annual vegetable or flower bed, take measures to control its spreading growth.

Companion Role with Insects

Research: Yarrow is a good insectary plant, attracting all sorts of predatory wasps and lady beetles. (52)

Appendix
Making Your Own Discoveries

We tend to forget that agricultural science hasn't always been in the hands of university researchers. The discoveries of prehistoric Indians, ancient Chinese farmers, Greek philosophers and British vicars form the basis of our most responsible food-raising practices. It was these people, ignorant of modern chemistry, genetics, plant pathology and intercropping, who bred the first crops, concocted the first insect repellents, developed rotation systems, irrigated, mulched, fertilized and even interplanted intensively for high yields. With the advent of agriculture schools, a more formal science took over and virtually ended lay research.

In the past century, scientists have given us tremendous insight into the ways plants, animals and the environment interact. They have bred hardy, high-yielding varieties. They have designed hundreds of tools and machines for faster, more efficient cultivation and harvesting. Yet, the record for practical, sustainable cropping methods is not so impressive. It must be said that while agronomy has taught us countless ways to exploit the land, it has introduced few ways to nurture it. Seldom are modern main-stream cropping practices as environmentally economical as those early instinctive ones. No wonder our modern agricultural ideal has collapsed, leading many of us to return again to the old ways.

Now, finally, science is directing its energies toward finding modern practices that are at least as environmentally sound as the best traditional ones. Work in companion planting and related topics such as allelopathy and covercropping has finally begun. But, valuable as the new work is, the effort is still far from adequate. If we are ever to use these practices to raise yields and significantly reduce pest, weed and disease problems, then much new knowledge will be needed.

The door is wide open for gardeners and farmers to contribute to this new science of companion planting. Aside from work at the Rodale Research Center and a few experimental stations, most interplanting research has little direct application to the organic vegetable garden or the small truck farm in North America. Interplanting potentials of relatively few garden vegetables or fruits have been investigated. Studies of wheat, sorghum, soybeans, rice and other major commercial food crops take precedence over garden favorites like lettuce and lima beans. The focus is on large-scale operations so that certain labor-intensive cultural procedures aren't even considered worth examining. These include hand weeding, mulching and interplanting among crops that are already growing. Where companion planting experiments are done with smaller operations in mind, quite often tropical subsistence farms are the models. Though there is much we can learn from these studies, something is bound to be lost in the translation from the tropical farm field plot to the temperate zone garden bed.

Given these gaps in existing information, we need to explore the effects of companion planting in the labor-intensive (lovingly tended) organic garden. There's a need for straightforward studies of cropping combinations using ordinary garden varieties of fruits, vegetables and herbs. We must identify the best associations that promote good soil nutrition, high yields, and pest, weed and disease management. Some of these crops might be more effective as mulches or green manures. For those crops that do interplant well, we need information on timing, spacing and culture.

Who is better equipped to provide this information than organic gardeners? Most of us are already experimenters of sorts. In an informal way, we note the comings and goings of insects, judge the merits of different varieties, and experiment with new designs, rotational patterns, spacings, compost recipes and all sorts of treatments. Interplanting or even companion planting may already be essential to our garden plan. In that case, we must simply formalize our approach and become more consistent in our efforts in order to come up with some valuable results.

It may seem unlikely that anything worthwhile could come out of a backyard experiment. Experimental procedures of this new science seem to cause the experts enough problems—how could someone who isn't a scientist ever design a meaningful study? Admittedly, intercropping studies are particularly complicated, and it's easy to plan a poor experiment that gives poor results.

The very general guidelines presented in this appendix will help you avoid some of the common mistakes specific to interplanting research, but don't rely only on what you read here. Read some of the scientific articles listed in the Bibliography at the end of this book. Research reports put out each year by the Rodale Research Center often cover experiments with intercrops, living mulches, repellent plants, sprays and other similar topics. (You can obtain a list of all the available research reports, along with their prices by writing to the Rodale Research Center, Box 323, RD 1, Kutztown, PA 19530.) Just sitting down with some of the better journals published in this field, such as *Experimental Agriculture, Journal of Applied Ecology, Agronomy Journal, HortScience* and *Annals of Applied Biology*, will give you a sense of the sorts of problems that are being investigated, and they'll also suggest ways to go about setting up your own experiment and analyzing the results. If you're not up to wading through all the jargon, figures and details typical of such articles, consult less esoteric publications such as those put out by state land grant

334

universities. *California Agriculture* and *Michigan Science in Action* have published excellent, readable, yet honest summaries of several interplanting studies done at the state schools. *Farmstead, The Grower* and other farm publications also cover interplanting topics occasionally.

Not all organic growers will be inclined toward garden research. Those of you who do devote time and energy toward experimenting are likely to be rewarded with some answers to your most vexing garden dilemmas. At the very least, you'll enjoy a deeper understanding of your garden's ecology.

Turning Observations into Experiments

Every time we do something new in our gardens—try out a new variety or a different method of cultivation or plant spacing—we are improving our gardening skills and increasing our level of experience, but we aren't usually doing research. Sure, research begins with observation, but along the way, a lot of careful planning and attention to certain experimental techniques are needed. It isn't enough to merely place a marigold plant beside a bean plant and wait for results. We need to know specifically what we want to find out—do marigolds increase the yield of beans? What specific varieties of both crops are we studying? Do marigolds reduce insect pests? If so, which pests and at what stages in their development? How many marigolds do we need to plant per bean plant for optimum results?

Be reasonable in your expectations as you select a topic for garden research. Choose something you can actually prove or disprove—and in some way measure—through observation and experimentation. Think back to your junior high school lessons on the scientific method and develop a hypothesis that, as clearly as possible, states the problem you wish to solve. Then restate the hypothesis as a series of treatments, in a number of plots or experimental areas.

Continuing with our example of beans and marigolds, if we narrow our study to a comparison of a certain species of marigold as an effective insect-repellent intercrop for Blue Lake beans,

(continued on page 338)

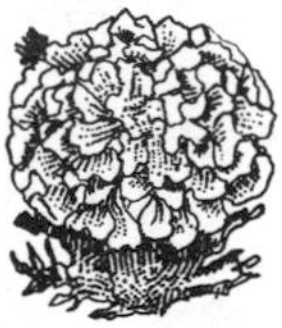

Suggestions for Garden Experiments

Below you'll find a few research ideas you might want to try, involving companion plants and related topics.

Question	Sample Experiment

Experiment 1

How effective are insect-repellent plants?

Compare the abilities of different species or varieties of repellent plants to repel one or more pests from a main crop.

Main crop: beans
Repellent crop: marigolds
(*Tagetes patula, T. minuta*)

Treatments:
  A: Monocropped plot
     (beans alone)
  B: Companioned plot
     (beans–*T. patula*)
  C: Companioned plot
     (beans–*T. minuta*)

Note: Use Latin square shown below.

C	A	B
A	B	C
B	C	A

Experiment 2

How many of a given repellent plant should I grow to effectively control a target pest on a given main crop?

Main crop: cabbage
Repellent crop: onions

Compare pest populations on intercropped plots where plants were set out at different densities.

Treatments:
A: Monocropped plot (cabbage alone)
B: Companioned plot (every cabbage plant surrounded by 4 onions)
C: Companioned plot (every cabbage plant surrounded by 12 onions)

Note: Use same Latin square given for first experiment.

Experiment 3

When should I plant each crop for maximum interplant effectiveness?

Main crop: corn
Companion crop: snap beans
Target pest: corn earworm

Compare different relative planting dates of the repellent and main crops.

Treatments:
A: Monocropped plot (corn alone)
B: Companioned plot (corn and beans planted simultaneously)
C: Companioned plot (corn planted 20 days before beans)

Note: Use same Latin square given for first experiment.

Experiment 4

How does a weedy border influence beneficial insect communities in the garden?

Main crop: broccoli

Compare the populations of certain beneficial insects in a bed surrounded by mowed lawn versus one surrounded by natural vegetation.

Treatments:
A: Monocropped plot with lawn border (mowed)
B: Monocropped plot with natural border (unmowed)

Note: Use Latin square shown below.

A	B
B	A

Experiment 5

How does a legume companion influence the yield or growth of a nonlegume main crop?

Main crop: cabbage
Companion crop: peas

Compare an intercropped planting with a monocropped one

Treatments:
A: Monocropped plot (cabbage alone)
B: Companioned plot (cabbage–peas)

Note: Use Latin square given for preceding experiment.

---

we might make the following hypothesis:

An interplanting of *Tagetes minuta* reduces Mexican bean beetle damage in Blue Lake beans.

Just by making a simple statement such as this, we have clarified many aspects of our experiment. We will compare one treatment or, in this case, one form of interplanting, with a monocropping of beans. Between-plant spacing and overall plant densities must remain the same in each treatment. The effectiveness of the treatment will be measured by damage to the main crop, not the number of Mexican bean beetles we spot, so we'll need to devise some way to quantify this so we can collect the data.

Our hypothesis can be rewritten as a set of treatments and a control:

Treatment 1: *Tagetes minuta* interplanted with Blue Lake beans

Control: Blue Lake beans monocropped

This study is satisfactory as it stands and might yield some interesting results. Yet, it might be more meaningful if we added another treatment. We could broaden our hypothesis to read:

An interplanting of *Tagetes minuta* is more effective than *T. patula* for controlling Mexican bean beetles on Blue Lake beans.

By looking at two different species of marigold, we would be able to decide which is the better one to use, and we'd have more opportunity to compare marigold companion cropping in general with monocropped beans. The control in this case is necessary so we can see how much insect damage occurs where no repellent plants exist.

Dozens of complex mechanisms are at work in interplanting, so some topics you wish to study may require a whole series of experiments, either carried out simultaneously or over a period of years. In order to avoid getting discouraged before you have really found any answers, *keep it simple*. Don't test more than two companion plants, spray recipes or allelopathic mulches. This will make it easier to design a reliable study and will keep your experimental area small and easy to care for. Select plants that you are familiar with and that tend to do well in your garden. If you're experimenting with plant-derived sprays or mulches, choose species that are easy to grow in large quantities so you'll have plenty of material to work with. For some ideas on experiments you might want to try, see the box, Suggestions for Garden Experiments.

As you gain more experience you may decide to expand your work to include studies of several factors at one time. This will be easier to do once you've mastered the basics of the agricultural experimental method and have already run a few garden experiments.

Designing the Experiment

The way you design a garden experiment depends on how much time, energy and land you're willing to devote to the project and on how reliable you want the results to be. Specific methods for arranging plants and making observations can lead to much more reliable answers much more quickly than the informal dabbling we routinely enjoy or the intuition and trial and error that our farmer-ancestors had to rely on. The scientific method enables us to observe systematically. It eliminates, or at least accounts for, outside influences and assures that our results will directly relate to the problem at hand.

Identifying Variables

No two living things are exactly alike. One Blue Lake bean seed may not behave the same way another does. Even though they are the same variety, each has a slightly different genetic code. To further complicate matters, everything in the environment is changing all the time. Temperature, rainfall, wind, even the tilt and rotation of the earth influence plant growth from one minute or hour or day to the next.

While all of these factors or variables delight the philosopher, they confound the scientist. The simplest experiment is rather complex just because you are dealing with living things. When work is being done outdoors, it is particularly complicated because there are so many living things involved!

When you plan an intercropping experiment, you must begin by considering all of the factors that might conceivably affect its outcome. For example, in our straightforward study of French marigolds as companion plants for Blue Lake beans, you may decide to set up one test plot of equally spaced bean plants. In the second plot, you space the beans at the same distance as the plants in the first but with marigolds intercropped in a row or per plant arrangement. To a greater or lesser degree, you can expect three basic types of variables to influence your results: genetic, location, and weather and season.

Each bean plant has a unique genetic makeup as does each marigold plant. They'll respond differently to stresses, and they'll have different yield potentials.

Where the plants grow has a profound effect on their health and productivity. Their proximity to other plants (and to what kinds of other plants) influences what nutrients are available, what pests and diseases are nearby, and even what sorts of beneficial insects and animals are available to feed on the pests. Surrounding vegetation can dramatically alter the microclimate of the test crop by raising or lowering temperatures and humidity. It can also deflect or channel breezes that might ultimately affect crop growth and populations of certain wind-borne diseases and pests.

Plants growing in different parts of the garden are bound to meet with different soil types. Soil temperature, drainage and subsoil conditions as well as the fertility and tilth of the plow zone (top 6 inches of soil) may be dramatically different within a few feet. Beans and marigolds planted in a slightly boggy area may develop more slowly or be more susceptible to certain pests than the test plants growing in a drier part of the garden.

Also related to location is the size of the experimental plots. Differences in plot size may influence pest populations and nutrient availability. You can't fairly compare a tiny control plot containing only a few test plants to a larger treatment plot containing many plants.

If plots have different slopes or shapes they'll start out with different advantages or disadvantages. Differences in slope affect light, moisture and other factors. Even the shape of the test plot can influence the plants' root growth and how much light they receive. Where plots contain more than one plant, edge effect becomes an important variable. Plants on the perimeter of the plot are influenced by different vegetation and different wind, light and moisture levels than those growing in the center. Soil compaction caused by walking around the test plot can drastically reduce root development in the border plants. This in turn can affect how well they ultimately grow and yield.

As anyone who has cultivated even one garden knows, daily and yearly weather changes often affect plants in drastic ways. We are aware of the ways a late spring slows plant growth or a wet summer favors certain crops. Yet often the effects are more subtle. A dry year might intensify the repellent qualities in marigold plants, while slowing the beans' growth and yield. It might also influence populations of pests and beneficial insects by making predators, parasites and alternative hosts more or less available. The results of our bean-marigold experiment could be quite different depending on the year or even the month we run it.

Controlling Variables

Once we've identified all the specific variables that will disturb our test, we need to devise ways to somehow reduce their effects. Most variables can be reduced even if they can't be totally eliminated. Genetic differences will be less of a problem if you're careful to use the same varieties (unless of course you're trying to compare relative merits of different varieties), purchased from the same seed company, in the same year. If you're using transplants, be sure they're uniform—the same size, shape and quality.

Location variables involving the effects of surrounding vegetation can be dealt with by keeping your experimental plots well away from hedges, outbuildings, windbreaks and the like. If you have space available, use it to establish "separate but equal" experimental areas, far enough apart not to influence one another, but with the same soil and other similar factors. If space is limited, you may wish to team up with a gardening neighbor and establish comparable plots in his or her yard. Sometimes, scientists set up a low fence of sheet plastic around each plot in order to minimize the influence adjacent plots might have on one another. Of course, barriers like that create certain edge effects (such as heat and humidity changes), which you must take into account when you analyze the data.

Test the soil in your experimental plots to be sure that fertility and tilth are about the same. Don't select one plot that is way out in the middle of an uncultivated field and another in a well-established garden bed. If possible, locate all experimental plots outside your ordinary garden area, so that garden cultivation, harvesting and pest control measures won't affect your research. Where major soil differences exist among plots, it may be a good idea to choose another area where the soil is more similar. If there's only a slight variation in the soil, blocking (explained later in this section) should allow you to overcome the differences somewhat. Adding compost, leaf mold or well-rotted manure, or planting a green manure crop will tend to make all soils more uniform over a period of time.

Experimental plots must, of course, be the same size. What size is best depends on the crops you're working with and the amount of uniform area you have available. Ideally, you want to use enough space to grow a diversity of individual plants, but keep it small enough to avoid problems of soil differences and the like. You also don't want to set up such large plots that you can't care for them or properly collect their data. Even plots as small as 9 square feet are satisfactory for most intercropping studies such as our bean-marigold experiment.

In scientifically conducted trials, edge effects are usually overcome by harvesting only from an inner core of the experimental plot. In the home garden experiment, limited space may only allow you to disregard a single row of border plants. If your test plot is very small, you may not want to throw out any data at all. Still, you can reduce edge effects somewhat by carefully choosing test sites and avoiding any of the more obvious structures such as walls and well-worn paths. Even the most conscientious garden researcher will not be able to completely control this variable, since even the act of walking by the border plants will affect them. Yet, what you can't control you can at least note and account for in carefully kept records.

Replication

Repeating individual treatments or entire experiments helps average out the differences caused by variables. It's the easiest way to overcome the distraction of certain variables without devoting a lot of time and space to the experiment. It works best where test plots have fairly similar soil conditions, but you want to minimize the role genetics, the weather and other effects play in the results.

Suppose we want to compare the weed control potentials of two plant residues, one of which is a neutral material such as shredded paper and another of which is allelopathic. One simple way to do this would be to mark off three small plots, each containing one plant of the main crop. Each plot would receive a treatment. Treatment Number 1 would receive one kind of mulch, Treatment Number 2 another mulch, and Treatment Number 3 would be the control—not mulched at all.

Obviously the results from just one plant per treatment in one experiment could be misleading and aren't very convincing in view of all the variables involved. Even if all three plants survive the experiment, genetic differences or the whim of circumstance could shift results one way or the other. Surely our experiment would be much better if we added more plants, either within each plot or in separate plots. So, we replicate the experiment by growing not just three plants but nine. We still have only two treatments and one control, but we've tripled the size of our experiment in order to get better results.

In a single way, our simple bean-marigold experiment can be improved by replication. This can be done by establishing identical test plots under similar conditions so that there are three plots of each treatment (including the control), or nine altogether.

No matter what the experiment, try to provide at least three replications of each treatment. If plots are small or spread out over a large area, more variables might be involved, so six or more replications are even better. Where space or time is limited, it's always better to repeat one treatment several times than to try more treatments. If you have room for 30 plants, it would be better to test 3 treatments 10 times, than to compare 3 plantings of 10 different treatments. The more repetitions, the more reliability— it's as simple as that.

Blocking

The larger the experimental area, the more difficult it is to find ways of replicating under similar conditions. More variables, particularly differences in soil or slope, are usually more significant in the bigger plots. One way to get around this is to divide the area into smaller uniform-size sections or blocks. You then test all treatments within each block. This enables you to make comparisons between blocks as well as within blocks. Just remember that each block will have a different soil makeup, slope or whatever. There are still many replications, but differences between treatments should be more consistent and measurable.

Randomization

Another technique for dealing with variables is randomization. Used in this sense, "random" means objective or unbiased. It not only helps smooth out variations in soil or other conditions, but it also forces us to overcome our own biases about what the experiment *should* prove. In deciding where to locate each repeated treatment, it's easy to let our expectations about the experiment get in the way. We need to find some way of assuring that the treatments we're somehow rooting for won't receive the best locations. Randomization does just this. It gives each treatment the same chance of being located in a given position. Randomization can also be applied to block design. By randomizing the placement of treatments within blocks, small unnoticeable variations within a mostly uniform block are ironed out.

In large-scale experiments where lots of treatments are being studied, researchers accomplish randomization by following random digit tables. They mark off plots in rows and place treatments according to numbers assigned from the table. In experiments involving just a few alternatives, like the ones you do in your backyard, drawing lots gives satisfactory randomization. For example, in our allelopathic mulching experiment, which has three treatments including the control, we would have nine slips of paper in a bag, three labelled 1, three labelled 2 and three labelled 3. As we move systematically from plot to plot, we would draw a slip at each location to determine which treatment is placed there. Where just two treatments are involved, you can accomplish randomizing with the flip of a coin.

Such randomizing techniques are ideal where shifts in slope, soil condition, surrounding vegetation and so on run from the top to the bottom of the experimental site. However, it often happens that two or more obvious differences occur as you move across and up and down the area. For example, you may have a site that slopes east to west and shifts from loamy to clay soil running north to south. Simple randomization does not assure an even distribution of all treatments across both gradients. By just drawing lots, all of one treatment may fall in a particular section. In a case like this, you can use the Latin square design to assure an even distribution across both variables. With this design, you can control variables running in two opposite directions. Plots are arranged in rows, with treatments assigned to individual plots according to the prescribed Latin square being used. The number of replications equals the number of different treatments. No single treatment occurs more than once in a given row.

In some circumstances, the Latin square is more efficient than the ordinary randomized design, yet it is limited in application. Use it only where the experimental site is roughly square and where three or more treatments are being studied, since it only allows for as many replications as there are different treatments.

Basic Latin Square Design

(three variables including the control)

Treatments A, B, AB

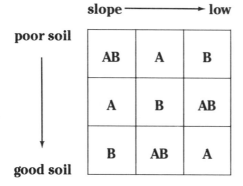

Treatment A: tomato alone

Treatment B: cabbage alone

Treatment AB: cabbage and tomato interplant

Note: When you use this Latin square design, substitute your own treatment crops for the tomatoes and cabbages used in this example. Then, follow the arrangement mapped out in the diagram when you plant your experimental plot.

Four by Four Latin Square Design

(*four variables including the control*)

Treatments A, B, C, D

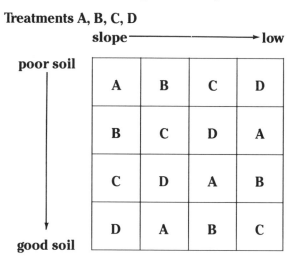

Treatment A: unmulched lettuce

Treatment B: lettuce mulched with chopped alfalfa

Treatment C: lettuce mulched with straw

Treatment D: lettuce mulched with chopped rye

Note: When you use this Latin square design, substitute your own treatments for the lettuce and mulch combinations used in this example. Then, follow the arrangement mapped out in the diagram when you plant your experimental plot.

Laying Out the Plots

Once you've located the experimental areas and you've carefully blocked off individual plots and assigned them specific treatments, you're ready for the next step—determining planting arrangements. The number of plants you fit into each plot depends upon the size of the plots and the optimum spacing for that particular crop. Often the main crop is planted at the same density and in the same pattern in all plots—both control and treatment. The companion cropping plan is then superimposed onto this main cropping design. Companions are squeezed in between rows or around individual main crop plants. This makes the total plant density higher in the intercropped plots, while maintaining the same number of main crop plants. In this type of setup, our Blue Lake beans might be planted 6 inches apart, in rows 12 inches apart in all 9 plots. In treatment plots, a row of marigolds might be planted between every two or three bean rows, or single marigold plants might be grown with groups of bean plants.

Such a high density design encourages inordinate competition among plants and doesn't always allow the companion and main crop to favorably interact. For this reason, some experimenters find it a fairer test to replace part of the main crop with the companion. Instead of simply adding the interplant to the basic cropping design, rows of the main crop of individual plants are sacrificed to make room for the companions. In our marigold-bean experiment, every fourth bean plant might be replaced by a marigold, or every fourth row, or perhaps just a single row in the center of the plot. A marigold border several plants deep might also bring interesting results.

This type of replacement system is suited to most interplanting studies. It works especially well with aggressive or perennial intercrops like mint, tomatoes, horseradish, Jerusalem artichokes or rye. You may want to use the uniform main-crop density system where you're concerned about maintaining the yield of a certain vegetable crop while interplanting with a smaller, less-competitive aromatic herb or other plant that has no significant food value. Unless you have unlimited garden space, you wouldn't want to devote half your bean patch to tansy. If the tansy can be squeezed in between bean plants, so much the better. You'll need to determine specific planting arrangements on the basis of each crop's growth habit, on what is known about the two plants abilities to "get along" and on the type of interaction you want to test. Most people in the scientific community feel that maximum benefits are achieved when the two crops are most closely spaced. However, it has also been shown that occasionally the spacing can be *so* close that competition becomes a problem. Repellent effects of some crops such as garlic may be expected to work only in close quarters. Other crops such as tansy or catnip are too aggressive to be closely interplanted. Companion plantings that supply alternate hosts or harbor beneficial insects can often be quite distant since such effects typically reach over a large area.

Collecting Data

Knowing what to look for and how to accurately describe what you see can be a most frustrating aspect of garden research. Unless you've clearly established what you are studying, you're likely to end up with very lengthy research notes that make for interesting reading but don't really provide the answers you thought you would find. If, for instance, you're trying to determine whether beans enhance corn growth, you must know exactly what "enhanced growth" is. Perhaps it is simply taller plants or plants with fewer pests. Or, is it more ears per plant or per plot? Could it be an earlier harvest? Is it bigger, heavier ears, perhaps more succulent ears or even better tasting ones?

Obviously, these qualities are each quite different and would involve very different measurements and sampling techniques. Although each experiment will have its own methods for collecting data, there are a few general rules that apply to most situations.

Measurements

In gathering data, all sorts of different measurements are taken. Quantitative data is the easiest to work with. You can record pest populations by counting the number of eggs, adults and/or larvae you find on plants or collect in traps or nets. To measure yields, you can count the number of pounds or bushels or perhaps individual vegetables you harvest per plot or per plant. In many professional experiments, growth rate is measured by periodically uprooting plants and weighing them before and after they've been dried in an oven. This obviously requires lots of plants and is impractical in the home garden experiment. You can come close to the professionals' accuracy by simply measuring the plant's height and possibly counting the number of branches or estimating leaf surface area. (To estimate leaf surface, snip one leaf off each sample plant, trace its outline on a piece of graph paper, and count the number of squares.) Qualitative data involving factors such as taste, appearance, marketability or insect damage is less accurate and is difficult to gather and interpret. Although you might use written descriptions to record such phenomena, in the long run, it's more accurate to devise a numerical scale that forces you to be specific and objective.

Such scales are only as good as the people who devise them. In order to come up with a clear set of categories, you must have a good idea of the range of diversity that exists in the test plots. Begin by surveying the treatments and controls, noting the worst and best plants. Then, make up a scale based on as many numbers as there are obvious classes. For instance, you might rate Mexican bean beetle damage to beans as follows:

0	0-10% plant's leaf area destroyed
1	10-25% plant's leaf area destroyed
2	25-50% plant's leaf area destroyed
3	50-75% plant's leaf area destroyed
4	75-100% plant's leaf area destroyed

When you record such measurements out in the garden, be careful to stay well within the bounds of each level on the scale. It's very easy to become subjective unless you consciously try to remain unbiased.

Sampling

Ideally, you should gather data from each plant in the experimental area. As long as you have kept the experiment fairly simple and the plots small, this is possible. However, where more than, say, 30 plants are involved, it's hard for a single investigator to keep track of per plant yields, pest populations, growth rates or other factors. When the scope of the experiment goes beyond a certain point, it's time to measure a smaller representative sample.

Samples will never exactly represent the total experimental population, but if they're carefully taken, they can come pretty close. Randomization is as important here as it is in the overall design of the experiment. Haphazardly choosing sample plants leaves the experiment wide open to the influence of your own biases. Try as you might to select the "typical" representatives, you're likely to be drawn to those that prove your point. Drawing lots will assure a fair, random sample. To do this, assign each plant a number. Decide how many plants you wish to sample (a percentage of the total population), and draw that many numbers. Don't forget to throw out border plants if you are controlling for edge effect.

Random sampling doesn't guarantee that samples will be taken from all portions of the plot. If you want to guarantee a well-distributed sample, systematic sampling is often preferred. Moving down the rows, collect data from every so many plants, until the entire plot has been covered. Select an interval that will not repeat the shape of the plot; if there are an even number of plants per row, then make the sampling interval an odd number.

You can also draw samples from a designated area within each plot. Often, investigators simply mark off an inner core within a larger plot or collect from plants running in a lattice or diagonal pattern.

Whatever process you use, be sure to select samples before the experiment is well underway. Neither random nor systematic sampling can be guaranteed to win out over your own biases. If you wait until the plants are established and data collection has begun, your selection may not be entirely objective.

Understanding Your Findings

Once the season has ended and the garden has been put to bed, you'll want to sit down with your experimental records and figure out just what, if anything, you have discovered. Experts rely on complex methods of statistical analysis. Such techniques are necessary for formal studies, but here, we'll be a bit less precise for the sake of simplicity. If the experiment has been straightforward, with few variables and good controls, simple analysis can be

Terms to Know

Treatment Total: Add together measurements from every plot (replication) receiving the same treatment.

Treatment Mean: Divide the treatment total by the number of plots (replications) receiving the same treatment.

Treatment Range: Subtract to find the difference between the largest and smallest measurements from plots (replications) receiving the same treatment.

Mean Range: Add together all treatment ranges from the experiment, then divide by the number of treatments.

---

amazingly accurate.

Begin by listing the measurements collected from each plot. These measurements might be the number of insect eggs or adults, crop yield, plant height and weight, or any other quantity. Organize the list in table form, listing measurements from each plot or replication under its appropriate treatment heading. Next, add together all the measurements for each treatment. This gives you the treatment total. The mean is found by dividing each treatment total by the number of replications done. Calculate the range of values for each treatment by subtracting the smallest measurement from the largest. Finally, find the mean range by averaging all the treatment ranges for the entire experiment.

Say, for the sake of example, that you are experimenting with tomatoes as companion plants for cabbage. You've measured the number of cabbage looper eggs per plant (test plants were chosen by random sampling, drawing lots or flipping a coin) at weekly intervals from the time the plants were set out until harvest. Your table might look something like this:

Treatment:
control (cabbage monocropped)

Day	Measurement (number of eggs per plant)		
	Plot A	Plot B	Plot C
0	0	2	0
7	8	6	12
14	15	23	18
21	17	25	19
28	13	20	16
35	15	19	17
42	7	8	8
TOTALS	75	103	90

Treatment total: 268
Treatment mean: 89.3
Treatment range: 28

Treatment:
cabbage/tomato interplant

Day	Measurement (number of eggs per plant)		
	Plot A	Plot B	Plot C
0	0	0	0
7	5	7	4
14	5	6	5
21	10	9	9
28	10	6	8
35	9	6	8
42	4	2	3
TOTALS	43	36	37

Treatment total: 116
Treatment mean: 38.7
Treatment range: 27

Mean Range for Experiment: 17.5

The data you end up with can give you some idea of the direction the experiment has taken, but you can't really draw any conclusions until you know how far off these numbers might be. Calculating the standard deviation helps you determine whether the differences you have observed between treatments are significant.

Figuring out the standard deviation is a rather complex exercise for those of us unschooled in statistical science. Lois Levitan, in her book *Improve your Gardening with Backyard Research* (Rodale Press, 1980), recommends a simpler, though admittedly less precise method for gardeners. To determine this standard deviation, refer to the Table of Mean Values. Find the appropriate r/σ value, which corresponds to the number of replications in the experiment. Divide the mean range of all treatments by this value. This gives the estimated standard deviation (SD).

In our imaginary experiment, three replications were used, so the r/σ value is 1.69. The mean range for the experiment is 17.5, so the SD is 17.5 divided by 1.69, or 10.4.

Once you've arrived at the standard deviation, you can use it to find out if treatment differences are significantly different. Our interplanted plots have less than half the cabbageworm eggs of the monocropped ones. But how much of this difference is due to chance? To find out, divide SD by the square root of the number of replications or samples ($\sqrt{n}$). This gives the standard error of the mean (SE) (SE=SD $\div \sqrt{n}$). We had three replications, so our n equals 3. That makes $\sqrt{n}$ equal to 1.7. Our standard deviation is 10.4. Therefore, the standard error of the mean (SE) is 10.4 divided by 1.7, or 6.1.

If the difference between any two treatment means is greater than three times the SE, you can conclude that the difference is significant. The difference between our imaginary treatment means is 89.3 minus 38.7, or 50.6. This is indeed significant, since it's well over three times the SE ($3 \times 6.1=18.3$).

From this hypothetical data, we could easily conclude that tomato interplanting did indeed help reduce the larvae of cabbage loopers. Future experiments might then deal with other interplants to see whether the reduction is due to repellent properties of the tomatoes or to the simple mixing of crops. We also might wish to look more closely at the tomato-cabbage interplanting to determine whether other pests are also repelled and whether overall damage, as well as pest population, is reduced to a satisfactory level.

In the "real world," experiments rarely produce such clear data. Don't let that discourage you. More often than not, researchers are left with unanswered questions and a confusing array of information that doesn't fit into a neat package. Still, you'll find that each well-planned, carefully executed and analyzed experiment brings some small discoveries and opens the way for new studies.

Table of Mean Values

n	Mean Value of r/σ
2	1.13
3	1.69
4	2.06
5	2.33
6	2.53
7	2.70
8	2.85
9	2.97
10	3.08
15	3.47
20	3.73
30	4.09
50	4.50
75	4.81
100	5.02
150	5.3
200	5.5
300	5.8
500	6.1
700	6.3

Source: Snedecor, G. W., and Cochran, W. G. 1967. *Statistical Methods.* 6th ed. Ames, Iowa: Iowa State University Press.

Glossary

Allelopathy: The process by which one plant releases chemicals or phytotoxins that inhibit the growth or development of another growing nearby. Allelopathy seems to occur widely in nature and has only recently been considered an important factor among cultivated plants and weeds.

Alternate hosts: Also called alternative hosts. Food in the form of plants or animals that insects rely on when their preferred food isn't available. Most insects are fairly limited in their diet, but almost none rely totally on one source of food. During part of the season, or part of their life cycle, crop pests may need to feed on weeds or other crops. In the same way, beneficial predatory and parasitic insects often require alternate insect food when their "favorite dinner" isn't around. Many beneficials require plant pollen and nectar to supplement their diet of pests. Ideally, you should eliminate alternate hosts of pests and maintain alternate hosts for beneficial insects.

Autoallelopathy: The process by which a plant produces chemicals (phytotoxins) that inhibit the growth of members of the same species. Thus, the roots of an apple tree might release substances that would harm other apple trees growing nearby.

Beneficial insects: Insects that work for the gardener's benefit by attacking pests, pollinating flowers or feeding on weeds. Surprisingly, most insects are beneficial, though not always in any dramatic way. Some insects have very passive roles as alternate hosts for predators and parasites.

Companion plants: Plants chosen for intercropping with a given crop because of its ability to enhance or complement the other's growth.

Cover crop: A legume or sod crop usually planted in the fall to protect the soil over the winter, and often plowed under as a green manure crop. Where erosion control is needed all summer, a crop might be directly planted into strips cut in the cover crop.

Ecosystem: A community of plants, animals and microorganisms in a given area. An agroecosystem is such a community specifically as it exists in a farm field.

Green manure: A crop grown to produce organic material that will be turned into the soil. Legumes such as alfalfa and clover, and grain crops such as rye, are typically used as green manure crops.

Interplanting: Also called intercropping. The practice of growing two or more crops at the same time in the same field or garden bed. Crops may be interplanted within rows or in alternate rows, blocks, circles or even mixed plantings that have no geometric pattern.

Monocropping: Also called monoculture. The practice of growing only one crop in a field or plot. Most large mechanized farms practice monocropping.

Parasitic insects: Insects that, as larvae, live in and feed on other insects. As adults, parasites eat mostly nectar and pollen and spend their time seeking out suitable victims on which to lay their eggs. When the young larvae hatch, they slowly consume their host, often leaving behind a hollow corpse. Most parasitic insects are small and rather hard to identify, but their distinctive cocoons on the backs of some caterpillars and the mummified pests they leave behind testify to their work. Tachinid flies, chalcid, braconid and ichneumonid wasps are parasites that help control many common garden pests.

Pheromones: Chemical substances released by insects and interpreted as signals by other individuals of the same species. Insect pheromones may serve as sex attractants, alarms, territory markers or other signals. Some plant chemicals mimic these pheromones, bringing about a certain behavior in certain insects.

Phytotoxins: Plant-produced chemicals that are harmful to other living things. Phytotoxins are responsible for allelopathic reactions. They give some plants protection from hungry insects or other animals.

Predatory insects: Insects that, during some stage of their growth, attack, kill and eat other insects. Predators range in size from tiny predatory mites to large ground beetles and hover flies. Lady beetles and lacewings are important, easily identified predators that help control all sorts of garden pests. They can be purchased from some garden suppliers and released in the garden. Unless the appropriate plant and insect hosts are available, predators will soon move on to other feeding grounds.

Bibliography

1. Agriculture Handbook 461, *Insecticides from Plants—A Review of the Literature, 1954-1971.* U.S. Department of Agriculture.

2. Altieri, Miguel A. 1981. Weeds May Augment Biological Control of Insects. *California Agriculture* 35(5-6):22-24.

3. Altieri, Miguel et al. 1982. Biological Control of Insect Pests. *American Horticulturist* 61(2):28-35.

4. Altieri, Miguel et al. 1978. A Review of Insect Prevalence in Maize (*Zea mays* L.) and Bean (*Phaseolus vulgaris* L.). *Polycultural Systems* 1:33-49.

5. Altieri, Miguel A. and Todd, James W. 1981. Some Influences of Vegetational Diversity on Insect Communities of Georgia Soybean Fields. *Protection Ecology* 3:333-38.

6. Altieri, Miguel; van Schoonhoven, A.; and Doll, J. 1977. The Ecological Role of Weeds in Insect Pest Management Systems: A Review Illustrated by Bean (*Phaseolus vulgaris*) Cropping Systems. *PANS* 23(2):195-202.

7. Altieri, Miguel A. and Whitcomb, W. H. 1979. The Potential Use of Weeds in the Manipulation of Beneficial Insects. *HortScience* 14(1):12-13.

8. Amonkar, S. V. and Banerji, S. 1971. Isolation and Characterization of Larvicidal Principles of Garlic. *Science* 174:1333-44.

9. Andow, David 1982. Effect of Agricultural Diversity on Insect Populations. *Proceedings of IFOAM Conference*, ed W. Lo.

10. Anon. 1982. Citrus Seeds: Bitter Bug Battler. *Science News* 12(15).

11. Anon. 1982. Grass Around Trees Inhibits Growth. *American Horticulturist* 61(7):10.

12. Anon. 1981. Intercropping Research Yields Needed Information. *Michigan Science in Action* 45:18-19.

13. Anon. 1979. Marigold Research, *IFOAM Bulletin*. 30 (3rd Quarter):4.

14. Anon. 1982. Organic Pest Control. *A Journal of Applied Technology* 1(3):7-10.

15. Anon. 1982. Plant Chemicals May be Contributing Factor for Crop Rotation. *Seed World* 120(6):32.

16. Anon. 1980. Substances in Fescue Inhibit Other Plants. *Research News* (Science and Education Administration, U.S.D.A.) NC-161.

17. Anon. 1978. Sugar Maples. *Avant Gardener* 10(20).

18. Anon. 1978. Weed Releases Substances that Reduce Crops' Yields. *Science Report* (College of Agricultural and Life Sciences, Univ. of Wisconsin-Madison).

19. Atsatt, Peter and O'Dowd, Dennis 1978. Mutual Aid Among Plants. *Horticulture* LVI(4):22-31.

20. Atsatt, Peter and O'Dowd, Dennis 1976. Plant Defense Guilds. *Science* 193:24-28.

21. Bach, Catherine E. 1980. Effects of Plant Diversity and Time of Colonization on Herbivore-Plant Interaction. *Oecologia* (Berlin) 44(3):319-26.

22. Bhowmik, P. C. and Doll, J. D. 1982. Corn and Soybean Response to Allelopathic Effects of Weed and Crop Residues. *Agronomy Journal* 74(4):601-6.

23. Bing, Arthur 1983. Research Reveals Weeds that Prevent Crop Seed Growth. *American Nurseryman* 157(7):91-94.

24. Blum, Murray S. 1983. Detoxication, Deactivation, and Utilization of Plant Compounds by Insects. *American Chemical Society.*

25. Buranday, R. P. and Raros, R. S. 1975. Effects of Cabbage-Tomato Intercropping on the Incidence and Oviposition of the Diamondback Moth (*Plutella xylostella*). *Phillipian Entomology* 2(5):369-74.

26. Burger, W. P. and Small, J. G. C. 1983. Allelopathy in Citrus Orchards. *Scientia Horticulturae* 20:361-75.

27. Cort, R. P. 1982. Effect of Non-Host Plants on Movements of Colorado Potato Beetles (*Leptinotarsa decemlineata*). Brookhaven National Laboratory, under contract with the U.S. Department of Energy. Available from National Technical Information Service. U.S. Department of Commerce, 5285 Port Royal Rd., Springfield, VA 22161.

28. Creasy, Rosalind 1982. *The Complete Book of Edible Landscaping.* San Francisco: Sierra Club.

29. Cromartie, W. J. 1975. The Effect of Stand Size and Vegetational Background on the Colonization of Cruciferous Plants by Herbivorous Insects. *Journal of Applied Ecology* 12:517-33.

30. Dempster, F. P. and Coaker, T. H. 1974. Diversification of Crop Ecosystems as a Means of Controlling Pests. *Biology in Pest and Disease Control.* Oxford, England: Blackwell Scientific Publications.

31. Doria, John J. 1981. Neem: The Tree Insects Hate. *Garden* 5(4):8-11.

32. Doutt, R. L. and Nakata, J. 1973. The Rubus Leafhopper and its Egg Parasitoid: An Endemic Biotic System Useful in Grape Pest Management. *Environmental Entomology* 2:381-86.

33. Drost, Dirk C. and Doll, Jerry D. 1980. Allelopathy: Some Weeds Use it Against Crops. *Crops and Soils Magazine* 32(6):5–6.

34. Eisner, T. 1964. Catnip: Its Raison d'Etre. *Science* 146:1318–20.

35. Ellis, Michael A.; Ferree, David C.; and Spring, David E. 1981. Investigation of Biological, Chemical, and Cultural Methods for Control of Collar Rot–A Research Update. *International Dwarf Fruit Tree Association* 14:121–25.

36. Feeny, P. P. and Bostock, H. 1968. Seasonal Changes in the Tannin Content of Oak Leaves. *Phytochemistry* 7:871–80.

37. Flaherty, D. 1969. Ecosystem Trophic Complexity and Willamette Mite *Eotetranychus willametei* (Acarina: Tetranychidae) densities. *Ecology* 50:911–16.

38. Forsyth, Adrian 1981. Flower Power Reconsidered. *Harrowsmith* 6(37):44–51.

39. Fukuoka, Masanobu. 1978. *The One-Straw Revolution.* Emmaus, Pa.: Rodale Press.

40. Fye, R. E. 1972. The Interchange of Insect Parasites and Predators Between Crops. *PANS* 18(2):143–45.

41. Ganser, Stephen 1980. Vegetable Production in a Living Sod. Rodale Research Report 80-2. Rodale Research Center, RD 1, Box 323, Kutztown, PA 19530.

42. Gibson, R. W. and Pickett, J. A. 1983. Wild Potato Repels Aphids by Release of Aphid Alarm Pheromone. *Nature* 302(5909): 608–9.

43. Gibson, Richard and Tingey, Ward 1979. Feeding and Mobility of the Potato Leafhopper Impaired by Glandular Trichomes of *Solanum berthaultii* and *S. polyadenium. Journal of Economic Entomology* 71:856–58.

44. Gliessman, Stephan R. and Altieri, Miguel 1982. Polyculture Cropping has Advantages. *California Agriculture* (July): 15–16.

45. Harborne, J. B. 1977. *Introduction to Ecological Biochemistry.* New York: Academic Press.

46. Harvey, R. G. and Linscott, J. J. 1978. Ethylene Production in Soil Containing Quackgrass Rhizomes and Other Plant Materials. *Soil Science Society of America Journal* 42: 721-24.

47. Hills, L. D. 1962. *The 1961 Tagetes Experiment.* Henry Doubleday Research Association, Convent Lane, Bocking, Brainetree, England.

48. Hofstetter, Robert 1980. Legume Sod Interplanting. Rodale Research Report 80-10. Rodale Research Center, RD 1, Box 323, Kutztown, PA 19530.

49. Hsiae, T. H. and Fraenkel, G. 1968. Selection and Specificity of the Colorado Potato Beetle for Solanaceous and Nonsolonaceous Plants. *Annals of Entomological Society of America* 61:493-503.

50. King, F. H. 1911. *Farmers of Forty Centuries,* reprinted. Emmaus, Pa.: Rodale Press.

51. Klein, R. R. and Miller, D. A. 1980. Allelopathy and Its Role in Agriculture. *Communications in Soil Science and Plant Analysis* (1):43-56.

52. Koehler; Barclay; and Kretchun 1983. Companion Plants. *California Agriculture* (September-October):14-15.

53. Korn, Larry; Snyder, Barbara; and Musick, Mark, eds. 1982. *The Future is Abundant.* Tilth, 13217 Mattson Rd., Arlington, VA 98223.

54. Lamberts, Mary Louise 1980. Intercropping with Potatoes. Master's thesis, Cornell University.

55. Latheef, M. A. and Irwin, R. D. 1979. The Effect of Companionate Planting on Lepidopteran Pests of Cabbage. *The Canadian Entomologist* 111:863-64.

56. Latheef, M. A. and Irwin, R. D. 1980. Effects of Companionate Planting on Snap Bean Insects. *Environmental Entomology* 9(2):195-98.

57. Latheef, M. A. and Ortiz, J. H. 1983. The Influence of Companion Herbs on Egg Distribution of the Imported Cabbageworm, *Pieris rapae*, on Collard Plants. *The Canadian Entomologist* 115:1031-38.

58. Latheef, M. A. and Ortiz, J. H. 1983. Influence of Companion Plants on Oviposition of Imported Cabbageworm, *Pieris rapae*, and Cabbage Looper, *Trichoplusia ni*, on Collard Plants. *The Canadian Entomologist* 115:1529-31.

59. Latheef, M. A. 1983. Personal communication.

60. Leather, Gerald R. 1983. Sunflowers (*Helianthus annuus*) are Allelopathic to Weeds. *Weed Science* 31:37-42.

61. Leius, K. 1967. Food Sources and Preferences of Adults of a Parasite, *Scambus buolianae* and Their Consequences. *Canadian Entomology* 99:865-86.

62. Levitan, Lois 1980. *Improve Your Gardening with Backyard Research*. Emmaus, Pa.: Rodale Press.

63. Lichtenstein, E. P.; Morgan, D. G.; and Mueller, C. H. 1964. Naturally Occurring Insecticides in Cruciferous Crops. *Journal of Agricultural Food and Chemistry* 12:158-61.

64. Lockerman, R. H. and Putnam, A. R. 1979. Evaluation of Allelopathic Cucumbers as an Aid to Weed Control. *Weed Science* 27(1):54-57.

65. Lolas, Petros C. and Cable, Harold D. 1982. Noncompetitive Effects of Johnsongrass (*Sorghum halepense*) on Soybeans (*Glycine max*). *Weed Science* 30:589-93.

66. Lundgren, L. 1975. Natural Plant Chemicals Acting as Oviposition Deterrents on Cabbage Butterflies. *Zoological Scripta* 4:253-58.

67. McMillian, W. W. et al. 1969. Extracts of Chinaberry Leaf as a Feeding Deterrent and Growth Retardant for Larvae of the Corn Earworm and Fall Armyworm. *Journal of Economic Entomology* 62(3):708-10.

68. Matthews, Diane 1981. The Effectiveness of Selected Herbs and Flowers in Repelling Garden Insect Pests. Rodale Research Report 81-28. Rodale Research Center, RD 1, Box 323, Kutztown, PA 19530.

69. Matthews, Diane 1980. The Effectiveness of Selected Insect Repellent Crops. Rodale Research Report 80-8. Rodale Research Center, RD 1, Box 323, Kutztown, PA 19530.

70. Maugh, Thomas H. 1982. Exploring Plant Resistance to Insects. *Science* 216(4547):722-23.

71. Merrill, R. 1976. *Radical Agriculture.* New York: Harper and Row.

72. Newman, Edward I. 1982. Possible Relevance of Allelopathy to Agriculture. *Pesticide Science* 13:575-82.

73. Oebker, N. and Hopen, H. 1974. Microclimatic Modification and the Vegetable Crop Ecosystem. *HortScience* 9(6): 564-68.

74. Olmstead, Carrie 1981. War on Weeds. *Michigan Science in Action* 44:16-18.

75. Owen, Jennifer 1984. Marigolds Among the Cabbages. *The Garden* (January):13-17.

76. Palti, Joseph 1982. Cultural Practices and Infectious Crop Diseases. New York: Springer-Verlan.

77. Patrick et al. 1963. Phytotoxic Substances in Arable Soils Associated with Decomposition of Plant Residues. *Phytopathology* 53:152-61.

78. Patrusky, Ben 1983. Plants in Their Own Behalf. *Mosaic* 14(2):33-39.

79. Perrin, R. M. 1975. The Role of Perennial Stinging Nettle *Urtica dioica* as a Reservoir of Beneficial Natural Enemies. *Annals of Applied Biology* 81:289-97.

80. Perrin, R. M. and Phillips, M. L. 1978. Some Effects of Mixed Cropping On Population Dynamics of Insect Pests. *Entomologia Experimentalis et Applicata* 24:585-93.

81. Peters, Elroy J. 1968. Toxicity of Tall Fescue to Rape and Birdsfoot Trefoil Seeds and Seedlings. *Crop Science* 8(November-December):650-653.

82. Philbrick, Helen and Gregg, Richard 1966. *Companion Plants and How to Use Them.* Old Greenwich, Conn.: Devin-Adair.

83. Pimentel, D. 1961. The Influence of Plant Spatial Patterns on Insect Populations. *Ecology* 54:61-9.

84. Poillion, William A. 1980-81. Succession Planting and Multiple Cropping in the Home Garden. *Louisiana Agriculture* 24(2):18-21.

85. Putnam, Alan R. and DeFrank, Joseph 1983. Use of Phytotoxic Plant Residues for Selective Weed Control. *Crop Protection* 2(2):173-81.

86. Putnam, Alan R. and Duke, William B. 1978. Allelopathy in Agroecosystems. *Annual Review of Phytopathology* 16: 431-51.

87. Putnam, Alan. 1983. Personal communication.

88. Reagan, John J. 1979. Same Ground, Two Crops. *The Furrow* 84(6):25-26.

89. Reagan, John J. 1983. Strip Intercropping: Worth a Look. *The Furrow* 88(6):18-19.

90. Reed, D. K. et al. 1970. Influence of Windbreaks on Distribution and Abundance of Brown Spot Scale in Citrus Groves. *Annals of Entomological Society of America* 63:792-94.

91. Rice, Elroy L. 1974. *Allelopathy.* New York: Academic Press.

92. Rice, Elroy L. 1983. *Pest Control with Nature's Chemicals.* Norman, Okla.:University of Oklahoma Press.

93. Rice, Elroy L. 1977. Some Roles of Allelopathic Compounds in Plant Communities. *Biochemical Systematics and Ecology* 5:201-6.

94. Ries, S. et al. 1977. Triacontanol: A New Naturally Occurring Plant Growth Regulator. *Science* 195:1339–41.

95. Riotte, Louise 1975. *Secrets of Companion Planting*. Charlotte, Vt.: Garden Way Publishing.

96. Risch, S. J. 1979. A Comparison by Sweep Sampling of the Insect Fauna from Corn and Sweet Potato Monocultures and Dicultures in Costa Rica. *Oecologia* (Berlin) 42:195-211.

97. Root, Richard B. 1973. Organization of Plant-Arthropod Association in Simple and Diverse Habitats: The Fauna of Collards (*Brassica oleracea*). *Ecological Monographs* 45(1):95-117.

98. Ryan, J.; Ryan, M. F.; and McNaeidhe, F. 1980. The Effect of Interrow Plant Cover on Populations of the Cabbage Root Fly *Brassicae* (Wiedemann). *Journal of Applied Ecology* 17(1):31-40.

99. Schultz, Brian et al. 1982. An Experiment in Intercropping Cucumbers and Tomatoes in Southern Michigan, U.S.A. *Scientia Horticulturae* 18:1-8.

100. Secoy, D. M. and Smith, A. E. 1983. Use of Plants in Control of Agricultural and Domestic Pests. *Economic Botany* 37(1):28-57.

101. Smith, Judith G. 1976. Influence of Crop Background on Natural Enemies of Aphids on Brussels Sprouts. *Annals of Applied Biology* 83:15-29.

102. Steenhagin, D. A. and Zimdahl, R. L. 1979. Allelopathy of Leafy Spurge (*Euphorbia esula*). *Weed Science* 27(1):1-3.

103. Stern, V. A. et al. 1969. Lygus Bug Control in Cotton Through Alfalfa Intercropping. *California Agriculture* 230(2):8-10.

104. Suryatna, E. S. and Harwood, R. R. 1976. Nutrient Uptake of Two Traditional Intercrop Combinations and Insect and Disease Incidence in Three Intercrop Combinations, presented at International Rice Research Institute Seminar, February 28, 1976.

105. Tahvanainen, Jorma O. and Root, Richard B. 1972. The Influence of Vegetational Diversity on the Population Ecology of a Specialized Herbivore, *Phyllotreta cruciferae* (Coleoptera: Chrysomelidae). *Oecologia* (Berlin) 10:321-46.

106. Theunissen, J. and Denouden, H. 1980. Effects of Intercropping with *Spergula arvensis* on Pests of Brussels Sprouts. *Entomologia Experimentalis et Applicata* 27(3):260-68.

107. Thresh, J. M., ed. 1981. *Pests, Pathogens and Vegetation*. London: Pitman Books.

108. Vandermeer, John 1981. The Interference Production Principle: An Ecological Theory of Agriculture. *Bio-Science* 31(5): 361-64.

109. van Emden, H. F., ed. 1973. *Insect/Plant Relationships*. New York: John Wiley and Sons.

110. van Emden, H. F., ed. 1974. *Pest Control and its Ecology*. London: Edward Arnold.

111. van Emden, H. F. 1965. The Role of Uncultivated Land in the Biology of Crop Pests and Beneficial Insects. *Scientific Horticulture* 17:121-36.

112. Villani, Michael 1983. Personal communication.

113. Volz, M. G. 1977. Infestations of Yellow Nutsedge in Cropped Soil: Effects on Soil Nitrogen Availability to the Crop and on Associated N Transforming Bacterial Populations. *Agro-Ecosystems* 3(4):313-23.

114. Walker, Chris and Lott, Jeanne 1980. Pesticides and the Home Gardener. *Calpirg Reports* 8(2):2-4.

115. Whittaker, R. H. and Feeny, R. P. 1971. Allelochemics: Chemical Interactions Between Species. *Science* 171(3973): 757-70.

116. Wilcox, Louis V., Jr. 1979. Companion Planting Primer–A Review of Garden Ecology. *Farmstead Magazine* 6(2):27-28.

117. Willey, R. W. 1979. Intercropping–Its Importance and Research Needs. *Field Crop Abstracts* 32(1):1-10, 74-85.

118. William, R. D. 1981. Supplementary Interactions Between Weeds, Weed Control Practices, and Pests in Horticultural Cropping Systems. *HortScience* 16(4):10-15.

119. Wolff, Anthony 1980. Plants vs. Insects. *Rockefeller Foundation Illustrated* 4(4):8-9.

120. Yih, Katherine 1983. Intercropping Vegetables. *The Grower* (February):12-16.

Index

Page numbers in *italic* type indicate illustrations.